**ICEK AJZEN**
University of Massachusetts
**MARTIN FISHBEIN**
University of Illinois

# Understanding Attitudes and Predicting Social Behavior

Prentice-Hall, Inc., Englewood Cliffs, New Jersey 07632

*Library of Congress Cataloging in Publication Data*

Ajzen, Icek.
   Understanding attitudes and predicting social behavior

   Bibliography: p. 248
   Includes index.
   1.  Attitude (Psychology)    2.  Prediction (Psychology)
3.  Social psychology—Addresses, essays, lectures.
I.  Fishbein, Martin, joint author.    II.  Title.
BF323.C5A37         301.1      79-26063
ISBN  0-13-936443-9
ISBN  0-13-936435-8 pbk.

*TO OUR MOST IMPORTANT OTHERS:*
*RACHEL, RON, AND ELIE*
*DEBORAH AND SYDNEY*

Printed in the United States of America

10   9   8   7   6   5   4   3   2   1

Prentice-Hall International, Inc., *London*
Prentice-Hall of Australia Pty. Limited, *Sydney*
Prentice-Hall of Canada, Ltd., *Toronto*
Prentice-Hall of India Private Limited, *New Delhi*
Prentice-Hall of Japan, Inc., *Tokyo*
Prentice-Hall of Southeast Asia Pte. Ltd., *Singapore*
Whitehall Books Limited, *Wellington, New Zealand*

# Contents

iii

CHAPTER 6

## Determinants of the Attitudinal and Normative Components   61

CHAPTER 7

## Theoretical Implications   78

Part 2

## APPLICATIONS   93

CHAPTER 8

## Overview   95

## CHAPTER 12

## Predicting and Understanding Consumer Behavior: Attitude-behavior correspondence    148

Martin Fishbein, Icek Ajzen

## CHAPTER 13

## Predicting and Understanding Voting in American Elections: Effects of external variables    173

Martin Fishbein, Icek Ajzen, Ron Hinkle

## CHAPTER 14

## Predicting and Understanding Voting in British Elections and American Referenda: Illustrations of the theory's generality    196

Martin Fishbein, Carol H. Bowman, Kerry Thomas, James J. Jaccard, Icek Ajzen

### CHAPTER 15

## Changing the Behavior of Alcoholics:
## Effects of persuasive communication    217

Martin Fishbein, Icek Ajzen, Judy McArdle

### CHAPTER 16

## Some Final Comments    243

# Preface

Our first co-authored book (Fishbein & Ajzen, 1975) described a theory of reasoned action dealing with the relations among beliefs, attitudes, intentions, and behavior. In that book we provided a general review of theory and research in the area of attitudes and attempted to integrate this diverse literature within our own theoretical framework. The book's emphasis was on theoretical and methodological issues and controversies.

The present book compliments the previous volume by focusing on the practical implications of our approach. It is designed to familiarize the reader with our theory and methods, and to show how the relatively small number of concepts comprising the theory of reasoned action can be used to predict, explain, and influence human behavior in applied settings. The theoretical foundation is detailed in the first of part of the book, as are the methods used to assess beliefs, attitudes, intentions, and behaviors. The second part describes, chapter by chapter, different applications of our approach to various problems of social significance, including choice of occupational orientation, consumer behavior, family planning, and voting in an election.

Given our practical objectives, we have made no attempt to present in-depth analyses of theory and research in these areas, but have instead focused on providing the tools and guidelines needed to use our approach effectively. Keeping this goal in mind we have taken care to define technical terms, to refer only to a few basic statistical concepts, and to avoid excessive use of professional jargon.

To the sophisticated reader, our account may at times appear a bit oversimplified, but we hope we have achieved our goal of presenting a simple description of our approach, unencumbered by qualifications that would be required in a more technical monograph.

This book, like our previous volume, is truly the result of a joint effort. We have reversed the order of the authorship to emphasize the equality of our contributions in the writing of both books. Every paragraph, every sentence, and virtually every word in the present book were written jointly in the course of many meetings in Champaign and Amherst. We thus take equal credit, and equal blame, for the contents of this book.

At the same time we acknowledge with great appreciation the contributions and assistance of many individuals. First and foremost, several of our students, former students, and associates were directly involved in the research described in the second part of this book. In fact, some of the studies reported are taken from Master's theses or Doctoral dissertations. We have acknowledged these contributions by listing the names of major investigators in the authorship of each applied chapter. Beyond these credits we would like to express our gratitude to the following individuals for their assistance at various stages of theory development, data collection and analysis: Jean Chung, Fred Coombs, Shel Feldman, Myron Glassman, John Hornick, Kalman Kaplan, George King, Thomas Kida, Susan Lehtinen, Richard Pomazal, Stephen Roberts, Angelica Robertson, and Mary Tuck. Special thanks are due to Joel Cohen, Leo Meltzer, and Amiram and Diane Vinokur who read parts of all the manuscript; their helpful comments are greatly appreciated. Also we wish to thank the following reviewers whose care and interest in the work we are grateful for: Professor Eugene Borgida, Department of Psychology, University of Minnesota, Minneapolis, Minnesota; Professor Clive Davis, Department of Psychology, Huntington Hall, Syracuse, New York; Professor Wayne Harrison, Department of Psychology, University of California, Riverside, California; and Professor Stuart Oskamp, Department of Psychology, Claremont Graduate School, Claremont, California.

Finally, we would like to express our indebtedness to Carol Marsh who invested a great deal of time and effort, typing and retyping various drafts of the manuscript.

Icek Ajzen

Martin Fishbein

# PART
# 1

## A Theory
## of
## Reasoned Action

# CHAPTER 1

## Introduction

This book is concerned with the prediction and understanding of human behavior. To solve applied problems and make policy decisions it is often necessary to forecast or predict people's behavior. Predictions may involve such diverse questions as the number of children people will have, whether or not they will buy a car in the next year, or for whom they will vote in a given election. In many instances, our goal goes beyond prediction in that we attempt to influence or change behavior. Although prediction is possible with little or no understanding of the factors that cause a behavior, some degree of understanding is necessary for producing change.

Investigators have usually assumed that there are very different causes for different behaviors. For example, the causes of political behavior are said to differ greatly from the causes of sexual behavior or consumer behavior. To explain voting behavior, investigators have examined such variables as party identification, socio-economic status, and attitudes toward political candidates. In contrast, attempts to explain family planning have relied on such factors as religious affiliation, the need to nurture, husband-wife dominance, etc. Moreover, even within a given domain there is often little agreement as to the crucial determinants of behavior. We are thus confronted with a multitude of concepts and theories that have, at one time or another, been proposed to explain the many behaviors of interest to the social scientist.

In this book we advocate a very different approach. We will try to show that it is possible to account for behavior of various kinds by reference to a relatively small number of concepts embedded within a single theoretical framework. Unlike most other explanations of social behavior, our approach is not restricted to a specific behavioral domain; it is just as applicable to buying behavior as it is to voting or family planning. Thus, the theory we will describe is designed to explain virtually any human behavior, whether we want to understand why a person bought a new car, voted against a school bond issue, was absent from work, or engaged in premarital sexual intercourse.

The first part of this book provides a general description of our theory and discusses the central concepts needed to understand and predict human behavior.

The second part illustrates the applicability and utility of the theory in a variety of behavioral domains.

## A THEORY OF REASONED ACTION

A complete description of our approach to behavioral prediction can be found in our previous book (Fishbein & Ajzen, 1975) which tried to show how the approach can serve to integrate diverse theories and lines of research in the attitude area. Our approach is the result of a research program that began in the late 1950s. While much of the early work was concerned with problems of attitude theory and measurement (Fishbein & Raven, 1962; Fishbein, 1963), work during the last 15 years has dealt with the prediction of behavior in laboratory and applied settings (e.g., Fishbein, 1967a; Ajzen & Fishbein, 1970; Fishbein, 1973; Fishbein & Jaccard, 1973; Ajzen & Fishbein, 1977).

Introduced in 1967 (Fishbein, 1967a), the theory has, over the years, been refined, developed, and tested (see Fishbein & Ajzen, 1975). On the following pages we will provide a preliminary outline of this theory. Generally speaking, the theory is based on the assumption that human beings are usually quite rational and make systematic use of the information available to them. We do not subscribe to the view that human social behavior is controlled by unconscious motives or overpowering desires, nor do we believe that it can be characterized as capricious or thoughtless. Rather, we argue that people consider the implications of their actions before they decide to engage or not engage in a given behavior. For this reason we refer to our approach as "a theory of reasoned action" (Fishbein, in press). The issue of reasoned versus automatic behavior will be taken up again in the concluding chapter, chapter 16, after the reader has had a chance to become familiar with our approach.

Our ultimate goal is to predict and understand an individual's behavior. The first step toward this goal is to identify and measure the behavior of interest. Once the behavior has been clearly defined, it is possible to ask what determines the behavior. As implied above, we make the assumption that most actions of social relevance are under volitional control and, consistent with this assumption, our theory views a person's *intention* to perform (or to not perform) a behavior as the immediate determinant of the action.

In a sense, then, we are suggesting that behaviors are not really difficult to predict. For example, to predict whether an individual will buy a video game, the simplest and probably most efficient approach is to ask him whether he intends to do so. This does not mean that there will always be perfect correspondence between intention and behavior. However, barring unforeseen events, a person will usually act in accordance with his or her intention.

The notion that intentions predict behavior does not provide much information about the reasons for the behavior. It is not very illuminating to discover that people usually do what they intend to do. Since our goal is to *understand* human behavior, not merely predict it, the second step in our analysis requires that we identify the determinants of intentions.

According to the theory of reasoned action, a person's intention is a function of two basic determinants, one personal in nature and the other reflecting social influence. The personal factor is the individual's positive or negative evaluation of performing the behavior; this factor is termed *attitude toward the behavior*. It simply refers to the person's judgment that performing the behavior is good or bad, that he is in favor of or against performing the behavior. People may differ, for example, in their evaluations of buying a video game, some having a favorable attitude and others an unfavorable attitude toward this behavior. The second determinant of intention is the person's perception of the social pressures put on him to perform or not perform the behavior in question. Since it deals with perceived prescriptions, this factor is termed *subjective norm*. To return to the act of buying a video game, we may believe that most people who are important to us think we should buy a video game or that they think we should not do so. Generally speaking, individuals will intend to perform a behavior when they evaluate it positively and when they believe that important others think they should perform it.

So far we have said little that does not conform to common sense, but even at this simple level our analysis raises some interesting questions. Consider the case of two women who hold positive attitudes toward using birth control pills and who perceive social pressures to not use the pill. What will be their intentions in this situation of conflict between attitude toward the behavior and subjective norm? To answer such questions, we need to know the relative importance of the attitudinal and normative factors as determinants of intentions. Our theory assumes that the relative importance of these factors depends in part on the intention under investigation. For some intentions attitudinal considerations may be more important than normative considerations, while for other intentions normative considerations may predominate. Frequently, both factors are important determinants of the intention. In addition, the relative weights of the attitudinal and normative factors may vary from one person to another.

The assignment of the relative weights to the two determinants of intention greatly increases the explanatory value of the theory. Let us return to the above example and imagine that one woman intended to use birth control pills while the other did not intend to do so. Since the two women held identical attitudes and subjective norms, their differing intentions could not be explained in terms of these factors alone. However, the different intentions would follow if the first woman's intention was determined primarily by attitudinal considerations and the second woman's intention was primarily under the control of her subjective norm.

For many practical purposes, this level of explanation may be sufficient. It is possible to predict and gain some understanding of a person's intention by measuring his attitude toward performing the behavior, his subjective norm, and their relative weights. However, for a more complete understanding of intentions it is necessary to explain why people hold certain attitudes and subjective norms. The theory of reasoned action also attempts to answer these questions.

According to the theory, attitudes are a function of beliefs. Generally speaking, a person who believes that performing a given behavior will lead to mostly positive outcomes will hold a favorable attitude toward performing the behavior, while a person who believes that performing the behavior will lead to mostly negative outcomes will hold an unfavorable attitude. The beliefs that underlie a person's attitude toward the behavior are termed *behavioral beliefs*. To illustrate, consider a man who believes that buying a video game would make his children happy, would permit his family to spend time together, and would provide interesting diversion at social gatherings with friends. A person holding such behavioral beliefs is likely to evaluate positively the act of buying a video game. In contrast, an individual is likely to hold an unfavorable attitude toward this behavior if he believes that buying a video game would provide only temporary amusement for his children, would add to the growing number of unused gadgets collecting dust in the attic, would be quite expensive, and would divert funds that could otherwise be invested in educational games.

Subjective norms are also a function of beliefs, but beliefs of a different kind, namely the person's beliefs that specific individuals or groups think he should or should not perform the behavior. These beliefs underlying a person's subjective norm  are termed *normative beliefs*. Generally speaking, a person who believes that most referents with whom he is motivated to comply think he should perform the behavior will perceive social pressure to do so. Conversely, a person who believes that most referents with whom he is motivated to comply think he should not perform the behavior will have a subjective norm that puts pressure on him to avoid performing the behavior. For example, suppose that in the area of buying household products a woman is motivated to comply with what she perceives to be the wishes of her husband, her children, her mother, and her close friends. If she believes that these referents think she should buy a video game, her subjective norm will exert pressure to perform this behavior. On the other hand, a woman who believes that her husband, children, mother, and close friends all think she should not buy a video game will perceive social pressure in the opposite direction. Thus, the subjective norm may exert pressure to perform or to not perform a given behavior, independent of the person's own attitude toward the behavior in question.

Figure 1.1 summarizes our discussion up to this point. The figure shows how behavior can be explained in terms of a limited number of concepts. Through a series of intervening constructs it traces the causes of behavior back to the per-

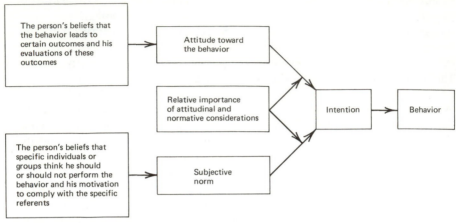

The person's beliefs that the behavior leads to certain outcomes and his evaluations of these outcomes → Attitude toward the behavior

Relative importance of attitudinal and normative considerations

The person's beliefs that specific individuals or groups think he should or should not perform the behavior and his motivation to comply with the specific referents → Subjective norm

Intention → Behavior

*Note*: Arrows indicate the direction of influence.

**FIGURE 1.1**
Factors determining a person's behavior.

son's beliefs. Each successive step in this sequence from behavior to beliefs provides a more comprehensive account of the causes underlying the behavior.

Note that although the theory of reasoned action makes reference to a person's attitude toward the behavior, it does not include such traditional attitudes as attitudes toward objects, people, or institutions. Our emphasis on attitudes toward behaviors, at the expense of attitudes toward objects or targets, questions a fundamental assumption underlying much research on social behavior. As we shall see in chapter 2, it has typically been assumed that a person's behavior toward some target is determined by his attitude toward that target. For example, failure to hire blacks has been attributed to prejudice against blacks. Consequently, it has been argued that blacks would be hired if prejudice could be reduced, that is, if people's attitudes toward blacks could be made more favorable.

According to our theory, the degree to which people like or dislike blacks may have little to do with whether or not they hire blacks. Instead, this behavior is assumed to be determined by the person's attitude toward *hiring* blacks (and by his subjective norm). A person who strongly dislikes blacks may nevertheless believe that hiring blacks will lead to more positive than negative consequences. His attitude toward hiring blacks will be positive, and he may therefore intend to hire blacks and actually do so.

Our analysis of behavior has also made no reference to various factors other than attitudes toward targets that social and behavioral scientists have invoked to explain behavior. Among these factors are personality characteristics, such as authoritarianism, introversion-extraversion, and need for achievement; demographic variables, including, sex, age, social class, and race; and such factors as social role, status, socialization, intelligence, and kinship patterns.

There is plenty of evidence that factors such as attitudes toward targets, personality traits, and demographic characteristics are sometimes related to the behavior of interest. Although we recognize the potential importance of such factors, they do not constitute an integral part of our theory but are instead considered to be *external variables*. From our point of view, external variables may influence the beliefs a person holds or the relative importance he attaches to attitudinal and normative considerations. For example, it would come as no surprise if it were found that an introvert held very different beliefs about attending a party than did an extravert. Further, since the extravert is likely to be more sensitive to social pressures, the subjective norm may be a more important determinant of his intention to attend the party than that of the introvert's intention.

It follows from these considerations that external factors may indeed influence behavior. The important point, however, is that there is no necessary relation between any given external variable and behavior. Some external variables may bear a relation to the behavior under investigation while others may not, and even when a relationship is discovered, it may change over time and from one population to another. Chapter 7 will provide a more detailed discussion of this issue. From our point of view, an external variable will have an effect on behavior only to the extent that it influences the determinants of that behavior shown in Figure 1.1. Whether or not an external variable can be shown to exert such effects on the determinants of behavior has little bearing on the validity of our theory. Although investigation of the effects of external variables can enhance our understanding of a given behavioral phenomenon, our theory deals mainly with the factors that intervene between external variables and behavior. The theory's validity depends not on support for hypotheses concerning the effects of external variables but on empirical support for the relationships specified in Figure 1.1.

One of the major disadvantages of relying on external variables to explain behavior is that different kinds of external variables have to be invoked for different behavioral domains. In fact, we mentioned at the beginning of this chapter that investigators have assumed different causes for different behaviors. Most of the factors they have proposed to explain behavioral phenomena of interest are what we have called external variables. This state of affairs has resulted in a proliferation of theories linking external variables to behavioral phenomena. From our point of view, such a multitude of theories is not only unnecessary, but it actually impedes scientific progress. We believe that the theory of reasoned action already outlined may provide a solution to this problem. It identifies a small set of concepts which are assumed to account for the relations (or lack of relations) between any external variable and any kind of behavior that is under an individual's volitional control.

The main purpose of this book is to show how the theory of reasoned action can be used to predict, explain, and influence human behavior. Since our approach has its roots in research on attitudes and related phenomena, we will begin with a brief historical review of the literature dealing with the relationship between attitude and behavior. Given our practical goal, however, we will neither provide a detailed description of the multitude of theories that have been proposed in the area of attitude formation and change, nor will we be concerned with the similarities and differences that may exist between these theories and our own. By the same token, we will try to avoid philosophical issues concerning the nature and definition of our concepts, and methodological controversies concerning their measurement.[1] Instead, following the historical perspective in chapter 2, we will concentrate on the set of concepts comprising the theory of reasoned action. Part 1 of this book will define these concepts and describe how they can be measured. In chapter 3 we will discuss how to define and measure the behavior of interest, as well as some of the implications that follow from choice of a behavioral criterion. The prediction of behavior from intention will be taken up in chapter 4, with particular emphasis on the question of correspondence between the measure of intention and the measure of behavior. Chapter 5 will describe the two determinants of intentions—attitude toward the behavior and subjective norm—and consider their relative contributions to the formation of a person's intention. In chapter 6 we will turn to an examination of the cognitive structure that underlies attitudes and subjective norms. We will discuss the effects of behavioral beliefs on attitudes toward the behavior and the effects of normative beliefs on subjective norms. The last chapter in part 1, chapter 7, will draw out some of the implications of the theory of reasoned action for attempts to change behavior and for the relation between behavior and such external variables as personality traits and traditional attitudes.

Chapters 3 through 7 are designed to provide a set of concepts and tools that we hope will enable the reader to answer questions about the causes of human actions. We will emphasize the practical aspects of our approach, providing guidelines for the student and practitioner who would like to apply this approach within a behavioral domain of interest. To facilitate the use of our approach, we have, in appendix A, summarized the steps involved in constructing an appropriate questionnaire, and in appendix B we show a questionnaire actually used in one of our investigations.

The utility of our approach, however, can best be demonstrated by discussing the results of actual research in applied settings. Part 2 of this book deals with

[1]Interested readers can find detailed discussions of these issues in Fishbein and Ajzen (1975).

applications of the theory of reasoned action to several socially relevant behaviors. Following a general overview (chapter 8), this part of the book illustrates how the concepts and tools developed in part 1 have been used to explain
and predict weight loss (chapter 9), occupational orientation (chapter 10),
family planning (chapter 11), consumer behavior (chapter 12), and voting behavior (chapters 13 and 14). Chapter 15 deals with behavioral change and shows
how our theory was used to influence the behavior of alcoholics by means of
persuasive communication. The final chapter (chapter 16) briefly discusses the
present status of the theory of reasoned action.

# CHAPTER
# 2

## Attitudes
## and
## Behavior

## A HISTORICAL PERSPECTIVE

The concept of attitude has played a major role throughout the history of social psychology. Many early theorists virtually defined the field of social psychology as the scientific study of attitudes (e.g., Thomas & Znaniecki, 1918; Watson, 1925). One of the first psychologists to employ the term "attitude" was Herbert Spencer (1862), who argued that "Arriving at correct judgments on disputed questions, much depends on the attitude of mind we preserve while listening to, or taking part in, the controversy" (Vol. 1, p. 1). This mentalistic view of attitude was later supplemented by the concept of motor attitude. As early as 1888, Lange showed that a person who was consciously prepared to press a telegraph key immediately upon receiving a signal had a quicker reaction time than did a person who was directed to attend to the incoming stimulus.

This line of research led to the conclusion that various mental and motor sets, attitudes, or states of preparedness influence people's thoughts and actions. By 1901, attitude was defined as "readiness for attention or action of a definite sort" (Baldwin, 1901). The first use of the attitude concept to explain social behavior, however, must be credited to Thomas and Znaniecki (1918) who viewed attitudes as individual mental processes that determine a person's actual and potential responses.

Very early, then, social scientists assumed that attitudes could be used to explain human action since they viewed attitudes as behavioral dispositions. With few exceptions, this assumption went unchallenged until the late 1960s. For example, in their introduction to social psychology, Krech, Crutchfield, and Ballachey (1962) argued that "Man's social actions—whether the actions involve religious behavior, ways of earning a living, political activity, or buying and selling goods—are directed by his attitudes" (p. 139).

## Early Attitude Measurement[1]

With the construct's increasing prominence came the need to develop valid techniques for the measurement of attitudes. While many investigators began constructing various types of instruments to assess attitudes in particular domains, the major breakthrough came when L.L. Thurstone (1929, 1931; Thurstone & Chave, 1929) applied psychometric methods to the problem. He argued that in all measurement we must restrict ourselves to some specified continuum along which the measurement is to take place. When comparing the attitudes of people, we want to be able to say that one person opposes abortion, approves of capital punishment, or likes Italians more (or less) than another person. For Thurstone, then, the crucial continuum in attitude measurement ranged from *positive* to *negative* or *favorable* to *unfavorable*. He thus defined attitude as "the affect for or against a psychological object" (Thurstone, 1931).

The problem of measurement was now reduced to obtaining a score which would identify a person's position on a bipolar affective dimension with respect to the attitude object. Thurstone proposed to accomplish this goal by assessing people's opinions or beliefs, which he considered to be verbal expressions of attitude. For example, a person who expresses the opinion that "there can be no progress without war" would seem to have a more favorable attitude toward war than a person who argues that "it is hard to decide whether wars do more harm than good," and the attitudes of both persons toward war clearly seem to be more positive than the attitude of a person who believes that "war is a futile struggle resulting in self-destruction." Thurstone thus assumed that differing opinion statements express differing degrees of favorableness or unfavorableness toward the attitude object, and he set out to develop techniques that would allow him to specify the location of any opinion statement on the evaluative continuum.

Thurstone developed different methods to assign scale values to opinion statements, but the most widely used is one that results in the "equal-appearing interval scale." The first step involves the collection of a large pool of belief items related to the attitude object under consideration. This pool of items is given to a sample of judges representative of the population whose attitudes are to be assessed. The judges are required to indicate the degree of favorableness or unfavorableness toward the attitude object that is implied by agreement with a given item. Specifically, they sort each item into one of eleven categories that they are to consider to be at equal intervals along the evaluative dimension ranging from *extremely unfavorable* through *neutral* to *extremely favorable*. The median or average value of the categories into which an item has been placed by the different judges is taken as that item's *scale value,* that is, its location on the evaluative dimension.

---

[1]In this chapter we can provide only brief descriptions of attitude measurement techniques. For more detailed discussion of attitude measurement, see Edwards (1957), Green (1954), and Fishbein and Ajzen (1975, chap. 3).

Two criteria are then used to select items for inclusion in the final attitude scale. First, items are eliminated from further consideration if there is large disagreement among the judges concerning the degree of favorableness they express *(criterion of ambiguity)*. Second, items are eliminated if they fail to discriminate among respondents with different attitudes *(criterion of irrelevance)*.[2] The final scale is comprised of approximately 20 items that have met both criteria and whose scale values are more or less equally spaced along the entire evaluative dimension. This scale can now be administered to assess the attitudes of different individuals. Each person is asked to check all items with which he agrees, and his attitude score is obtained by computing the median or mean scale value of the endorsed items. Thus, a person who agreed with three statements whose scale values were 2.5, 3.1, and 3.7, respectively, would have an attitude score of 3.1.

It is important to realize that Thurstone scaling can be used to assess attitudes not only on the basis of the endorsement of belief statements but also on the basis of expressed intentions or actual behavior with respect to the attitude object. Clearly, scale values can be assigned to intentions and actions in the same way that they are assigned to beliefs, and it is thus possible to infer a person's attitude from expressions of belief, statements of intention, observations of behavior, or any combination of these.

The theory underlying Thurstone's scaling method has important implications, which have often been overlooked, for the relation between attitude and behavior. In Thurstone scaling, the attitude score represents a person's evaluation of an object implied by a *set* of his beliefs, intentions, or actions. The implications are clearly stated by Thurstone (1931):

> It is quite conceivable that two men may have the same degree or intensity of affect favorable toward a psychological object and that their attitudes would be described in this sense as identical but that they arrived at their similar attitudes by entirely different routes. It is even possible that their factual associations about the psychological object might be entirely different and that their overt actions would take quite different forms which have one thing in common, namely, that they are about equally favorable toward the object (p. 263).

Thus, as early as 1931, Thurstone made it clear that although a person's attitude toward an object should be related to the pattern of his behavior with respect to the object, there is no necessary relation between attitude and any given behavior.

The development of Thurstone's scaling methods resulted in their widespread use in the assessment of attitudes. The amount of work involved in constructing

---

[2]Although essential to the construction of a valid Thurstone scale, the criterion of irrelevance is seldom applied. To test items on this criterion, a second sample of respondents indicate their own agreement or disagreement with items that have met the criterion of ambiguity. An item passes the criterion of irrelevance if it is most likely to be endorsed by respondents whose attitudes are located at the same position on the attitude dimension as the item itself.

a Thurstone scale, however, led investigators to look for simpler procedures. In 1932, Rensis Likert proposed the method of summated ratings which was widely adopted, since it greatly simplified matters by dispensing with the use of judges. After again collecting a large pool of opinion items, the investigator decides whether agreement with each item implies a favorable or unfavorable attitude toward the object in question. Neutral or ambiguous items are immediately eliminated. The remaining items are administered directly to a sample of subjects representative of the target population. Typically, subjects are asked to respond to each item in terms of a five-point scale, defined by the labels *agree strongly, agree, undecided, disagree,* and *disagree strongly.*

A preliminary estimate of each respondent's attitude is obtained as follows: First, responses to each item are scored from 1 to 5. Strong agreements with favorable items are given a score of 5, and strong disagreements with these items are given a score of 1. Scoring is reversed for unfavorable items, so that disagreement with an unfavorable item results in a high score. The person's preliminary attitude score is obtained by summing across all his item scores. For a set of 100 items, these attitude scores could range from 100 to 500; the higher the score, the more favorable the attitude.

To be retained in the final attitude scale, an item must meet the *criterion of internal consistency,* that is, it must discriminate between people with positive and negative attitudes.[3] The 20 or so most discriminating items, usually 10 favorable and 10 unfavorable, constitute the Likert scale. This scale can now be given to a new sample of subjects whose attitude scores are computed in the manner described earlier with reference to the preliminary attitude score.

Like Thurstone scaling, the Likert scaling procedure thus results in a single score that represents the degree to which a person is favorable or unfavorable with respect to the attitude object. Further, a given attitude score can again reflect different patterns of beliefs, intentions, or actions.

## Early Attitude Research

As these standard scaling procedures became available, attitude surveys began to proliferate. Much of this early attitude research was descriptive in nature, comparing the attitudes of different segments of the population. For example, men were found to oppose prohibition more than women and Jewish students were found to be more in favor of birth control and communism than were Protestant or Catholic students (for a review, see Bird, 1940, ch. 6).

There were, however, those who questioned the use of unidimensional, evaluative scales for the measurement of attitudes. In the first comprehensive review of the attitude area, Gordon W. Allport (1935) surveyed the multitude of definitions that had been proposed by other theorists and suggested a definition of his

---

[3]In practice, an item is said to meet the criterion of internal consistency if the item score correlates significantly with the preliminary attitude score.

own which would be "sufficiently broad to cover the many kinds of attitudinal determination which psychologists today recognize." According to Allport, "An attitude is a mental and neural state of readiness, organized through experience, exerting a directive or dynamic influence upon the individual's response to all objects and situations with which it is related."

Conceding that most definitions of attitude regard readiness for response as their essential feature, and that they provoke behavior which is favorable or unfavorable toward the attitude object, Allport nevertheless argued that the evaluative dimension alone could not capture the complexity of the attitude concept. He reasoned that

> Two radicals may be equally in favor of change, but disagree in the *modus operandi* of reform. Two people equally well disposed toward the church may differ in their sacramental, liturgical, esthetic, social, Protestant, or Catholic interpretation of the church. Is the degree of positive or negative affect aroused by the concept of "God" as significant as the *qualitative* distinctions involved in theistic, deistic, pantheistic, agnostic, intellectualistic, or emotional attitudes? When one speaks of attitudes toward sex, it is obviously only the qualitative distinctions that have any intelligible meaning. . . . All of these objections to the unidimensional view argue strongly for the recognition of the *qualitative* nature of attitudes. (Allport, 1935, p. 820).

Allport's arguments concerning the complexity of attitudes were perhaps the first sign of what was later to become the predominant view of attitudes, namely, that attitudes are comprised not only of affect but also of cognition and conation. This multicomponent view of attitude will be discussed below.

Relation Between Attitude and Behavior

Despite the concern expressed by Allport, early research seemed to confirm the validity of unidimensional attitude scales by showing that people who behave in different ways also differ predictably in their attitudes. Thus, investigators found that union members have more favorable attitudes toward labor unions than does management, that pacifists have more negative attitudes toward war than do nonpacifists, and that northerners are more favorable toward blacks than are southerners. However, the "behavioral" criterion in these studies can best be viewed as a behavioral syndrome rather than as a specific behavior toward the stimulus object. The finding that groups known to differ in their behaviors also differ in their measured attitudes nevertheless was taken as evidence confirming the assumption of a close link between attitude and behavior. Given this assumption, most investigators turned their attention to studies of attitude formation, organization, and change.

From time to time, however, investigators tried to test the assumption that attitudes serve as behavioral predispositions. The first and best-known study is

Richard LaPiere's (1934) investigation of racial prejudice. In the early 1930s, LaPiere accompanied a young Chinese couple in their travels through the United States. Calling upon 251 restaurants, hotels, and other establishments, they were refused service only once. About 6 months later, LaPiere sent a letter to each establishment visited, asking the same question: "Will you accept members of the Chinese race as guests in your establishment?" Of the 128 establishments that replied, over 90% answered "No."

These findings, for the first time, raised serious doubts about the assumption of a strong relation between attitude and behavior. Negative results were soon reported by other investigators. For example, Corey (1937) used a Likert scale to measure students' attitudes toward cheating and attempted to predict actual cheating on a given set of tests. Over a period of five weeks, Corey's students took five true-false examinations. Each week's test papers were returned unmarked after the students' scores had been recorded. The students then graded their own papers during the following class session. The difference between the true score and the score each student reported for himself, summed over the five tests, constituted the primary behavioral criterion. This measure of cheating behavior was found to be completely unrelated to the students' attitudes toward cheating.

As those negative results began to accumulate, it became necessary to consider possible explanations for the failure of attitudes to predict behavior. The first explanation was offered by Doob (1947) who, relying on behavior theory, defined attitude as an implicit mediating response to a stimulus object. Just as a person must learn the mediating response (i.e., attitude) in the presence of the stimulus object, he must also learn to make a specific overt response to the attitude. Thus, Doob saw no innate relationship between attitude toward an object and any given behavior with respect to that object. Two people may learn to hold the same attitude toward a given stimulus, but they may also learn to emit different responses, given the same learned attitude. Although the attitude may initially predispose them to behave in the same ways (positively or negatively), the behaviors they ultimately come to exhibit will depend on the nature of the reinforcements they receive.

Note the similarity between Doob's position and Thurstone's view described earlier. Both theorists argued that the same attitude can be expressed in different actions. While knowledge of a person's attitude can tell us little as to whether she will perform some particular behavior, it can tell us something about her overall pattern of behavior.

**Multicomponent view of attitude.** Most investigators, however, were unwilling to give up the assumption that there is a direct link between attitude toward an object and any given action with respect to that object. Instead, they considered alternative explanations for the failure of attitudes to predict behavior. One such explanation seemed to follow naturally from the concern, first expressed by

Allport (1935), that unidimensional affective or evaluative measures did not do justice to the complexity of the attitude concept. Despite the fact that most attitude measurement was unidimentional, the prevailing conceptions of attitude were much more elaborate. For example, in their influential textbook, Krech and Crutchfield (1948) defined attitudes as "an enduring organization of motivational, emotional, perceptual, and cognitive processes with respect to some aspect of the individual's world." This multifaceted description of attitude was further developed in the writings of such theorists as Cartwright (1949), Smith (1947), and Katz and Stotland (1959) who conceptualized attitudes in the framework of the age-old trilogy of cognition, affect, and conation.

By the late 1950s, this multicomponent view of attitude was adopted almost universally and attitudes were viewed as complex systems comprising the person's beliefs about the object, his feelings toward the object, and his action tendencies with respect to the object. Given this inclusive view of attitude as encompassing all the person's experiences with respect to the object, it would be difficult to assume anything other than a strong relationship between attitude and behavior. At the same time, however, this multicomponent view of attitude was used to explain the low empirical relations between measures of attitude and overt behavior.

Figure 2.1 shows Rosenberg and Hovland's (1960) schematic representation of the three-component view of attitude. Note that all responses to a stimulus

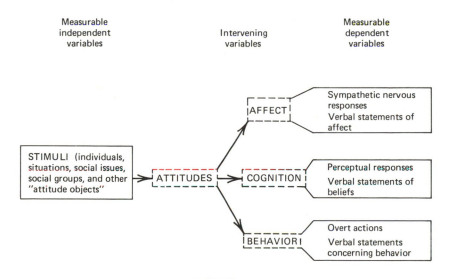

**FIGURE 2.1**
Three-component view of attitude.
(From Rosenberg & others, Attitude Organization and Change.
New Haven: Yale University Press. © 1960 Yale University Press, Inc.)

object are mediated by the person's attitude toward that object. The different responses, however, are classified into three categories: cognitive (perceptual responses and verbal statements of belief), affective (sympathetic nervous responses and verbal statements of affect), and behavioral or conative (overt actions and verbal statements concerning behavior). Corresponding to each of these response classes is one component of attitude.

Figure 2.1 also implies that a complete description of attitude requires that all three components be assessed by obtaining measures of all three response classes. It follows that measures of attitude based on only one or two response classes are incomplete and that use of such incomplete measures to predict overt behavior does not represent a fair test of the relation between attitude and behavior. The repeated finding of a low relation between attitude and behavior was explained by arguing that most measures of attitude merely assess the affective component. It was not made clear, however, whether the prediction of behavior required assessment of all three components or whether it would be sufficient to obtain an index of the conative or behavioral component.

**Additional attitude measurement techniques.** Although they criticized attempts to predict behavior from attitude scales which they viewed as tapping only the affective component, investigators did little to develop independent measures of the cognitive and conative components, or to use whatever measures were available in an effort to improve behavioral prediction. Indeed, it is interesting to note that the major contributions to attitude measurement during the 1940s and 1950s were the development of two new scaling techniques which, like the Thurstone and Likert scales, result in a single score representing a person's evaluation of the attitude object. Louis Guttman's (1944) scalogram analysis was designed to test whether a set of beliefs or intentions can be ordered along a single (evaluative) dimension. The items are said to form a Guttman scale if they can be ordered so that respondents who endorse an item in one position on the scale (e.g., an item put in the fourth position) also endorse all items that are lower in order (i.e., items in positions 1, 2, and 3). When this condition is met, the result is a set of items that form a unidimensional cumulative scale, and the respondent's attitude is indexed by the most extreme item he is willing to endorse.

By far the most important new contribution to attitude measurement, however, was the development of the semantic differential by Charles Osgood and his associates (Osgood, Suci, & Tannenbaum, 1957). Designed originally to measure the meaning of a concept, Osgood, et al. recognized that the semantic differential could be used to measure attitudes. In this context, the semantic differential consists of a set of bipolar evaluative adjective scales, such as *good-bad, harmful-beneficial, pleasant-unpleasant, positive-negative.*[4] Typically, the adjectives in a

[4]As with other scaling techniques, items have to be selected to meet certain criteria. Osgood, Suci, and Tannenbaum used a sophisticated technique known as factor analysis to identify evaluative adjective scales. This technique ensures that, as in Likert scaling, each item selected discriminates between people with positive and negative attitudes.

given pair are placed on opposite ends of seven-place graphic scales, and respondents are asked to evaluate the attitude object by rating it on each scale. Thus, attitude toward war might be assessed by means of the following evaluative semantic differential.

War

harmful ____ : ____ : ____ : ____ : ____ : ____ : ____ beneficial

good ____ : ____ : ____ : ____ : ____ : ____ : ____ bad

pleasant ____ : ____ : ____ : ____ : ____ : ____ : ____ unpleasant

awful ____ : ____ : ____ : ____ : ____ : ____ : ____ nice

Responses are scored from $-3$ on the negative side of each scale (e.g., *harmful, bad*) to $+3$ on the positive side (e.g., *pleasant, nice*), and the sum across all scales is a measure of the respondent's attitude toward war.

Clearly, despite the important contributions of these techniques to attitude measurement, neither the Guttman scale nor Osgood's semantic differential goes beyond the assessment of evaluation or affect. Indeed, as late as 1967, Triandis pointed out that "there is a gap between those who are primarily concerned with the *measurement* of attitudes and those who have written *theoretically* about attitudes. The former frequently rest their case after providing us with a single score, whereas the latter make a large number of theoretical distinctions but do not provide us with precise and standard procedures for measurement" (Triandis, 1967, p. 228).

On closer examination, we see that the multicomponent view of attitude cannot provide an adequate explanation of the low attitude-behavior relation. We noted earlier that Thurstone and Likert scales rely on beliefs or intentions (i.e., cognition or conation) to infer a person's attitude. This implies that in providing a measure of affect the standard scaling procedures already take into account cognitions, conations, or both. Whether our measures are based on statements concerning beliefs, feelings, intentions, or behaviors, the results will be much the same. It follows that separate assessment of all three components is unlikely to lead to improved behavioral prediction.

A cursory review of the literature will confirm these arguments. If nothing else, however, the multicomponent view of attitude generated a considerable body of research dealing with the relationships among cognition, affect, and conation, Rosenberg (1956), for example, showed that a person's evaluation of an object is strongly related to his expectations or beliefs that the object furthers or hinders the attainment of valued goals. He proposed an expectancy-value model of attitude to describe the relationship between affect and cognition. A similar model, developed by Fishbein (1963), will be discussed in a subsequent chapter. The point to be made is that this line of research confirmed Thurstone's (1931) claim that a person's evaluation of an object, although not necessarily related to any given belief, is strongly related to the total set or pattern of his beliefs about the object.

Parallel findings were reported with respect to the relation between affect and conation. Systematic research on the conative component was stimulated by the pioneering work of Harry Triandis (1964). After developing a measuring instrument known as the behavioral differential, Triandis identified several dimensions or types of interpersonal intentions (e.g., intentions to interact with superiors or subordinates, to show admiration, to give friendship) and explored their relations to a measure of affect. He found that some types of intention (e.g., to admire or respect) were highly related to affect, while for others (e.g., intention to subordinate or marry) the relation was lower. However, later research (Fishbein, 1964) showed that when the entire set of intentions is taken into consideration, a strong relation between affect and conation is obtained.

Additional evidence that global measures of cognition, affect, and conation are highly interrelated can be found in the work of D.T. Campbell (1947), Bettelheim and Janowitz (1950) and Ostrom (1969). More important, Ostrom's study also showed that separate assessment of cognition, affect, and conation with respect to the church did not improve the prediction of various religious behaviors.

**Consistency theories.** Interest in the relationships among beliefs, feelings, and behavioral tendencies led to the development of various theories of attitude organization and change. Known collectively as "consistency theories," they assume that individuals strive toward consistency among their beliefs, attitudes, and behaviors.[5] Most of these theories grew out of Fritz Heider's (1944, 1958) work on social perception and causal attribution, but the theory that attracted most attention was Leon Festinger's (1957) theory of cognitive dissonance. According to this theory, inconsistency between two cognitive elements—whether they represent beliefs, attitudes, or behavior—gives rise to dissonance. Assumed to be unpleasant, the presence of dissonance is said to motivate the individual to change one or more cognitive elements in an attempt to eliminate the unpleasant state. For example, if a person's behavior is inconsistent with his attitude he should try to reduce his dissonance by changing either his attitude or his behavior.

Most of the research designed to test dissonance theory has investigated the effects of inducing a person to behave in a way that is inconsistent with his beliefs or attitudes. While studies of this kind showed that people tend to bring their beliefs and attitudes into line with their actions, they provided no information about the extent to which attitudes influence behavior. In fact, in his presi-

[5]For reviews of these theories, see Kiesler, Collins, and Miller (1969); Abelson et al. (1968); Fishbein and Ajzen (1975, chap 2).

dential address to the social psychology division of the American Psychological Association, Festinger (1964) noted that he could find only three studies dealing with the effect of attitude change on behavior. None of these studies supported the expectation that a change in attitude would be followed by a change in behavior.

In short, although consistency theories have contributed to our understanding of attitude organization and change, they have done little to explain the observed inconsistencies between attitude and behavior.

**Pseudo-inconsistency.** In 1963, Donald Campbell analyzed the nature of attitudes and other behavioral dispositions. Like Thurstone (1931) and Doob (1947) before him, Campbell recognized that attitudes should be related to global patterns of behavior with respect to an object but not necessarily to any given action. Unfortunately, Campbell's analysis has often been misinterpreted to imply that low empirical relations between attitude and behavior do not represent true inconsistencies. It is therefore instructive to consider Campbell's position in greater detail.

A fundamental assumption of Campbell's analysis was that verbal expressions of attitude, and overt behavior with respect to the attitude object, are both manifestations of the same underlying disposition. He made it very clear, however, that verbal statements and overt actions could be inconsistent with each other yet at the same time serve as valid indicants of, and hence be entirely consistent with, an underlying attitude.

Consider, for example, the LaPiere (1934) study mentioned earlier, in which restaurant and hotel managers were found to accept a Chinese couple in a face-to-face confrontation but in reply to a letter stated that they would not accept Orientals in their establishments. Despite the inconsistency between the managers' words and deeds, Campbell argued that when taken together, these two responses were entirely consistent with a moderately unfavorable attitude toward Orientals.

Refusing to accept an Oriental couple in a face-to-face situation is obviously more difficult and would express a more negative attitude than saying, in response to a letter, that one would not accept Orientals. According to Campbell, verbal responses and overt actions can be viewed as items on an attitude scale and, as in Guttman scaling, they can be ordered along an evaluative dimension. True inconsistency occurs only when responses to the items fail to exhibit a cumulative pattern, that is, when respondents who are willing to perform a relatively difficult act expressing a favorable (or unfavorable) attitude are unwilling to perform less difficult acts expressing the same attitude.

It can thus be seen that there was nothing inconsistent in the *pattern* of responses exhibited by the hotel and restaurant managers: They rejected Orientals verbally (an easy expression of prejudice) but not in the more difficult face-to-face situation. Inconsistency between attitudes and the pattern of overt behavior would be indicated only if some of the managers had exhibited the reverse pattern, that is, if in response to the letter some had said they would accept Orientals but had refused service in the face-to-face situation.

Campbell thus concluded that in many studies, the reported failure of attitudes to predict behavior represented "pseudo-inconsistencies" that have little bearing on the attitude-behavior relation. The negative findings reflect inconsistencies among different indicants or expressions of an underlying attitude but not the absence of a relation between the underlying attitude and the *pattern* of a person's behavior.

Contrary to Campbell's intent, many investigators interpreted this analysis to mean that there are no "real" inconsistencies between words and deeds and that, therefore, attitudes are related to specific actions. This misunderstanding is particularly surprising in light of Campbell's argument that, just as we have to use many expressions of opinion to infer an underlying disposition, such as attitude, we must observe many different behaviors in order to see the disposition reflected in overt action. "The unreliability and invalidity of overt behavior measures should . . . be remembered . . ., and in no case should a single overt behavior be regarded as the criterion of a disposition" (Campbell, 1963, p. 162). It is difficult to see how Campbell's analysis can be viewed as supporting the conclusion that attitudes are related to specific behaviors. Although they should be related to patterns of behavior, attitudes cannot be expected to predict single actions.

## RECENT DEVELOPMENTS

Our historical review of the controversy surrounding the relationship between attitude and behavior may make it appear that this issue was in the forefront of attitude research throughout the years. Actually, the problem received relatively little attention. Most investigators simply worked on the assumption that attitudes explain and predict behavior and devoted much of their effort to descriptive attitude surveys or to controlled experiments dealing with attitude formation and change; investigations directed at the attitude-behavior relation were few and far between. Nevertheless, these isolated studies proved to be rather embarrassing since they reported little evidence that attitudes could predict behavior. With the accumulation of negative results came a growing concern for the validity of the attitude concept. Some theorists (e.g., DeFleur & Westie, 1963; Deutscher, 1966) questioned the need for a construct that refers to a behavioral disposition. Instead, they proposed to view verbal and overt behavior as different response systems and the relationship between them as an empirical question.

These concerns were reinforced by Wicker's (1969) influential review of the relevant literature. Although Wicker was able to identify fewer than 50 studies in which "at least one attitudinal measure and one overt behavioral measure toward the same object [were] obtained for each subject," they collectively led to a clear conclusion. In Wicker's words, "It is considerably more likely that attitudes will be unrelated or only slightly related to overt behaviors than that attitudes will be closely related to actions" (p. 65).

Other Variables Explanation

By the early 1970s the low empirical relation between attitude and behavior could no longer be neglected. Some investigators (e.g., Abelson, 1972) simply concluded that attitudes cannot predict behavior. Others, taking a more moderate position, have suggested that certain behaviors are so dependent on the situational context as to be virtually unpredictable from measures of attitude (see Schuman & Johnson, 1976). For the most part, however, attitudes continued to be regarded as primary determinants of a person's responses to an object. At the same time, there was a growing recognition among investigators that there is no one-to-one correspondence between attitude and any given behavior. The most popular view to emerge was that

> ...attitudes always produce pressure to behave consistently with them, but external pressures and extraneous considerations can cause people to behave inconsistently with their attitudes. Any attitude or change in attitude tends to produce behavior that corresponds with it. However, this correspondence often does not appear because of other factors that are involved in the situation. (Freedman, Carlsmith, & Sears, 1970, pp. 385-386)

Reliance on other factors to explain observed attitude-behavior inconsistencies is commonly known as the "other variables" approach. According to this view attitude is only one of a number of factors that influence behavior, and other variables must also be taken into account. Among the variables suggested are conflicting attitudes; competing motives; verbal, intellectual, and social abilities; individual differences, such as personality characteristics; normative prescriptions of proper behavior; alternative behaviors available; and expected or actual consequences of the behavior (see Ehrlich, 1969; Wicker, 1969 for discussions). However, we have no systematic way of deciding which of the many "other variables" might be relevant for a given behavior. In fact, as Wicker (1969) has pointed out, "Often these factors are mentioned in discussion sections by investigators who failed to demonstrate attitude-behavior consistency.... The arguments for the significance of each factor are often plausible anecdotes and *post-hoc* explanations" (Wicker, 1969, p. 67). Perhaps more important, the addition of other variables—even if found to improve prediction of behavior—does little to advance our understanding of the attitude-behavior relation itself (cf., Schuman & Johnson, 1976).

A different and more interesting interpretation of the other variables approach is that the relation between attitude and behavior is *moderated* by other variables. For example, Fazio and his associates (Fazio & Zanna, 1978; Regan & Fazio, 1977) have reported attitude-behavior relations of moderate magnitude when respondents were given direct experience with the attitude object or with the behavior. In the absence of such direct experience, the relation between attitude and behavior was found to be relatively weak. Other moderating variables that have been suggested include actual or considered presence of others, possession of skills required to perform the behavior, internal consistency of the attitude, confidence with which the attitude is held, and occurance of unforeseen extraneous events. Although not all of these factors have been found to moderate the attitude-behavior relation in a systematic fashion, they have often been invoked in attempts to explain why attitudes are found to predict behavior in some situations but not in others. The significance of moderating variables and their place in the theory of reasoned action will be considered in our discussion of the stability of intentions (see chapter 4).

## CONCLUSION

Social scientists have in recent years shown a growing interest in the relationship between attitudes and action (e.g., Brannon, 1976; Calder & Ross, 1973; Liska, 1975; Schneider, 1976; Schuman & Johnson, 1976). The attitude-behavior problem has ramifications far beyond its practical implications in that it has led to re-examinations of our definition and measurement of attitudes. Although it is possible to discern, in the last few years, a trend to return to the unidimensional definition of attitude as evaluation or affect with respect to a psychological object (see, for example, Schneider, 1976; Schuman & Johnson, 1976), there is still widespread consensus that, in addition to affect, attitudes also contain cognitive and conative components. In fact, most investigations concerned with attitude formation and change make no distinctions among beliefs, feelings, and intentions; virtually all verbal responses—and sometimes even overt actions—are considered to be indicants of a person's "attitude," and measures of these variables are often used interchangeably.

This view of attitudes is accompanied by general agreement that attitude, no matter how assessed, is only one of the many factors that influence behavior. It follows that in order to predict behavior accurately we have to take additional variables into account, either as independent contributors to behavior or as moderators of the attitude-behavior relationship. While re-affirming the importance of attitudes, this position also accommodates the findings of low or inconsistent empirical relations between attitude and behavior.

In this book we present ideas and data that are clearly at variance with this view of the attitude construct. We restrict the term "attitude" to a person's evaluation of any psychological object and we draw a clear distinction between beliefs, attitudes, intentions, and behaviors. In the following chapters we discuss each of these concepts and describe the relations among them, as postulated by our theory of reasoned action. In contrast to the currently accepted view that there is no close link between attitude and behavior, our approach suggests that appropriate measures of attitude are strongly related to action. Like Thurstone, Doob, and Campbell we take the position that attitudes toward an object can predict only the overall pattern of behavior; they are of little value if we are interested in predicting and understanding some particular action with respect to the object. To predict a single behavior we have to assess the person's attitude toward the behavior and not his attitude toward the target at which the behavior is directed. In other words, according to our approach any behavioral criterion can be predicted from attitude—be it a single action or a pattern of behavior—provided that the measure of attitude corresponds to the measure of behavior. A recent review of the attitude-behavior literature (Ajzen & Fishbein, 1977) supports this position.

The attitude-behavior problem has led not only to a re-examination of the attitude concept but also to a growing recognition that, in marked contrast to the amount of effort invested in the development of reliable and valid attitude measures, very little attention has been paid to the assessment of behavior (see Fishbein, 1967a, 1973; Fishbein & Ajzen, 1974; Schuman & Johnson, 1976). Clearly, adequate conceptualization and measurement of behavior is essential for an understanding of the attitude-behavior relation. Accordingly, we begin our discussion of the theory of reasoned action in chapter 3 by reviewing the nature and measurement of behavioral criteria.

# CHAPTER
# 3

## How to Define
## and
## Measure Behavior

Social scientists are called upon to answer many different kinds of questions. As a small sample consider the following concerns: Why do people smoke? How can we increase sales of a product? How can we get people to contribute money to a campaign fund or charity? Why did people vote for Nixon rather than for McGovern? What can we do to reduce population growth? How can we increase the productivity of employees or reduce absenteeism?

Each of these questions focuses on a different type of behavior, and to find answers we must identify an appropriate behavioral criterion. At first glance it may appear easy to define and measure the behavior of interest. Indeed, most investigators have devoted little thought to this issue; behavior is typically viewed as a given factor that requires no further elaboration. On closer examination, however, we find that defining and measuring behavior is not as simple as it first appears.

## BEHAVIORS VERSUS OUTCOMES

People sometimes fail to distinguish between behaviors and occurrences that may be the outcomes of those behaviors. For example, success on exams and weight reduction have been used to measure behavior. In point of fact, neither of these criteria is a measure of behavior. Success on exams is a possible outcome of such specific actions as attending lectures, reading books, memorizing materials, or even copying answers from another person's test paper. Similarly, losing weight may be the result of such actions as eating low calorie foods, skipping meals, or jogging two miles a day.

More important, outcomes such as passing an exam or losing weight may also be influenced by factors other than the person's own behavior. The exam's difficulty level or a clerical error may determine success or failure on the exam, and loss of weight may sometimes be due to physiological factors like metabolic rate or to prolonged illness rather than to any particular actions performed by the in-

29

dividual. It follows that in order to understand how outcomes are produced, we may have to study not only the effects of the person's actions but also the effects of extraneous factors that influence occurrence of the outcomes in question.

Good examples of this problem can be found in industrial settings where management is concerned with understanding and predicting productivity and sales. Since we are dealing here with outcomes rather than behaviors, it is necessary to consider factors other than the behaviors of employees (to predict productivity) or consumers (to predict sales). These other factors may include such things as technology, availability of resources, efficiency of subcontractors, effective distribution, and availability of the product.

The first step in defining a criterion, then, is to decide whether we are dealing with a behavior or with an outcome. If we are interested in an outcome, the situation is a bit more complicated than in the case of a behavior. Many different behaviors can lead to the same outcome, and we may actually be more interested in one or more of these behaviors than in the outcome itself. Whenever the outcome itself is of interest, actions leading to the outcome have to be identified. Bear in mind, however, that factors other than these actions may also have to be considered. Although outcomes are legitimate topics of investigation, the main concern of this book is with behavior. To the extent that a person's behavior controls certain outcomes, our approach is also relevant for the prediction and understanding of those outcomes.

## SINGLE ACTIONS VERSUS BEHAVIORAL CATEGORIES

Another problem is that people often treat inferences from behaviors as if they were themselves behaviors. Note that in our preceding discussion of success on an exam and weight reduction we could have referred to studying, cheating, dieting, and exercising instead of listing specific actions. These general terms represent inferences from one or more specific behaviors. If we observe that a person is skipping meals we may infer that he or she is dieting. Inferences about such things as dieting or studying thus involve general classes or categories of behavior. The distinction between specific behaviors and general categories of behaviors has frequently been overlooked. Obviously, it is impossible to observe behavioral categories directly, although it is possible to observe specific actions that are assumed to be instances of the general class. For example, we cannot observe "aggression," but we can observe specific actions that have been defined as aggressive or not aggressive. The same is true for "studying;" we can only observe such specific behaviors as reading books and taking notes. The assumption is that these specific actions are instances of studying.

## Single Actions

A single act is a specific behavior performed by an individual. To be able to measure a single action, we have to define it clearly enough so that we can determine whether or not it has been performed. The apparent simplicity of this requirement is deceptive. Although there would probably be little disagreement among observers asked to record whether or not a given individual attended church, they might disagree if they were asked to judge whether the individual listened to the sermon. Similarly, observers would have little difficulty deciding whether a person bought a package of Kent cigarettes, but they might encounter problems in judging whether he or she read the health warning on the package.

The problem, then, is to define the action in such a way that there is high agreement among observers concerning its occurrence. To assess the extent of agreement among observers, an index of *inter-judge reliability* can be computed. Before deciding to use a specific action as a behavioral criterion, it is necessary to demonstrate that the action in question has high inter-judge reliability.

## Behavioral Categories

Behavioral categories involve sets of actions rather than a single action. They can refer to a relatively narrow range of behaviors, such as raising funds for a political candidate, dieting, and exercizing, or to a broader range, such as assistance in a candidate's campaign, health maintenance, and recreational activity. Perhaps the broadest range of behaviors is considered when you are interested in all positive or negative behaviors with respect to some object or person.

As noted above, behavioral categories cannot be directly observed. Instead they are inferred from single actions assumed to be instances of the general behavioral category. For example, dieting must be inferred from such behaviors as eating, drinking, or taking diet pills. Similarly, raising funds for a political candidate is inferred from such single actions as making face-to-face requests for contributions, asking for contributions on the telephone, sending out invitations to a fund-raising dinner, placing a political advertisement in a newspaper, or writing a fund-raising letter. The first step in constructing a general behavioral criterion, then, involves selecting a set of single actions deemed relevant to the category in question. Needless to say, it must be shown that each action can be observed with high inter-judge reliability.

Since a general behavioral category is comprised of many different single actions, observation of any one act will rarely provide an adequate measure of the category in question. In fact, when measuring only one or two single actions, it is probably more appropriate to refer to each of the acts than to a general behavioral category. Not only are one or two single actions too small a sample to represent the general category, the particular action or actions selected may not be valid indicants of the intended category. In fact, this problem is encountered irrespective of the number of single actions under consideration. It is not clear, for example, whether drinking coffee without sugar is a valid indication of diet-ing—the behavioral category which it is assumed to represent. Many individuals may drink their coffee without sugar simply because they like it that way, not because they are on a diet. Eating or not eating low calorie foods may appear to be a more adequate measure of "dieting." On closer examination, however, it becomes obvious that this action may also be insufficient evidence for the general class. A person who eats low calorie foods may be found to snack between meals and drink large quantities of beer; a person who does *not* eat low calorie foods may avoid snacks between meals and eat only two meals a day. It follows that dieting could not be inferred only from the consumption of low calorie food. To obtain an adequate measure of a behavioral category, such as dieting, it is neces-sary to observe a set of single actions and in some way combine these observa-tions to arrive at a general measure.

Computation of a simple index can be illustrated with respect to dieting. Table 3.1 shows 10 single actions that were selected as indicants of this behav-ioral category. The first step is to decide for each action whether a person who performs it is (+1) or is not (−1) on a dietary program.[1] These values appear in front of each action in Table 3.1. The respondent's performance (+1) or nonper-formance (−1) of each action is then recorded. Hypothetical performance data for two respondents are shown in Table 3.1. For example, it can be seen that Respondent A snacks between meals and does *not* drink coffee without sugar while Respondent B does drink coffee without sugar but does *not* snack between meals.

For each action, a score is computed by multiplying the action's value by the respondent's performance. The resulting score takes on a value of +1 whenever the respondent's behavior indicates that he is on a diet and a score of −1 when it indicates that he is not on a diet (see Table 3.1). For example, since Respondent A snacks between meals, his score for this action is a −1. In contrast, Respon-dent B does not snack between meals and he therefore receives a score of +1 for this act. The general index of dieting is computed by summing the scores for the set of single actions. It can be seen in Table 3.1 that Respondent A has a lower dieting index (−6) than Respondent B (+2). Clearly, the higher a person's score on the dieting index, the more dieting behavior that person displays.

---

[1]Obviously, an action for which it is impossible to make this decision cannot serve as an indicant of the behavioral category (dieting) and it should be eliminated. Note also that we could make other judgments about the implications of performing each of the specific ac-tions. For example, we could judge whether performance of a given action indicates a favor-able or unfavorable attitude toward a target such as "weight reduction" or "high calorie foods." When such judgments are made, the resulting index is not a measure of the be-havioral category of dieting but is instead a behavioral measure of attitude toward the target in question. This issue will be discussed in greater detail in chapter 7.

TABLE 3.1
Computation of an Index for Dieting Behavior

| VALUE | SINGLE ACTIONS | RESPONDENT A | | RESPONDENT B | |
|---|---|---|---|---|---|
| | | *Performance* | *Score* | *Performance* | *Score* |
| −1 | Snack between meals | +1 | −1 | −1 | +1 |
| −1 | Eat ice cream | +1 | −1 | −1 | +1 |
| +1 | Drink coffee without sugar | −1 | −1 | +1 | +1 |
| +1 | Drink low calorie beverages | −1 | −1 | −1 | −1 |
| +1 | Eat only two meals a day | +1 | +1 | −1 | −1 |
| −1 | Eat starchy food | +1 | −1 | −1 | +1 |
| −1 | Eat dessert with dinner | +1 | −1 | −1 | +1 |
| −1 | Drink beer | +1 | −1 | +1 | −1 |
| +1 | Take diet pills | −1 | −1 | −1 | −1 |
| −1 | Eat bread | −1 | +1 | −1 | +1 |
| | | Dieting index: | −6 | | +2 |

These considerations suggest a difference between single actions and behavioral categories that is worth noting. Whereas it is reasonable to ask whether a person does or does not eat bread, it may not be very meaningful to ask this question with respect to being on a diet. As we have seen, people vary in terms of the degree to which they diet, and classifying an individual as being on a diet or not is an arbitrary decision. For example, it would be possible to decide that a person is on a diet if he performs at least one dieting behavior, (i.e., if he has any score other than −10). Alternatively he could be classified as a "dieter" if his score is greater than zero, or if his score is at least +4. Because of this problem it is preferable not to categorize respondents, but to use the score provided by the index as a quantitative measure of the behavioral category.

Note that among the set of single actions comprising the index, there may be some that are really not very good indicants of the general behavioral category. For example, we mentioned earlier that drinking coffee without sugar may provide little information about dieting. Formal procedures are available to identify and eliminate such inappropriate observations.[2] However, if one selects a relatively large number of acts (perhaps 10 or more) that appear to be relevant for the general behavioral category, an index based on the total set of these behaviors will usually provide an adequate measure of the general action under consideration.[3]

[2]The formal selection procedures are adaptations of the standard attitude scaling methods (Likert, Thurstone, or Guttman scaling) discussed in chapter 2.

[3]Evidence for the validity of very general, unselected behavioral indices can be found in Fishbein and Ajzen (1975).

## BEHAVIORAL ELEMENTS:
## ACTION, TARGET, CONTEXT, AND TIME

Once we have decided upon the behavior of interest (be it a single action or a behavioral category), our next step is to measure it. Clearly, the way we make our observations influences the kind of data we obtain. People usually realize that it is important to consider the _target_ at which a behavior is directed. Thus, a person who drinks Budweiser may not drink Schlitz. Similarly, very different results may be obtained when the target is a general category (e.g., beer) as opposed to a single instance of the category (e.g., Budweiser). These considerations make it clear that a behavioral criterion involves not only an action but also the target at which the action is directed.

Less recognized is the fact that a behavioral criterion also involves a _context_ and a _time_. For example, a person who drinks beer in a local pub may not drink beer at home, and a person who drinks beer in the evening may not drink beer in the morning. It follows that context and time are also parts of the behavioral criterion.

We saw earlier that a behavioral criterion may involve either a single action or a category of behaviors. The same is true for the target, context, and time elements: We may be interested in a single target or a range of targets, a single context or a range of contexts, a single point in time or a broader time period. Behavioral observations should be guided by these decisions to ensure that the behavioral measure will correspond to the criterion of interest.

The problem is that in practice such correspondence is often not attained. For example, to assess whether or not a person buys beer, we may decide to observe his buying behavior in a local supermarket. The criterion we actually obtain is a measure of whether the person buys beer _in that supermarket,_ and is not a measure of whether he buys beer. A person who does not buy beer in the supermarket in question may buy it in some other supermarket or in a liquor store.

This problem tends to arise because a single action is always performed with respect to a given target, in a given context, and at a given point in time. Although we may often be interested in the performance of an action with respect to a given target, we usually have little interest in a specific context or a specific point in time. For example, we may ask whether a person drinks Falstaff, and we may not care where or when he drinks it. It follows that we will have to consider all contexts in which the behavior may reasonably occur and that we will have to make our observations over a reasonable period of time.

The fact that what an investigator thinks he is measuring often does not correspond to his actual behavioral criterion can perhaps best be illustrated by looking at laboratory research on racial discrimination. To obtain an appropriate measure of an individual's discriminatory behavior with respect to, say, blacks, we would have to observe the extent to which he performed different actions falling within the behavioral category of "discrimination," and these observations would have to be made with respect to a representative sample of black individuals, in a variety of contexts, and over a reasonable period of time.

In marked contrast, in the typical laboratory study, the investigator creates a situation where he can observe whether the subject performs a particular behavior with respect to one or two black individuals. The behavioral criterion is thus not discrimination toward blacks but rather the performance of a single action (e.g., administration of electrical shocks), with respect to a specific target (a particular black individual), in a given context (e.g., a "learning experiment"), within a limited time period.

## MULTIPLE CHOICE AND MAGNITUDE

So far we have dealt only with the performance of single actions, although we have noted that it is possible to combine such actions into an index representing a general behavioral category. Single-act criteria can take on different forms. One possibility we have noted is to simply record whether or not a given behavior has been performed. Another procedure is to specify a set of behaviors and to record which of the alternatives has been performed.

The first procedure implies that the person has a choice between two alternatives: performing the behavior or not performing it. The second procedure views the person as having more than two alternatives among which he can choose. For example, instead of simply observing whether or not a person drove his car to work, it is possible to record, on the following checklist, which of the available modes of transportation he used to get to work:

_____ own car or truck
_____ passenger in another person's car or truck
_____ bus
_____ taxi
_____ motorcycle
_____ bicycle
_____ walk

Note that the multiple choice procedure can be viewed as a set of single actions, each of which is or is not performed. In contrast to the actions used to construct a behavioral category, the alternative actions in the multiple choice procedure cannot be combined into a single index but must instead be treated as separate behaviors.

A third procedure for recording single actions attempts to quantify the extent to which the behavior has been performed. For example, rather than observing whether or not a person donated money to the United Fund, the amount of money donated may be recorded. Similarly, it is possible to observe not only whether a person bought Pepsi-Cola but how much Pepsi-Cola (in liters) he bought.

It can be shown that such measures of magnitude are in many ways comparable to the multiple choice procedure. Instead of recording the amount of money donated or the number of liters of Pepsi purchased, it is possible to divide these behaviors into several categories of magnitude, as in the following examples:[4]

| | | | |
|---|---|---|---|
| _____ none | | _____ none | |
| _____ $1 - $10 | | _____ less than 1 liter | |
| _____ $11 - $25 | | _____ 1 - 2 liters | |
| _____ $26 - $50 | | _____ 2.1 - 4 liters | |
| _____ $51 - $100 | | _____ more than 4 liters | |
| _____ $101 - $1000 | | | |
| _____ more than $1000 | | | |

Viewed in this way, measures of magnitude (like multiple choice criteria) can be viewed as involving a set of single actions, each of which is or is not performed. Thus, a person may be said to have or have not donated $50, $100, etc.

## REPEATED OBSERVATIONS

In many situations, we may be concerned not so much with behavior on a single occasion but with a person's behavior over time. Investigators frequently observe how often a behavior is performed over a given number of occasions. For example, we may record the number of days on which a person took the bus to work in the month of March. Similarly, we might consider the occasions on which a person bought beer and record how often the beer bought was Schlitz.

These two examples illustrate measures of absolute and relative frequency. The absolute frequency is simply the number of times the person performed a behavior. The relative frequency is the proportion or percentage of times he performed it; that is, relative frequencies measure how often a person performed a behavior in relation to the number of opportunities he or she had to do so. For example, the number of days a person rode the bus to work in the month of March provides a measure of absolute frequency, since it simply indicates the extent to which the person made use of the bus as a mode of transportation for getting to work. It does not serve as a measure of relative frequency, since it

[4]Obviously, the choice of alternatives is arbitrary and will depend on the type of behavior under consideration.

does not reflect the number of opportunities the person had for performing the behavior. Compare two individuals: one who went to work every day in March and another who was sick and missed a week of work. Clearly, the number of times that they used the bus to get to work does not reflect this difference in opportunities. To obtain a measure of *relative* frequency, it would be necessary to compute the percentage or proportion of times that each person took the bus when he went to work. In contrast, the number of times a person bought Schlitz out of ten occasions on which he bought beer does provide a measure of relative frequency, since the number of opportunities is taken into account.

As in the case of magnitude, it is also possible to view absolute and relative frequencies as a multiple choice among alternatives, where each alternative represents a single frequency or a range of frequencies. This can be seen in the following illustrations.

| *Person rode the bus to work on* | *Person bought Schlitz when buying beer* |
|---|---|
| _____ no days in March | _____ never |
| _____ 1 - 5 days in March | _____ 1 out of 6 times |
| _____ 6 - 10 days in March | _____ 2 out of 6 times |
| _____ 11 - 15 days in March | _____ 3 out of 6 times |
| _____ 16 - 20 days in March | _____ 4 out of 6 times |
| _____ 21 - 25 days in March | _____ 5 out of 6 times |
|  | _____ 6 out of 6 times |

Again, each of these alternatives can be treated as a single action which is either performed or not performed by a given individual.

It can be seen that it is useful to distinguish between measures of magnitude, frequency, and relative frequency of a behavior. Which of these measures is appropriate depends on the particular problem. If we want to know how much of the behavior occurred, we need to obtain a measure of magnitude. If we want to know how often a person performed the behavior in question, we can simply measure its frequency. Finally, if we are interested in the proportion of times that the behavior occurred, a measure of relative frequency is called for. We have noted that each of these criteria can be viewed as involving sets of single actions, and the individual is classified as having performed or not performed each action.

## SELF-REPORTS OF BEHAVIOR

So far we have dealt only with direct observations of behavior. Clearly, many behaviors are not directly accessible to an observer and it may be necessary to rely on the actor's self-report. For example, it is very difficult, if not impossible, to observe whether a woman uses an intrauterine device or whether a voter casts his ballot for one candidate or another. Although self-reports of behavior are usually quite accurate, their accuracy cannot be taken for granted. If it is difficult or impossible to observe the behavior directly, we must decide whether a self-report is acceptable. Although there are no clear guidelines for making this decision, self-reports are obviously inadequate if there are strong reasons to suspect their accuracy.

When self-reports of behavior can be used, they have certain advantages over direct observations. Most obviously, they require less effort, time, and money. They are especially convenient when we want to observe a given behavior repeatedly or when we are interested in a general behavioral category. In the case of repeated observations we can simply ask the respondent to indicate how often he has performed the behavior in question, for instance, on how many Sundays during the past year he attended church. In the case of observations of behavioral categories the procedure is somewhat more complex. To obtain a self-report measure of a behavioral category, it is first necessary to identify a set of behaviors relevant to the category in question. The respondent is then presented with a list of these behaviors and asked to report whether or not he or she performed each behavior. Following the procedures described previously for direct observations, these data are then used to construct a self-report index of the behavioral category (see Table 3.1).

Although it is possible to ask a person directly whether he engaged in the behavioral category (e.g., whether he diets), this is not an adequate measure of the behavioral category. As we noted earlier with respect to dieting, the investigator's decision to classify a person as dieting or not is highly arbitrary and subjective. The same is true of self-classifications. Of two people who behave in identical ways, one may classify himself as being on a diet, the other may not. Such a measure may be useful if we are interested in people's self-perceptions, but it does not provide useful information about their behavior.

Finally, it is worth nothing that, in contrast to direct observations of behavior, self-reports can be obtained free of specific targets, contexts, or time. For example, a respondent can be asked to indicate whether he contributed money to any charity in the past year or if he bought a record in the last six months. Such behavioral criteria are very difficult to observe but are easily measured by means of self-reports.

## SUMMARY AND CONCLUSION

We have seen that many problems are inherent in defining and measuring a behavioral criterion. We noted first that it is important to distinguish between behaviors and outcomes which may be only partly determined by those behaviors.

Our analysis of behavioral criteria showed that they are comprised of four elements: the action, the target at which the action is directed, the context in which it occurs, and the time at which it is performed. Each of these elements can be very specific or more general. We discussed the difference between single actions and general categories of behavior which must be inferred from such single actions. Similarly, we have seen that a behavioral criterion may involve a single target or a range of targets, a single context or a range of contexts, and a single point in time or a broader time period.

Single observations always involve a single action, with respect to a given target, in a given context, at a given point in time. The behavioral criterion becomes more general when different actions of an individual are observed. It is also possible to broaden it by observing one or more actions with respect to different targets, in different contexts, and at different points in time. The nature of the behavioral criterion is defined by the kinds of observations that are made. This fact is often overlooked with the result that the investigator's actual criterion may be more specific than he realizes. Thus, an investigator may be interested in a general category of behaviors directed at a class of individuals, but he may measure a single action directed at a given person, in a specific context.

Sometimes we are interested not only in whether or not a behavior has been performed but also in the extent to which it has occurred. Thus, we may obtain measures of magnitude, absolute frequency, or relative frequency. We noted that all of these measures can be viewed as sets of multiple alternatives, with each alternative representing a single action.

In a sense, then, all behavioral criteria can be viewed as measures of one or more single acts. Generally speaking, we can refer to a single action criterion, a behavioral category criterion (which is an index based on a set of single actions), or a multiple-choice criterion (which usually involves a set of mutually exclusive and exhaustive single action alternatives).

Finally, we have discussed some of the possible limitations and advantages of self-report measures of behavior. A major advantage of self-reports is that they provide an easy means of defining each of the four elements at any level of generality. In chapter 4 we shall see that the precise definition of the elements comprising the behavioral criterion is an essential prerequisite for predicting and understanding behavior.

# CHAPTER
# 4

## Predicting
## Behavior
## from
## Intention

In chapter 1 we made the assumption that most behaviors of social relevance are under volitional control and are thus predictable from intentions. From our point of view, intention is the immediate determinant of behavior, and when an appropriate measure of intention is obtained it will provide the most accurate prediction of behavior.

Moreover, our discussion in chapter 3 suggested that all behavior involves a choice, be it a choice between performing or not performing a given action or a choice among several qualitatively or quantitatively different action alternatives. To use a person's intention to predict his choice, we can present him with the available alternatives and ask him which alternative he intends to perform. For example, he could be asked to respond to the following item:

_____ I do

_____ I do not     intend to vote in the forthcoming election.

Or, using the following response format, he could be asked to check the brand of toothpaste he intends to buy when he next shops for toothpaste.

| | | | |
|---|---|---|---|
| _____ Colgate | | _____ Pepsodent |
| _____ Crest | | _____ Ultra-Brite |
| _____ Aim | | _____ Other |
| _____ Gleem | | _____ I never buy toothpaste |

Alternatively, he could be asked to respond to the following question measuring donation to the United Fund:

I intend to donate $_____ to the United Fund this year.

The measures discussed above may be called *choice intentions*. When the respondent is expressing his choice intention he is essentially saying that he is more likely to perform one of the alternatives than any of the others, and it is expected that the respondent will in fact perform the alternative he has indicated. Although from a theoretical point of view, intentions determine behaviors, this should not be taken to mean that a measure of intention will always be an accurate predictor of behavior. A number of factors will influence the strength of the observed relationship between intention and behavior. One such factor is the degree of correspondence between the measure of intention and the behavioral criterion. Another factor is the degree to which the intention remains stable over time.

## CORRESPONDENCE BETWEEN INTENTION AND BEHAVIOR

To predict a behavioral criterion from intention, it is essential to ensure that the measure of intention corresponds to the measure of behavior. Like behaviors, intentions can be viewed as consisting of action, target, context, and time elements. Intention and behavior correspond to the extent that their elements are identical.

### Correspondence for Single-Action Criteria

A single-action criterion is simply a record of whether a person has or has not performed a given behavior. We saw that a person's intention with respect to a single-action criterion could be measured by asking him whether he did or did not intend to perform the behavior in question. For many purposes, however, it is preferable to obtain a more precise measure of the likelihood that the person will engage in the behavior. Thus, a respondent might be asked to indicate her subjective probability that she will vote in the forthcoming election, as follows:

I intend to vote in the forthcoming election.

probable _____:_____:_____:_____:_____:_____:_____ improbable
     extremely  quite   slightly  neither/  slightly  quite  extremely
                                nor

Alternatively, she could be asked to estimate, in percentage points, how likely it is that she would vote in the forthcoming election, as in the following illustration:

There is a _____% chance that I will vote in the forthcoming election.

A measure of the likelihood that a person will engage in a given behavior may be termed *behavioral intention*. Note that in the above example the respondent's probability of not voting in the forthcoming election would be 100% minus the percent that she indicated. That is, knowing a person's behavioral intention to perform a given behavior also provides information about her intention to not perform that behavior.

It is possible to measure a person's behavioral intention with respect to each action alternative available to him. In the preceding example concerning the purchase of toothpaste, the respondent could be asked to indicate his subjective probability that he will buy each brand of toothpaste listed. Similarly, with respect to monetary donations to the United Fund, the person could be asked to provide estimates of the likelihood that he will contribute less than $5, $6 to $10, and more than $10.

Our discussion thus far has centered on the action elements of intentions and behaviors. It should be recalled, however, that a single-action criterion also involves a target at which the action is directed, the context in which the action occurs, and the time of its occurrence. To ensure correspondence, the elements of the intention have to be identical to those of the behavior.

Imagine that we want to predict, for each respondent in a sample, whether he or she will buy a color television set. Further, suppose we decide to wait a year before measuring whether the behavior has occurred. It can be seen that this criterion specifies an action (buying), a target class (color television sets), and a time period (the year in question), but it leaves the contextual element unspecified. The only measure of intention that corresponds exactly to this behavioral criterion is a measure of the person's intention "to buy a color television set within the next year." If we had decided to return in six months to record the behavior, the corresponding intention would be the intention "to buy a color television set within the next six months."

It may be instructive to consider another example of intention-behavior correspondence. Suppose we want to predict voting behavior in the forthcoming presidential election. We interview residents of voting age, living in a given precinct, a week before the election in order to assess their intentions to vote, and on the day of the election we go to the polling station for the precinct and observe whether or not the residents interviewed showed up to vote.

Note that although we are interested only in whether a person voted in the election, our actual behavioral criterion is a single action (voting), toward a given target (presidential election), in a given context (a specific polling station), during a particular time period (election day). A measure of intention corresponding exactly to this criterion could be obtained as follows:

I will go to the _____ polling station on Tuesday, November _____
to cast my vote in the presidential election.

likely ____ : ____ : ____ : ____ : ____ : ____ : ____ unlikely

The formulation of this intention may appear unnecessarily pedantic, but consider what would happen if we simply assessed intention "to vote in the

forthcoming presidential election." Many residents might give an affirmative reply to this question, but they might not come to the precinct's polling station.
Instead, they may be registered, and thus vote, elsewhere or they may cast an
absentee ballot. This more general measure of intention might thus lead us to
conclude that there is a low relation between intention and behavior. However,
had we used the more precise measure of intention which corresponded exactly
to the behavior we were going to observe, individuals who planned to vote elsewhere or to cast an absentee ballot would probably have stated a negative intention. Consequently, the accuracy of our prediction would be greatly improved.[1]

### Correspondence for Multiple-Choice Criteria

A multiple-choice criterion records which of a number of behavioral alternatives
a person performed. These alternatives can refer to qualitatively different behaviors (e.g., buying different makes of automobiles) or to different quantities
of the same behavior (e.g., amount of money donated, frequency with which a
given product is purchased, or amount purchased).

   We saw earlier that it is possible to measure a person's choice intention by
asking him to indicate which of the behavioral alternatives he intends to perform. Choice intentions can be measured either in an open-ended format (e.g.,
"How much money do you intend to contribute?") or in a closed format which
specifies the range of alternatives available.

   Of course, as in the case of single-actions, a choice intention is expected to
predict the actual choice only if there is correspondence between the two measures. Each behavioral alternative is defined in terms of certain action, target,
context, and time elements. To ensure correspondence, the measure of choice
intention has to specify alternatives which involve exactly the same elements as
the multiple-choice criterion.

   To return to the example of an election, suppose you do not want to predict
merely whether a person will or will not vote in a forthcoming election but for
whom he will vote. Since this behavior cannot be directly observed, the criterion
will have to be a self-report. Thus, following the election, respondents could be
asked to check one of the following alternatives:

In the 1976 presidential election


_____ I voted for Gerald Ford.
_____ I voted for Jimmy Carter.
_____ I voted for some other candidate.
_____ I did not vote.

---

[1]Parenthetically, the second more general measure of intention (which specifies only action and target) would correspond to the behavioral criterion if the criterion had been a self-
report of whether or not a person voted in the presidential election.

This criterion specifies an action (voting), several targets (the candidates), and a general context and time (the 1976 presidential election). A measure of choice intention would correspond to this criterion if it involved exactly the same elements. Thus, some time prior to the election, the respondents might have been asked to answer the following questions by checking one of the alternatives.

In the 1976 presidential election

_____ I will vote for Gerald Ford.
_____ I will vote for Jimmy Carter.
_____ I will vote for some other candidate.
_____ I will not vote.

Alternatively, the respondents could simply be asked to indicate for whom they were going to vote in the 1976 presidential election, using an open-ended format.

Such open-ended formats are also typically used when the criterion is a measure of magnitude or frequency. Here, too, the question of correspondence between intention and behavior is crucial. Imagine, for example, that an investigator interested in helping behavior comes to your door on a Friday evening and asks you if you would help him out by getting your friends to fill out a 20-page questionnaire dealing with their sexual behaviors. He further tells you that the completed questionnaires would have to be returned to him by noon on the following Monday. As his behavioral criterion, he records how many questionnaires you actually take.

To illustrate some of the difficulties involved in establishing correspondence in this case, imagine that some time prior to the behavior under consideration you completed a questionnaire which, among other things, asked you to indicate whether or not you would help an investigator in his research. Clearly, this measure of intention shows little correspondence to the criterion. Whereas the criterion is the number of copies of a particular questionnaire the respondent took in response to a request made by a given individual at a given point in time, the measure of intention makes no reference to any of these specific elements. To obtain a measure of intention that corresponds to the criterion, respondents could be asked to state how many copies of the particular questionnaire they would take in response to a request made by the investigator on a Friday night. Obviously, a person's behavior (and his intention) will be influenced by such factors as the kind of questionnaire he is asked to distribute, the timing of the request, how many days he can take to fulfill the request, and who is making the request. Only if the intention corresponds to the behavior in all of these components will there be a strong relationship between the two.

**Behavioral intentions versus choice intentions.** So far we have considered only the use of choice intentions to predice multiple-choice criteria. Earlier in the chapter we saw that it is possible to measure the person's behavioral intentions (i.e., subjective probabilities) with respect to each of the action alternatives. This set of behavioral intentions can also be used to predict the choice. Imagine, for example, that a person had indicated the following subjective probabilities prior to the 1976 presidential election.

| | |
|---|---|
| I will vote for Gerald Ford. | 30% chance |
| I will vote for Jimmy Carter. | 40% chance |
| I will vote for some other candidate. | 5% chance |
| I will not vote. | 25% chance |

It stands to reason that the person will perform that alternative to which he assigned the highest subjective probability; in this case, he is most likely to have voted for Jimmy Carter.

Note that a person's intention to perform *one* of the behavioral alternatives cannot always be used to predict his choice.[2] For example, a person who indicates a 40% chance that he will buy Shell gasoline the next time he needs gas may in fact do so if the probabilities for any other brand are even lower, but he may buy Exxon gasoline if his subjective probability for Exxon is, say, 45%.

An analogous problem arises in the prediction of behavioral magnitudes or frequencies. Knowing that a person has a 40% likelihood of donating $100 to the United Fund tells us little about the amount of money he will actually donate because it does not tell us which amount of money has the highest subjective probability. To carry this one step further, measuring a person's behavioral intention "to donate money to the United Fund" is also unlikely to predict the amount of money actually donated. As a general rule, then, a person's intention to perform a given behavior cannot be used to predict the extent, magnitude, or frequency of that action.

### Correspondence for Behavioral Categories

Our discussion in chapter 3 showed that measures of behavioral categories represent the degree to which an individual engages in a general class of behaviors. We also noted that asking a person to classify himself as performing or not performing the behavioral category (e.g., dieting) does not provide a meaningful classification, since such judgments are arbitrary. It follows that a measure of intention to diet or to perform some other general category may not be a good predictor of the behavioral index computed on the basis of a set of single actions.[3]

---

[2]One important exception is the single-action criterion which may be viewed as a choice between performing and not performing the behavior. Here, a person's intention to perform the behavior is the complement of his intention to not perform the behavior. That is, the probability of performing the behavior is one minus the probability of not performing the behavior, and knowing one probability is sufficient to predict the choice.

[3]If the behavioral criterion is a report of whether the person views himself as dieting or not dieting, this measure of intention should provide accurate prediction.

A measure of intention that corresponds to a behavioral category is obtained as follows. We measure the respondent's intentions with respect to each of the single actions comprising the behavior index, making sure that the elements of each intention correspond to those of the behaviors. For example, if we were going to observe whether a person had snacked between meals over a two-month period, we would assess his intention to snack between meals in that two-months period. We can then compute an intentional index in a manner similar to that described in chapter 3 for computing the behavioral index.

In sum, we have seen that it is important to ensure a high degree of correspondence between intention and behavior, whether the criterion is a single action or a behavioral category. Lack of correspondence on any of the four elements (action, target, context, and time) can reduce the accuracy of prediction.

## STABILITY OF INTENTIONS

We have argued that a measure of intention which corresponds to the behavior will lead to accurate prediction. This argument has important implications for any attempt to understand and influence human behavior. Given a one-to-one relation between intention and behavior, knowledge of the determinants of intentions is both necessary and sufficient for understanding and influencing human action. However, a measure of intention will not *always* be a good predictor of behavior. It should be obvious that intentions can change over time and a measure of intention taken some time prior to observation of the behavior may differ from the intention at the time that the behavior is observed. The longer the time interval is, the greater the likelihood is that events will occur which will produce changes in intentions. Generally speaking, therefore, the longer the time interval, the less accurate the prediction of behavior from intention, that is, the lower the observed relation is between intention and behavior.

Predicting Behavior

Since intentions can change over time, it is important to measure the intention as close as possible to the behavioral observation in order to obtain an accurate prediction. In many instances, however, it may be neither feasible nor of practical value to measure the intention in close proximity to the behavior. Imagine, for example, that we are trying to predict the behavior of a soldier on the battlefield. We could hardly approach soldiers in the midst of a battle and try to assess their intentions. In other cases, it may be important, for planning purposes, to make predictions months or years in advance. Long-range predictions are usually not concerned with the behavior of any given individual but rather with projecting or forecasting behavioral trends in relatively large segments of the population. For example, market researchers are interested not so much in the likelihood that a given individual will buy a car in a given calendar year but in the number or proportion of people who will buy cars in that year. By the same token, the military is concerned not with predicting the enlistment behavior of a given individual but rather with the number of volunteers that will enlist at some future time.

The distinction between predicting behavior at the level of the individual and at the aggregate level is important because aggregate intentions are apt to be much more stable over time than are individual intentions. A great variety of events can produce changes in the intentions of individuals. Among such unexpected events are sudden illness; a fortuitous inheritance; injury; natural disasters, such as tornadoes, floods, or earthquakes; loss of job; unexpected pregnancy; and economic recession. Similarly, if a person's intention is based on the expectation that another person will behave in a certain way or on the expectation that some event will occur, and the expectation is not confirmed, this information may also lead to a change in intention.

Since such idiosyncratic events are likely to balance out, intentions at the aggregate level will tend to be relatively stable. For example, one person may have intended to buy a new car but, because an expected rise in salary does not occur, she changes her intention. Another person might be involved in an accident and, although he did not intend to buy a new car, he finds himself in the position where he has to buy one. Although the behaviors of these individuals could not have been predicted, the changes in intention would have had no effect on the accuracy of the aggregate prediction. In fact, there is considerable evidence that even when individual predictions are relatively poor, prediction of behavior from intention at the aggregate level is often remarkably accurate (see chapters 11 and 12).

One exception to this rule is the case of an external event that changes the intentions of a large proportion of the population in the same direction. For example, large increases in air fares tend to reduce people's intentions to travel by plane. Similarly, the outbreak of war in the Middle East greatly reduced people's intentions to visit that area.

**Conditional intentions.** To make accurate long-range predictions (at either the aggregate or the individual level) we could try to identify likely extraneous events whose occurrence would change intentions. Consider, for example, an automobile manufacturer who is planning his production for the coming year. A sample of potential car buyers is interviewed in August, and their intentions to buy the car in question during the following calendar year are assessed. Note that the manufacturer is trying to predict behavior 4 to 16 months in advance. While many different factors may change any given individual's intention, one potential extraneous event might influence the intentions of a large number of people—namely, an increase in the price of gasoline.

Assume that a large increase in the price of gasoline occurred in January. The manufacturer would be well advised to reinterview his respondents (or a new sample of individuals) in order to assess any changes in intentions that may have taken place. For purposes of illustration, imagine that this is impossible. If the manufacturer had foreseen the possibility of a large increase in the price of gasoline, he could have obtained an additional measure of intention that was conditional upon the occurrence of this event. That is, in the initial interview, he could also have asked his respondents how likely it was that they would buy the car if the price of gasoline increased by 20% or more. In the case of such an increase in the price of gasoline, this conditional intention would lead to more accurate prediction of behavior than the original measure of intention.[4]

There are many long-range predictions that could be improved by means of conditional intention measures. To return to the previous examples, prediction of air travel could be improved by measuring intentions conditional upon increased air fares, and prediction of travel to foreign countries could be improved by taking into account events that might occur in those countries (e.g., war, a change in government, re-valuation of currency).

Even relatively short-range predictions could be improved by means of conditional intentions. To give just one example, attendance at concerts or theaters might be predicted with greater accuracy by measuring intentions conditional upon the weather.

Note that in all of these examples we considered only events known to the general public and thus also to the investigator. Although it is true that consideration of such events as illness, loss of job, and unexpected company could also improve prediction, they are of little practical value for the prediction of a person's behavior.[5] To find out if somebody was taken ill, lost his job, or had unexpected company one would have to observe or interview him. Clearly, if it is possible to re-interview respondents to obtain this information prior to the behavioral observation, it is also possible to simply re-assess the person's intention at that time. Since this more recent measure of intention would have already been influenced by these events, as well as by any other events that may have occurred, it will provide a more accurate prediction than any conditional intention.[6]

## Moderating Effects of Other Variables

In chapter 2 we mentioned the argument voiced in recent years that the strength of the attitude-behavior relationship is moderated by "other variables," such as direct experience with the attitude object, presence of other people, possession of skills required to perform the behavior, and occurrence of unforeseen extrane-

[4]The conditional intention measure not only improves prediction, it also can help the manufacturer in his initial decisions concerning production of the car.

[5]They may, however, be useful for predicting the percentage of people who perform the behavior, that is, at the aggregate, as opposed to the individual, level.

[6]Although information about the occurrence of idiosyncratic events does not aid prediction of a person's behavior, it may help explain that behavior after the fact.

ous events. Since most investigators make no distinction between attitudes and intentions (see chapter 2), these variables would also be expected to moderate the intention-behavior relation.

In marked contrast, we are claiming that intentions should always predict behavior, provided that the measure of intention corresponds to the behavioral criterion and that the intention has not changed prior to performance of the behavior. From our point of view, other variables may appear to have moderating effects on the strength of the intention-behavior relation if the second of these requirements is not met. This can easily be seen in the case of unforeseen extraneous events. Clearly, when such events occur, they will tend to change intentions and thus reduce the relationship between a previous measure of intention and subsequent behavior. It follows that the intention-behavior relation will tend to be strong in the absence of unexpected events but weak in their presence. However, as noted above, if the intention is measured *after* the extraneous events have occurred (or if those events are taken into account) a strong intention-behavior relation will be obtained.

Similar considerations apply to the other "moderating variables." Take, for example, the case of direct experience with the behavioral target. An intention formed without such direct experience may change greatly when the person is actually confronted with the target of the behavior. In contrast, a person who has interacted with the target in the past will have developed more realistic expectations, and his intention is likely to remain relatively stable.[7]

A concrete example may help illustrate this point. Imagine a young woman who is quite attractive but who, on first encounter, appears a bit reserved and rejecting. Suppose Mr. A has interacted with her on several past occasions and has come to realize that her coldness is only a front. Mr. B on the other hand is only superficially acquainted with her. Let us assume that because both men are attracted to the woman, each forms the intention to ask her out. In their conversations with her prior to extending an invitation each man is confronted with her typical reserve. Their reactions, however, may differ greatly. Mr. A expects a certain coolness, is unperturbed, and carries out his intention. Mr. B, who does not realize that the reserve is only superficial, is taken aback, perhaps offended, and quickly changes his intention. Mr. B's behavior is consistent with his new intention *not* to ask the woman for a date, but it is unrelated to his initial intention as measured on a previous occasion.

It can be seen that direct experience may help preserve a stable intention and hence a strong intention-behavior relation. Note, however, that direct experience need not necessarily lead to the development of more realistic expectations. Direct experience will therefore not always influence the stability of intentions (or attitudes) and hence will not always moderate the strength of the intention-behavior relationship.

---

[7]The same arguments apply to the stability of a person's *attitude* toward the target or toward a behavior with respect to the target. Here, too, direct experience may influence the stability of the attitude and hence moderate its relation with behavior.

To summarize briefly, we have seen that in order to ensure accurate prediction of behavior, intentions that are not stable have to be measured immediately prior to observation of the behavior. When this cannot be done, the measure of intention should be taken as close in time as possible to the behavior. Further, it is sometimes possible to improve prediction by measuring conditional intentions. These conditional intentions take into account extraneous events, foreseen by the investigator, that might produce changes in intentions. Finally, we saw that long-range prediction from intentions will usually be accurate at the aggregate level, even when the measure of intention does not permit accurate prediction of individual behavior.

## PREDICTION OF OUTCOMES

We noted in chapter 3 that investigators are sometimes interested in predicting outcomes rather than behaviors. The case of predicting weight loss will be discussed in chapter 9. Unlike behaviors, outcomes are not completely under a person's volitional control. For example, whether a woman will have a child in the next two years depends not only on her own actions but also on such factors as her husband's behavior, the availability of contraceptives or abortions, and the couple's fecundity.

It may appear that the simplest way to predict this outcome would be to measure the woman's intention to have a child in the next two years. Note, however, that use of such a measure is based on two assumptions: that the outcome in question will result from the performance of certain behaviors and that the intention to produce the outcome will lead to the performance of those behaviors. When these assumptions are met, then the intention to produce an outcome will predict its occurrence. When they are not met, we cannot expect a strong relationship.

A more promising approach is to identify the behaviors and other factors that control the outcome. To predict its occurrence one could then measure the person's intentions to perform each of the identified behaviors and assess the presence or absence of the other factors.

## SUMMARY AND CONCLUSION

In this chapter we have considered some of the issues involved in using intentions to predict behavior. We have noted that although intentions are assumed to be the immediate antecedents of actions, the observed relation between intention and behavior depends on two factors: First, the measure of intention has to correspond to the behavioral criterion in action, target, context, and time;

second, a measure of intention will predict behavior only if the intention does not change before the behavior is observed. These considerations apply whether the criterion is a single action, a choice between multiple alternatives, a behavioral category, or an index based on repeated observations. In fact, we saw that each of these criteria can be viewed as consisting of one or more single actions.

The investigator can ensure high correspondence between intention and behavior by obtaining an appropriate measure of intention. The intention's stability, however, is not under his control. We saw that many variables assumed to moderate the strength of the intention-behavior relation may do so by influencing the stability of the intention. To maximize behavioral prediction the intention should be assessed just prior to the behavior. When this is not feasible, it may sometimes be possible to improve long-range prediction by measuring intentions conditional upon the occurrence of certain events. We also noted that long-range prediction is less problematic in the case of aggregate data than it is at the individual level.

Finally, we have considered the prediction of outcomes, as opposed to behaviors. Although it is possible to measure intentions to achieve the outcome, the predictive validity of intentions depends on the extent to which they lead to the performance of behaviors that control the outcome.

# CHAPTER
# 5

## Determinants
## of
## Behavioral
## Intentions

Our discussion in the previous chapters has shown that although different kinds of behavioral criteria can be assessed, they can all ultimately be reduced to one or more single actions. It follows that in order to understand a person's behavior, it is necessary to consider the factors that determine these single actions. For example, to understand a person's choice among behavioral alternatives, it is not enough to understand why he performed a given alternative, but we must also be able to explain why he did not perform the remaining alternatives.[1]

In chapter 4 we saw that a single action can be predicted from the corresponding behavioral intention. In fact, within our theoretical framework, the person's intention to perform a given behavior is the immediate determinant of that behavior. We thus turn to an examination of the factors that determine behavioral intentions. According to the theory of reasoned action, two major factors determine a person's behavioral intentions: a personal or attitudinal component and a social or normative component.

## ATTITUDE TOWARD A BEHAVIOR

The attitudinal component refers to the person's attitude toward performing the behavior under consideration. Although, as we saw in chapter 2, investigators have defined attitude in many different ways, from our point of view an attitude toward any concept is simply a person's general feeling of favorableness or unfavorableness for that concept. To assess a person's attitude toward a behavior, we could use any of the standard scaling procedures described in chapter 2.

A relatively simple method in frequent use is the semantic differential (Osgood, Suci, & Tannenbaum, 1957). Using this method, respondents could be

[1]This implies that although a measure of choice intention may lead to very accurate behavioral *prediction,* knowledge of a person's choice intention will not contribute very much to our *understanding* of the person's choice. To understand the choice we must consider the factors influencing his intentions to perform or not perform each of the alternatives available.

asked, for example, to rate "my voting in the forthcoming election" by checking each of the following *evaluative* scales:[2]

My voting in the forthcoming election is

good ____ : ____ : ____ : ____ : ____ : ____ : ____ bad.
     (+3)   (+2)   (+1)   (0)   (−1)   (−2)   (−3)

foolish ____ : ____ : ____ : ____ : ____ : ____ : ____ wise.
       (−3)   (−2)   (−1)   (0)   (+1)   (+2)   (+3)

pleasant ____ : ____ : ____ : ____ : ____ : ____ : ____ unpleasant.
        (+3)   (+2)   (+1)   (0)   (−1)   (−2)   (−3)

The response to each scale can be scored from +3 to −3 (as indicated), and the sum of these scores is used as the attitude measure. Alternatively, the respondent could be asked to provide a direct indication of his attitude in the following manner:

My attitude toward my voting in the forthcoming election is

favorable ____ : ____ : ____ : ____ : ____ : ____ : ____ unfavorable.

These measures of attitude, like all standard attitude scaling methods, result in a single score which represents a given person's general evaluation or overall feeling of favorableness or unfavorableness toward the behavior in question. It should be recognized that the definition of attitude as a bipolar evaluation does not capture the full complexity that has come to be associated with the attitude concept. However, there is widespread agreement that evaluation is the most essential part of attitude and our definition therefore does justice to the attitude concept. In contrast to our relatively simple definition, we saw in chapter 2 that many practitioners and laymen have tended to view attitudes as a complex of feelings, beliefs, motivations, perceptions, and intentions. Consistent with this multidimensional definition, they have attempted to measure attitudes by asking a great number of questions designed to assess the presumed constituents of attitude. Although such an approach can provide descriptive information of considerable interest, much of this information may be of little value or irrelevant for an assessment of the attitude's most crucial aspect, namely, evaluation. We therefore suggest that attitudes be viewed as overall evaluations and that they be measured by a procedure which locates respondents on a bipolar evaluative

[2]A common mistake has been for investigators to use clearly nonevaluative (e.g., potency or activity) scales or to use scales that appeared to be evaluative without empirical evidence for this assumption.

dimension. Thus, when we use the term *attitude toward a behavior,* all we mean is a person's judgment that performing the behavior is good or bad, that he is in favor of or against performing the behavior. Clearly, other things equal, the more favorable a person's attitude is toward a behavior, the more he should intend to perform that behavior; the more unfavorable his attitude is, the more he should intend to not perform the behavior.

Other investigators have often attempted to include the reasons for, and the consequences of, a person's evaluation within their definitions and measures of attitude. Thus, they have assessed perceptions, beliefs, motivations, intentions, etc. While we do not deny the importance of such factors, we believe that no useful purpose is served by treating them as part of attitude. Instead, we prefer to treat them as separate concepts that can be related to attitudes.[3]

### Correspondence Between Attitude and Intention

The first step in predicting and understanding behavioral intentions, then, is to obtain a measure of the person's attitude toward his own performance of the behavior in question. Of course, just as the measure of intention must correspond to the behavioral criterion in action, target, context, and time elements, so too must the attitude correspond to the intention. For example, the attitude corresponding to a person's intention to "take a vacation this summer" is his evaluation of "my taking a vacation this summer."

Note that the attitude refers specifically to the person's *own* performance of the behavior rather than to its performance in general. Although a person may be in favor of "taking a vacation this summer" he may be opposed to *his* taking such a vacation and he thus may not intend to do so. To take a more obvious example, consider a woman's intention to use or not use birth control pills. Although she may favorably evaluate "using birth control pills," her evaluation of "*my* using birth control pills" may be quite negative for a variety of reasons (e.g., she may want to get pregnant).[4]

Lack of correspondence can occur in less subtle ways. Evaluations of "my taking a vacation" and of "my taking a vacation this year" also fail to correspond to the intention to take a vacation this summer. Clearly, a person's attitude toward taking his vacation *this year* may differ greatly from his attitude toward taking his vaction *this summer.*

An intention can involve very general action, target, context, and time elements or very specific elements. From a theoretical point of view it makes no difference how specific or general the intention is. (The level of generality is

---

[3]Although our discussion has dealt with the definition and measurement of attitudes toward behaviors, everything we said applies to any attitude: toward persons, issues, objects, institutions, etc.

[4]Although it is important to ensure that the attitude measure always assesses the person's evaluation of *his* performing the behavior, it may be unnecessary to use the format, "*my* performing behavior *X*" if this is clearly implied by the context in which the measure is obtained.

determined by the behavioral criterion of interest.) What is important when using a measure of attitude to predict and understand intentions is to make sure that the measures of attitude and intention correspond to each other. Thus, corresponding to the general intention to socialize is the attitude toward socializing. But if we want to predict intentions "to attend the forthcoming Christmas party for factory employees," then we have to assess each person's attitude toward "my attending the forthcoming Christmas party for factory employees."

## SUBJECTIVE NORM

The second or normative component of our theory deals with the influence of the social environment on intentions and behavior. It refers to the person's subjective norm, that is, his perception that most people who are important to him think he should or should not perform the behavior in question.

The concept of subjective norm is much more restricted than the sociological view of norms. In our theory, "subjective norm" refers to a specific behavioral prescription attributed to a generalized social agent. In contrast, sociologists have used "norm" to refer to a rather broad range of permissible, but not necessarily required, behaviors. Norms are typically viewed as "socially agreed upon rules, the definition of what is right and proper" (Webster, 1975, p. 16). The subjective norm, however, refers to the person's *perception* that important others desire the performance or nonperformance of a specific behavior; this perception may or may not reflect what the important others actually think he should do.

The following format can be used to assess a person's subjective norm:

Most people who are important to me think

I should ____ : ____ : ____ : ____ : ____ : ____ : ____ I should not
perform behavior *X.*

According to our theory, the more a person perceives that others who are important to him think he should perform a behavior, the more he will intend to do so. That is, other things constant, people are viewed as intending to perform those behaviors they believe important others think they should perform. Conversely, if they believe important others think they should not perform a behavior, they will usually intend not to do so.

### Correspondence Between Subjective Norm and Intention

In addition to measuring the person's attitude toward the behavior, then, it is also necessary to assess his subjective norm in order to predict and understand intention. Again, the measure of subjective norm has to correspond to the intention in action, target, context, and time elements. To return to an earlier example, the following subjective norm would correspond to the intention to take a vacation this summer:

Most people who are important to me think

I should ____ : ____ : ____ : ____ : ____ : ____ : ____ I should not
take a vacation this summer.

### Relative Importance of Attitude and Subjective Norm

In most instances, we are likely to find that people hold favorable attitudes toward behaviors their important others think they should perform and negative attitudes toward behaviors their important others think they should not perform. In these cases, the two components are in agreement, and prediction of intention is relatively straightforward.

Sometimes, however, the two components may not be in agreement. That is, a person may hold a favorable attitude toward performing a behavior and believe that his important others think he should not perform it or vice versa. Here, the person's intention will depend on the relative importance of the two components for the person. Consider, for example, a student who has an unfavorable attitude toward his attending church but who believes his important others think he should attend church. If we knew that the student pays more attention to attitudinal than to normative considerations, we could predict that he would intend to not go to church. On the other hand, if he pays more attention to normative considerations, he should intend to go to church.

According to our theory, each component is given a weight reflecting its relative importance as a determinant of the intention under consideration. A given component may have a very high weight or no weight at all. These relative weights may change from one behavior to another and from one person to another. The weighted components are summed to predict the intention.

**Variations in weights as a function of behavior.** For some behaviors, normative considerations (the perceived prescriptions of important others) are more important in determining behavioral intentions than are attitudinal considerations (the person's favorable or unfavorable evaluation of his performing the behavior). For other behaviors the reverse may be true. In fact, variations in any of the four elements defining the behavior (i.e., action, target, context, and time) may influence the relative importance of the attitudinal and normative components. For example, there is some evidence that attitudinal considerations are more important for competitive behaviors than for cooperative behaviors while normative considerations are more important for cooperative than for competitive actions. Similarly, there is evidence that subjective norms are important determinants of intentions to buy some products but not others.

**Variations in weights due to individual differences.** The relative importance of the two components can also be influenced by demographic variables (e.g., age, sex, status), personality traits (e.g., authoritarianism, introversion-extraversion), and other individual differences. For example, for some behavioral intentions, women may place more emphasis on attitudinal considerations than men do while the reverse may be true for other behavioral intentions. In a similar fashion, individuals high in authoritarianism may place more weight on the subjective norm than individuals low in this trait.

Ideally, the weights of the attitudinal and normative components would be available for each individual with respect to each behavior. Unfortunately, at the present time no adequate procedures are available to assess such individual weights.[5] However, it is possible to estimate the relative importance of each component for a group of individuals with respect to a single behavior or for a given person with respect to a set of behaviors.[6] These estimates can then be used in the prediction of intention.

## THE MEDIATING ROLE OF INTENTIONS

We have argued that a person's intention to perform a behavior is determined by her attitude toward the behavior and by her subjective norm. In the previous chapter we saw that behavioral intentions are, in turn, the immediate determinants of behavior. Although these statements may appear to imply that one can go directly from the two components to the behavior, this is not necessarily the case. We saw in chapter 4 that the obtained relation between intention and behavior is not always perfect since various events can intervene between the measurement of intention and the observation of behavior. Assuming that appropriate measures are obtained, the attitudinal and normative components should always predict the intention; their ability to predict the behavior will depend on the strength of the intention-behavior relation. The effects of attitude and subjective norm on behavior are thus mediated by the behavioral intention.

Imagine, for example, that men's intentions to use condoms are not very accurate predictors of actual behavior. If this were the case, attitudes toward "my using condoms" and appropriate subjective norms should still predict the intentions, but they would not be expected to predict the behavior. Thus, the failure

[5]There is evidence that a person's subjective report of his own relative weights does not provide satisfactory estimates.

[6]To obtain these estimates we can perform a multiple regression analysis; the standardized regression coefficients serve as estimates of the weights for the theory's two components.

of attitudes and subjective norms to predict whether or not a man actually uses condoms cannot be taken as evidence against the theory. Any failure to predict the intention, however, would call the theory into question.

### Intentions to Attain Outcomes

The mediating role of intentions can perhaps best be illustrated with respect to the attainment of outcomes. Our discussion so far has dealt only with attitudes and subjective norms concerning the performance of single behaviors. It is also possible, however, to measure a person's attitude toward his attaining a given outcome and his subjective norm with respect to attaining the outcome. After assigning relative weights to these two components, they can be used to predict the person's intention to attain the outcome in question—assuming that the measures of the two components correspond to the intention.

To give one example, a student's intention to pass a test should be predictable from her attitude toward her passing the test in question and her perception that other people who are important to her think she should or should not pass this test.

In chapter 4, however, we saw that the occurrence of an outcome may have little to do with a person's intention to attain that outcome. Knowing that a student intends to pass a test may not provide accurate prediction of her actual performance on the test. It follows that success on the exam will also be unrelated to the person's attitude and subjective norm. Obviously, the failure to predict performance on the exam from attitudes and subjective norms would, in this case, be entirely consistent with the theory.

## SUMMARY AND CONCLUSION

In this chapter we have seen that a person's behavioral intention is determined by his attitude toward the behavior and by his subjective norm. The attitudinal component is his favorable or unfavorable evaluation of his performing the behavior while the normative component refers to his perception that most people who are important to him think he should or should not perform the behavior. This implies that a person will usually intend to perform those behaviors he positively evaluates and which he believes important others think he should perform. The relative importance of the two components in determining intentions may vary from one behavior to another and from one individual to another.

We emphasized the necessity of ensuring correspondence between the measure of intention and the measures of the attitudinal and normative components. Given correspondence, a weighted sum of the two components should provide accurate prediction of the intention. The extent to which the two components also permit accurate prediction of behavior depends on the strength of the intention-behavior relation.

# CHAPTER
# 6

Determinants
of the
Attitudinal
and
Normative Components

The theory we have presented so far suggests that a person's behavior is determined by his intention to perform the behavior and that this intention is, in turn, a function of his attitude toward the behavior and his subjective norm. We have also argued that if our only purpose is to predict behavior, it is sufficient to measure corresponding behavioral intentions. Consideration of attitudes and subjective norms constitutes the first step toward an understanding of *why* people behave the way they do. So long as there is a strong empirical relation between intention and behavior, the factors that determine intentions also provide an explanation of behavior.

For many purposes it may be quite sufficient to explain intentions and behavior by reference to attitudes and subjective norms. A deeper understanding of the factors influencing behavior, however, requires that we look for the determinants of the attitudinal and normative components. We shall see that this search will lead to a consideration of the beliefs individuals hold about themselves and their environment, that is, to the information they have about themselves and the world in which they live. We assume that human beings use or process this information in a reasonable fashion in their attempts to cope with their environment. Beliefs are thus viewed as underlying a person's attitudes and subjective norms, and they ultimately determine intentions and behavior.[1]

## DETERMINANTS OF ATTITUDE TOWARD A BEHAVIOR

There seems to be agreement among investigators that attitudes toward any object are determined by beliefs about that object. Generally speaking, we form beliefs about an object by associating it with various characteristics, qualities, and

---

[1]Beliefs also underlie attitudes and subjective norms concerning the attainment of outcomes. Anything we say in this chapter about the determinants of attitudes toward behaviors and subjective norms concerning behaviors can also be applied to the determinants of attitudes and subjective norms concerning attainment of outcomes.

attributes. Automatically and simultaneously we acquire an attitude toward that object. More specifically, we learn to like (or have favorable attitudes toward) objects we believe have positive characteristics, and we acquire unfavorable attitudes toward objects we associate with negative characteristics.

As an illustration, consider Table 6.1, which shows the beliefs about Toyotas held by two individuals. It can be seen that Person 1 associates Toyotas with mainly positive characteristics, while Person 2 associates Toyotas with more negative than positive characteristics. Given these beliefs, it stands to reason that the first person's attitude toward Toyotas would be more favorable than the second person's attitude.

In the course of a person's life his experiences lead to the formation of many different beliefs about various objects, actions, and events. These beliefs may be the result of direct observation, they may be acquired indirectly by accepting information from outside sources, or they are self-generated through inference processes. Some beliefs may persist over time, others may be forgotten, and new beliefs may be formed.

Although a person may hold a large number of beliefs about any given object, it appears that he can attend to only a relatively small number of beliefs—perhaps five to nine—at any given moment. According to our theory, these *salient* beliefs are the immediate determinants of the person's attitude. It is, of course, possible for more than nine beliefs to be salient and to determine a person's attitude; given time and incentive, a person may take a much larger set of beliefs into account. We are here merely suggesting that under most circumstances, a small number of beliefs serve as the determinants of a person's attitude. Clearly, salient beliefs are also subject to change; they may be strengthened or weakened or replaced by new beliefs.

The implication of this discussion is that in order to understand why a person holds a certain attitude toward an object it is necessary to assess his salient beliefs about that object. Perhaps the simplest and most direct procedure involves asking the person to describe the attitude object, using a free-response format. For example, he could be asked to list "the characteristics, qualities, and attributes" (Zajonc, 1954) of the object in question. Since salient beliefs are upper-

TABLE 6.1
Two Hypothetical Belief Systems Concerning Toyotas

| PERSON 1 | PERSON 2 |
| --- | --- |
| Toyotas are reliable. | Toyotas are inexpensive. |
| Toyotas are inexpensive. | Toyotas are small. |
| Toyotas are economical. | Toyotas are ugly. |
| Toyotas are small. | Toyotas are uncomfortable. |
| Toyotas are well-designed. | Toyotas are economical. |
|  | Toyotas are unreliable. |

most in the individual's mind, we can assume that the first five to nine beliefs he emits are his salient beliefs about the object.

It is possible, however, that only the first two or three beliefs emitted are salient for a given individual and that additional beliefs emitted beyond this point are not primary determinants of his attitude (i.e., are not salient). Unfortunately, it is impossible to determine with any precision the exact point at which a person starts to emit nonsalient beliefs. Recommending use of the first five to nine beliefs is therefore merely a rule of thumb.

### Correspondence Between Beliefs and Attitudes

So far we have dealt with attitudes in general, be they attitudes toward persons, things, institutions, behaviors, attainment of outcomes, events, or any other object. In fact, from our point of view the meaning of the term *attitude* is independent of the object of the attitude. In chapter 5 we saw that a person's attitude toward a behavior is his positive or negative evaluation of his performing the behavior. By the same token, his attitude toward a person, institution, or event is his positive or negative evaluation of the person, institution, or event in question. Quite simply, an attitude is an index of the degree to which a person likes or dislikes an object, where "object" is used in the generic sense to refer to any aspect of the individual's world.

Perhaps more important, irrespective of the object under consideration, the attitude is determined by the person's salient beliefs about that object. For example, a person's attitude toward "the church" is a function of his beliefs about the church, whereas his attitude toward "my attending church" is determined by his beliefs about his attending church. These considerations demonstrate that just as intentions must correspond to the behavioral criteria and attitudes must correspond to intentions, beliefs must correspond to attitudes if they are to permit either prediction or understanding of those attitudes.

From this point on our discussion will focus primarily on attitudes toward behaviors since, within the theory of reasoned action, these are the only attitudes that are directly relevant for predicting and understanding human behavior. When eliciting the salient beliefs that determine attitudes toward behaviors, it is essential to ensure correspondence in action, target, context, and time elements. For example, to elicit the beliefs underlying a person's attitude toward (his) buying a car in the next six months, we could ask him the following questions:

1. What do you believe are the advantages and disadvantages of your buying a car in the next six months?
2. What else do you associate with your buying a car in the next six months?

The respondent is asked to briefly list the beliefs that come to mind.

By way of comparison, to obtain salient beliefs that underlie the person's attitude toward (his) buying some particular make of car, say a Pinto, in the next six months, we would have to phrase the questions in terms of the advantages and disadvantages of his buying a Pinto in the next six months. Clearly, the perceived consequences of buying a Pinto may be very different from the advantages and disadvantages of buying a car in general. Similarly, beliefs about buying a Pinto may also differ greatly from beliefs about buying a Vega or a Mustang.

These examples illustrate lack of correspondence in the target element. The same issues can be raised with respect to the action, context, and time elements. Beliefs about buying a car are not the same as beliefs about renting a car; the consequences of buying a Pinto from a local Ford dealer may differ greatly from the consequences of buying a Pinto from a used car dealer; and beliefs about buying a car in the next six months can be very different from beliefs about buying a car in the next five years. It can be seen that the set of salient beliefs that underlie a person's attitude will be very different depending upon the definition of the behavior involved; changing any one of the four elements defining the behavior can call out completely different sets of salient beliefs.

In this context it is worth considering a problem that has arisen particularly in research on consumer behavior. Attempting to understand the reasons for purchasing one brand rather than another, market researchers have often asked such questions as the following: "In thinking about buying an automobile, what characteristics are important to you?" Two problems are associated with this question. First, it will tend to elicit beliefs about the attributes of automobiles, rather than beliefs about *buying* automobiles. Second, the beliefs elicited concern automobiles in general and they may be irrelevant for understanding the person's attitude toward buying any particular make of car (see chapter 12).

Predicting Attitude from Beliefs

We have argued that a person's attitude toward a behavior is determined by the set of salient beliefs he holds about performing the behavior. The first step toward an understanding of attitude requires elicitation of the salient beliefs. Once this has been accomplished, we must ask how the different salient beliefs combine in determining the attitude toward the behavior.

Consider a woman's salient beliefs about using birth control pills. If she associates this behavior with positive consequences she should hold a favorable attitude toward her own use of birth control pills; if she associates it with negative consequences, her attitude should be unfavorable. Suppose a woman has emitted the beliefs shown in Table 6.2. It can be seen that this woman associates five consequences with using birth control pills. To understand her attitude toward the behavior we first have to know how she evaluates each of these consequences. These evaluations are simply her attitudes toward the consequences in question, but in chapter 5 we saw that attitudes can be measured by means of one or more bipolar evaluative scales.

**TABLE 6.2**
A Woman's Beliefs about Using Birth Control Pills

| MY USING BIRTH CONTROL PILLS | OUTCOME EVALUATIONS | BELIEF STRENGTH | PRODUCT |
|---|---|---|---|
| 1. causes me to gain weight. | −2 | +3 | −6 |
| 2. is convenient. | +1 | +3 | +3 |
| 3. enables me to regulate the size of my family. | +2 | +2 | +4 |
| 4. gives me guilt feelings. | −1 | +2 | −2 |
| 5. regulates my menstrual cycle | +3 | +1 | +3 |
| | | Total | +2 |

To illustrate, the woman could be asked to evaluate each of the five outcomes she listed on a seven-point, good-bad scale, as follows:

causes me to gain weight

good __(+3)__ : __(+2)__ : __(+1)__ : __(0)__ : __(−1)__ : __(−2)__ : __(−3)__ bad
extremely  quite  slightly  neither/  slightly  quite  extremely
nor

Column 1 of Table 6.2 shows the hypothetical results. The respondent in our example felt that causing her to gain weight was quite bad, while enabling her to regulate the size of her family was quite good.

The next step is to assess how confident the person is that the behavior does indeed lead to each of the consequences, that is, to measure the strength of her beliefs. To this end, we must take a closer look at the definition of belief. Earlier we mentioned that a belief associates an "object" with some "attribute." In the case of behavioral beliefs, the object is the behavior of interest and the associated attribute is usually a consequence or outcome of the behavior. With respect to any behavior-outcome association, people may differ in terms of the perceived likelihood that performing the behavior will lead to (or is associated with) the outcome under consideration.

To measure the strength of a person's belief we can ask her to indicate the likelihood (i.e., her subjective probability) that performing a behavior will result in a given outcome or is associated with some other attribute. To return to our previous example, we could ask our respondent to make the following estimate:

The chances are _____ in 100 that my using birth control pills will cause me to gain weight.

Alternatively, we could use the following scale:

How certain are you that using birth control pills will cause you to gain weight?

_____ not at all certain (0)
_____ slightly certain (+1)
_____ quite certain (+2)
_____ extremely certain (+3)

In fact, the values given in Column 2 of Table 6.2 assume use of such a measure. It can be seen that the respondent is extremely certain that using birth control pills causes her to gain weight and that using them is convenient. She is only slightly certain that using birth control pills regulates her menstrual cycle.

According to our theory, a person's attitude toward a behavior can be predicted by multiplying her evaluation of each of the behavior's consequences by the strength of her belief that performing the behavior will lead to that consequence and then summing the products for the total set of beliefs. These computations are illustrated in Column 3 of Table 6.2, and there it can be seen that the woman's attitude toward using birth control pills is predicted to be slightly positive (+2).

In conclusion, attitudes are based on the total set of a person's salient beliefs. People usually believe that performing a given behavior will lead to both positive and negative consequences; their attitudes toward the behavior correspond to the favorability or unfavorability of the total set of consequences, each weighted by the strength of the person's beliefs that performing the behavior will lead to each of the consequences.

This expectancy-value model of attitude has several interesting implications. It is apparent that two individuals who associate the same set of consequences with performing a given behavior may hold different attitudes toward the behavior if they evaluate the consequences differently or if the strength of their beliefs differs. By the same token, people who have different sets of salient behavioral beliefs (i.e., who associate different consequences with performing the behavior) may nevertheless have the same attitudes.

A related implication is that one or more of a person's beliefs can change and yet his attitude may remain the same. For example, even though one salient belief may be replaced by another, they may both have the same belief strength and evaluation. Alternatively, two beliefs might change simultaneously, with the net result being no change in attitude.[2]

One final implication relates to the fact that, in our model, salient beliefs are not weighted for their importance in determining the attitude. It has sometimes been argued that, in addition to obtaining measures of probability and evaluation, each outcome should be rated for its importance. Despite the intuitive plausibility of this position, it has consistently been found that including such measures of importance in the prediction of attitude actually lowers the accuracy of the prediction. From our point of view this finding is not surprising. Out-

[2]Attempts to produce attitude change often fail to recognize that information directed at changing one belief may also produce changes in other beliefs, leaving the attitude unaffected.

comes that are important are typically evaluated more positively or negatively (i.e., their evaluations are more polarized) than outcomes that are unimportant. Further, people usually have more information about things that are important to them and therefore they tend to be more certain and to have stronger beliefs about important than about unimportant outcomes. These arguments suggest that our measures of probabilities and evaluations take enough of importance into account to make redundant any independent assessment of importance. In other words, we assume that all salient beliefs are important, and any differences in their degree of importance is taken into account by the measures of belief strength and outcome evaluation.[3]

**Modal behavioral beliefs.** So far we have dealt only with the procedures involved in predicting a person's attitude from a consideration of his or her own salient beliefs. The advantage of this approach is that we obtain the individual's *own* beliefs and these beliefs can be used to provide insight into the basis for that person's attitude.[4] On the other hand, the elicitation procedure usually produces sets of beliefs that differ from respondent to respondent in terms of content and number. This makes it difficult to compare the beliefs of different individuals and to submit their responses to quantitative analyses.

To overcome these difficulties, we can identify the set of beliefs that are salient in a given population. These *modal salient beliefs* can be ascertained by eliciting beliefs from a representative sample of the population; the beliefs most frequently elicited by this sample constitute the modal set for the population in question. As described earlier, we would ask the sample of respondents to list the advantages, disadvantages, or anything else they associate with performing the behavior under investigation.[5]

Once the respondents have listed their beliefs, we have to make decisions concerning the number and kind of beliefs to be included in the model set. The first step is analagous to a content analysis of the various beliefs emitted by different individuals. It involves organizing the responses by grouping together beliefs that refer to similar outcomes and counting the frequency with which each outcome in a group was elicited.

Table 6.3 shows a partial list of beliefs concerning the use of birth control pills that might have been elicited by a sample of 100 respondents and that were organized in the manner described. At this point, we have to decide whether to

---

[3]Note particularly that investigators have sometimes measured importance in place of evaluation. Clearly, an important outcome can be either positive or negative, and the two measures are not interchangeable. For a more complete discussion of these issues, see Fishbein and Ajzen (1975).

[4]Recall that beyond the first few, not all beliefs emitted are necessarily salient, and the elicitation procedure may produce some beliefs that do not function as determinants of attitude.

[5]To be sure that the respondents list both advantages and disadvantages, it is suggested that these questions be asked separately. (See appendix A.)

**TABLE 6.3**
Organization of Salient Beliefs

| BELIEF GROUPINGS | USING BIRTH CONTROL PILLS | FREQUENCY | BELIEF NUMBER |
|---|---|---|---|
| | gives me guilt feelings | 20 | 1 |
| 1 | is immoral | 25 | 2 |
| | affects my sexual morals | 15 | 3 |
| | affects my sexual behavior | 10 | |
| | increases the frequency with which I have intercourse | 8 | 4 |
| 2 | | | |
| | decreases the frequency with which I have sex | 4 | |
| 3 | regulates my menstrual cycle | 40 | 5 |
| | controls my period | 10 | |
| | takes away the worry of becoming pregnant | 45 | 6 |
| 4 | means I won't get pregnant | 15 | |
| | enables me to regulate time intervals between pregnancies | 30 | 7 |
| | makes me vomit | 6 | |
| | makes me nauseous | 12 | 8 |
| | makes me throw up | 3 | |
| 5 | causes me to gain weight | 5 | |
| | gives me a headache | 4 | 9 |
| | gives me cramps | 2 | |

consider the outcomes in a given group as a single belief or as separate beliefs. Table 6.3 was constructed such that it illustrates some of the problems concerning these decisions. In some instances, the differences between beliefs within a given group are merely semantic. The outcomes "makes me vomit" and "makes me throw up" clearly refer to the same effect. In other cases, this decision is not so easy as is illustrated by the outcomes "makes me vomit" versus "makes me nauseous." Respondents could be referring to the same or to different outcomes.

To make the decision you have to use your common sense, since no clear rules can be provided. However, a useful rule of thumb is to ask yourself whether the two outcomes in question could have been reasonably emitted by the same person. If so, you should return to the original responses and see whether individual respondents did in fact list both consequences. To return to our example, if many of the women who said that using the pill makes them vomit also said that it makes them nauseous, the two outcomes would be treated as separate beliefs just as they would be in the case of identifying the salient beliefs of a single individual. However, if only very few individuals listed both outcomes, we could decide that different women used different labels to refer to the same outcome and treat them as one outcome as we did in Table 6.3.

Another decision illustrated in the table concerns the last three outcomes. Although they are not identical, all three refer to relatively minor side effects of using the pill. Despite the fact that each outcome by itself was mentioned by only a few respondents, when taken together they suggest a salient belief in the population concerning the side effects of using birth control pills. In order to capture this belief, a statement such as "my using birth control pills leads to minor side effects" can be included in the modal set.

Table 6.4 shows the results of organizing the responses into outcome categories. The nine outcomes (starred), as well as a few additional examples, are listed in order of frequency with which they were emitted. Note that in most cases, the wording used for a given category is the most frequently mentioned outcome in that category.

The final decision to be made concerns which of these beliefs to include in the modal salient set. One possibility is to take the 10 or 12 most frequently mentioned outcomes. This procedure results in a set of beliefs which is likely to include at least some of the beliefs emitted by each respondent in the sample. Another possibility is to use those beliefs that exceed a certain frequency. We might decide that we want all beliefs mentioned by at least 10% or 20% of the sample. In our example, this would result in selecting the first 14, or the first 9 beliefs, respectively. Perhaps the least arbitrary decision rule is to choose as many beliefs as necessary to account for a certain percentage (e.g., 75%) of all beliefs emitted. In our example, the total number of beliefs emitted is 463. Of

**TABLE 6.4**
Identification of Modal Salient Beliefs

| NO. | USING BIRTH CONTROL PILLS | FREQUENCY |
|---|---|---|
| 1 | *takes away the worry of becoming pregnant | 60 |
| 2 | is using the best method available | 58 |
| 3 | *regulates my menstrual cycle | 50 |
| 4 | enables me to regulate the size of my family | 45 |
| 5 | *enables me to regulate time intervals between pregnancies | 30 |
| 6 | *is immoral | 25 |
| 7 | *affects the frequency of my sexual behavior | 22 |
| 8 | *makes me nauseous | 21 |
| 9 | *gives me guilt feelings | 20 |
| 10 | leads to major side effects | 18 |
| 11 | is convenient | 18 |
| 12 | *affects my sexual morals | 15 |
| 13 | increases my sexual pleasure | 12 |
| 14 | *leads to minor side effects | 11 |
| 15 | is expensive | 5 |
| 16 | produces children with birth defects | 3 |
| | various idiosyncratic beliefs with frequencies below 3 | 50 |
| | Total | 463 |

*Outcomes identified in Table 6.3

this total, 75% is 347. To meet the 75% criterion, we would need to take the first 10 beliefs.

This completes the selection of modal salient beliefs. We can now construct a questionnaire based on the set of beliefs identified. As we noted earlier with respect to the individual's own salient beliefs, the statements have to be phrased such that the beliefs correspond to the attitude toward the behavior. The respondents are asked to evaluate each of the outcomes and to indicate their subjective probabilities that their performing the behavior would lead to each of the outcomes. Above we have seen how evaluations of outcomes can be assessed by using a bipolar evaluative scale. Note that the outcomes respondents should be asked to evaluate are the entire statements contained in Table 6.4. Thus, the appropriate outcomes are "takes away the worry of becoming pregnant," not "becoming pregnant," "increases my sexual pleasure," not "sexual pleasure," etc.

The strength of each belief should be measured by means of a bipolar scale, such as the following:

My using birth control pills affects my sexual morals.

likely ___ : ___ : ___ : ___ : ___ : ___ : ___ unlikely
  (+3) (+2) (+1)  (0)  (−1) (−2) (−3)

Whereas a person is expected to attach some degree of likelihood to the outcomes she emits herself, she may disagree that performing the behavior will lead to one or more of the *modal* outcomes. Thus, if a woman states that "my using the pill is immoral," it is reasonable to use a unipolar scale to assess how certain she is, as we illustrated earlier. However, when the same statement is presented to a woman who did not emit it herself, she may well judge it to be unlikely. Clearly, it would be inappropriate not to give her the opportunity to say that the statement is false. It is for this reason that it is essential to use a bipolar scale in order to assess the strength of modal beliefs.

Use of a bipolar scale has an additional important advantage. Disagreement that a behavior leads to a negative outcome will, as it should, contribute positively to the attitude toward the behavior (whereas this is not the case with a unipolar belief scale). Consider, for example, a woman who has a negative evaluation (e.g., −3) of "leads to major side effects," and who believes it is quite unlikely (−2) that her using birth control pills will lead to major side effects. Since, as we saw earlier, beliefs and evaluations are multiplied to predict the attitude, this particular belief would make a contribution of +6 to the woman's attitude toward her using birth control pills.[6]

---

[6]Note that use of bipolar scales treats this belief as equivalent to the belief that "using birth control pills does *not* lead to major side effects." Further, it assumes that the woman would have a positive evaluation of "*not* leading to major side effects." Use of a unipolar belief scale does not have the same implications.

In conclusion, we have seen that it is possible to obtain a standard set of salient beliefs for a given population. Although these modal salient beliefs do not necessarily represent the behavioral beliefs held by any given individual, they provide a general picture of the beliefs that are assumed to determine the attitudes for most members of the population under investigation. Within the modal set will be many of the beliefs that are salient for a given individual. By measuring belief strength and evaluations with respect to the modal salient beliefs we can not only *predict* a given individual's attitude but we also obtain information about the *determinants* of his attitude.[7]

In addition, use of the modal set of beliefs enables comparisons across individuals. Table 6.5 illustrates the kinds of comparisons that can be made between the beliefs of users and nonusers of birth control pills. The hypothetical example shows that, on the average, users are predicted to have more favorable attitudes toward the behavior than nonusers (+18.9 versus +12.1). Examination of the beliefs provides insight into the reasons for the different attitudes.

By looking at the products of belief strength and evaluation, it can be seen that two beliefs contribute most to the difference: the beliefs that using the pill "regulates my menstrual cycle" and that it "is using the best method available." Further examination shows that these two beliefs contribute to the difference in attitudes in different ways. Although users and nonusers both believe that using the pill regulates their menstrual cycles, users have a significantly more favorable evaluation of this outcome than nonusers. In contrast, users and nonusers have the same evaluations of "using the best method available," but in

**TABLE 6.5**
Mean Modal Salient Beliefs of Users and
Nonusers of Birth Control Pills

| MY USING BIRTH CONTROL PILLS | BELIEF STRENGTH | | OUTCOME EVALUATION | | PRODUCT | |
|---|---|---|---|---|---|---|
| | *Users* | *Nonusers* | *Users* | *Nonusers* | *Users* | *Nonusers* |
| takes away the worry of becoming pregnant | +2.2 | +2.1 | +2.5 | +2.6 | + 5.5 | + 5.5 |
| is using the best method available | +2.7 | +1.4* | +2.6 | +2.4 | + 7.0 | + 3.4* |
| regulates my menstrual cycle | +1.5 | +1.3 | +2.4 | + .3* | + 3.6 | + .4* |
| enables me to regulate the size of the family | +2.0 | +1.9 | +1.8 | +1.9 | + 3.6 | + 3.6 |
| affects my sexual morals | −2.6 | + .4* | + .3 | −2.0* | − .8 | − .8 |
| | | | Total | | +18.9 | +12.1* |

*significant difference between users and nonusers

[7]Although we can use standard sets of nonsalient beliefs if our sole purpose is to *predict* attitudes, we have to realize that such beliefs may have little to do with the determinants of any person's attitude.

comparison to nonusers, users believe more strongly that using the pill is the best method available.

One other point of interest is illustrated in our hypothetical example. It can be seen that users and nonusers differ in their beliefs that using the pill affects their sexual morals and in their evaluations of this outcome. Nevertheless, this belief contributes little to the difference in attitudes since the product of belief strength and evaluation is the same for users and nonusers.

This example shows that by comparing the modal salient beliefs of people who perform a behavior with the beliefs of people who do not, we can obtain valuable information about the reasons for the differences in behavior.

## DETERMINANTS OF SUBJECTIVE NORMS

We saw that a person's attitude toward a behavior is determined by her beliefs about performing the behavior. Her subjective norm is also a function of beliefs but in this case they are not behavioral beliefs but normative beliefs. In chapter 5 we defined *subjective norm* as a person's belief that most of her important others think she should (or should not) perform the behavior in question. Our theory thus implies that, in forming a subjective norm, an individual takes into account the normative expectations of various others in her environment. That is, she considers whether specific individuals and groups think she should or should not engage in the behavior and she uses this information to arrive at her subjective norm.

Note that a belief such as "my having an abortion would please my husband" is not a normative belief but a belief about performing the behavior in question. As such, it constitutes one of the determinants of the woman's attitude toward her having an abortion. In contrast, the belief "my husband thinks I should have an abortion" is a normative belief, since it is a belief about another person and it concerns that person's behavioral prescription. This normative belief constitutes one of the determinants of the woman's subjective norm.

Although this distinction may appear somewhat arbitrary, there are many cases where a person may hold one type of belief but not the other. For example, I may believe that buying a gift for my friend would please him without believing that he thinks I should buy him a gift. Conversely, I may believe that my doctor thinks I should take a vacation, but it is unlikely that one of my salient beliefs about taking a vacation would be the belief that doing so would please my doctor.

In sum, while some beliefs about performing a behavior may involve a referent, only the person's belief that the referent thinks he should (or should not) perform the behavior is a normative belief. Normative beliefs are thus similar to subjective norms, except that they involve specific individuals or groups rather than a generalized important other.

Clearly, not every possible referent will be relevant or important; only the *salient* referents will influence the person's subjective norm. As in the case of behavioral beliefs, we can elicit a person's salient normative beliefs in a free-response format. For example, with respect to having an abortion, the respondent could be asked to list referents in response to the following question:

> If you considered having an abortion, there might be individuals or groups who would think you should or should not perform this behavior. If any such individuals or groups come to your mind when you consider having an abortion, please list them below.

In formulating this question, it is again essential to ensure correspondence in behavioral elements. That is, the behavior involved in the subjective norm should be exactly replicated in eliciting normative beliefs. For example, if the subjective norm is concerned with whether important others think I should wear jeans at work, then normative beliefs must be elicited with respect to wearing jeans at work and not with respect to wearing jeans in general or wearing jeans at home. Clearly, very different referents may be salient when the same action is considered in different contexts. The same is true for variations in the action, target, and time elements. Table 6.6 shows a hypothetical set of referents elicited by a woman in response to the question concerning abortion.

Once the salient referents have been identified, we can measure the person's normative beliefs, using the same scale as the one previously used to measure subjective norms. For example, a woman's normative belief about her church would be measured as follows:

My church thinks that

I should (+3) : (+2) : (+1) : (0) : (−1) : (−2) : (−3) I should not
have an abortion.

Column 1 of Table 6.6 shows the woman's hypothetical normative beliefs for her five salient referents. As can be seen, she believes that her husband feels very

**TABLE 6.6**
A Woman's Normative Beliefs about Having an Abortion

| REFERENTS | NORMATIVE BELIEF | MOTIVATION TO COMPLY | PRODUCT |
|---|---|---|---|
| My husband | +3 | +3 | 9 |
| My mother | −1 | +1 | −1 |
| My church | −3 | +1 | −3 |
| My brother | 0 | 0 | 0 |
| My doctor | −1 | +2 | −2 |
| | | Total | +3 |

strongly that she should have an abortion, while all other referents are either neutral or think she should not have an abortion.

Knowing a person's beliefs about the relevant referents is, however, not sufficient to predict or understand her subjective norm. In order to do this, we must also assess her general motivation to comply with each of her referents. This can be done by means of a scale such as the following:[8]

In general, how much do you want to do what your husband thinks you should do?

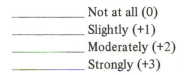

_____ Not at all (0)
_____ Slightly (+1)
_____ Moderately (+2)
_____ Strongly (+3)

In Column 2 of Table 6.6 it can be seen that our hypothetical woman shows considerable differences in her motivations to comply with her various referents. While she is strongly motivated to comply with her husband, she is not at all motivated to comply with her brother.

According to our theory, a person's subjective norm can be predicted from the index we obtain if we multiply her normative beliefs by the corresponding motivations to comply and then sum the products. By taking into account the motivation to comply, we ensure that important referents are given proportionately more weight in the prediction of the subjective norm. Since people have little or no motivation to comply with an unimportant referent, the weighted sum of normative beliefs should correspond to the belief concerning the expectations of most important others (i.e., the subjective norm).

These computations are illustrated in Column 3 of Table 6.6; it can be seen that the woman's subjective norm is predicted to be slightly positive (+3). That is, we would predict that she would have a relatively weak belief that most of her important others think she should have an abortion.

## Modal Normative Beliefs

Our discussion thus far has dealt only with predicting a person's subjective norm from her own normative beliefs and motivations to comply. As in the case of behavioral beliefs, it will often be useful to construct a standard set of modal normative beliefs. This can be done by asking a representative sample of the population under study to list the other people or groups who would approve or disapprove of the respondents' performing the behavior.[9] To obtain a list of

---

[8]Note that this is a unipolar scale, since people are unlikely to be motivated to do the opposite of what their salient referents think they should do.

[9]To construct a list of modal salient referents for use in a standard questionnaire concerning abortion, the following three questions are recommended: 1. Are there any people or groups who would approve of your having an abortion? 2. Are there any people or groups who would disapprove of your having an abortion? 3. Does anybody else come to mind when you think about having an abortion? (See appendix A.)

salient referents we select the most frequently mentioned individuals or groups. In the final standard questionnaire we assess normative beliefs and motivations to comply with respect to each of these modal salient referents. We can then compare the normative beliefs and motivations to comply of people who perform a given behavior with those of people who do not perform the behavior. In this fashion, we gain additional insight into the normative considerations that account for behavioral differences.

In sum, subjective norms are based on the total set of salient normative beliefs, each weighted by motivation to comply. This implies that there is no necessary relation between any single normative belief and the subjective norm. In fact, as can be seen in Table 6.5, although three of the five normative beliefs are negative, the overall subjective norm is predicted to be positive. By the same token, if a given normative belief were to change, this does not mean that a change in subjective norm would have to follow. As in the case of attitudes, one salient referent could be replaced by another but the normative beliefs (and motivations to comply) might stay the same and a change in one salient normative belief could be cancelled by a complimentary change in a second normative belief. It should also be evident that two people with the same set of referents may have different subjective norms, and people with different sets of referents may have the same subjective norms.

## THE MEDIATING ROLE OF ATTITUDES AND SUBJECTIVE NORMS

We have argued that with the aid of appropriate elicitation and measurement procedures, it is possible to predict a person's attitude toward a behavior from a weighted sum of his beliefs about performing the behavior and to predict his subjective norm from a weighted sum of his normative beliefs. Since attitude toward a behavior and subjective norm are the determinants of intention, it should theoretically be possible to predict intention directly from the two sets of beliefs. In practice, however, this will hold only if the following conditions are met. First, we must show that the set of behavioral beliefs do indeed predict the attitude toward the behavior and that the set of normative beliefs are predictive of the subjective norm. These predictions may break down if beliefs, attitudes, and subjective norms lack correspondence or if the beliefs, evaluations, or motivations to comply are otherwise inappropriately measured. Second, the attitude toward the behavior and the subjective norm must be shown to predict the intention. Inappropriate measures or lack of correspondence may again impair the observed relation.

Of course, it must also be recognized that inaccurate prediction may not be the result of inappropriate measures but rather reflect the failure of the theory, at least in the context of the behavior under investigation. Finally, even if the two sets of beliefs are found to permit accurate prediction of intentions, the degree to which they predict behavior will depend on the strength of the intention-behavior relation.

These considerations make it clear that our theory cannot be tested by examining only the relations between beliefs and either intentions or behavior.

## SUMMARY AND CONCLUSION

In this chapter we have argued that a person's attitude toward a behavior is determined by his salient beliefs that performing the behavior leads to certain outcomes and by his evaluations of those outcomes. Similarly, we saw that a person's subjective norm is determined by his beliefs that specific salient referents think he should (or should not) perform a given behavior and by his motivations to comply with those referents. Attitude toward a behavior and subjective norm are both considered to be a function of the weighted sum of the appropriate beliefs. As we have emphasized repeatedly, it is essential to ensure correspondence between measures of belief on the one hand and measures of attitude and subjective norm on the other. We emphasized that only salient beliefs serve as determinants of attitudes and subjective norms, and we discussed procedures for eliciting individual as well as modal salient beliefs.

# CHAPTER
# 7

## Theoretical
## Implications

Chapters 4 through 6 can be viewed as representing different levels of explanation for people's behavior. At the most global level, a person's behavior is assumed to be determined by his intention. At the next level, we showed that these intentions are themselves determined by attitudes toward the behavior and subjective norms. The third level explained attitudes and subjective norms in terms of beliefs about the consequences of performing the behavior and about the normative expectations of relevant referents. In the final analysis, then, a person's behavior is explained by reference to his beliefs. Since a person's beliefs represent the information (be it correct or incorrect) he has about his world, it follows that a person's behavior is ultimately determined by this information.

We have seen that behavior involves a choice between two or more alternatives. To completely understand behavior, it is therefore necessary to identify the beliefs related to the performance of each behavioral alternative. For example, to fully understand why an individual chooses to ride a bus to work each Monday (rather than riding a bicycle or motorcycle, taking a cab, riding as a passenger in someone else's car, or driving his own car) it would be necessary to consider his beliefs about using each of these alternative modes of transportation. Often, however, our goal is not complete understanding of a behavioral choice but the solution of an applied problem. If we are interested in increasing use of public transportation (in this case, the bus) we do not need to know why people do or do not ride bicycles or drive cars. Instead, we need to identify the factors that determine use of public transportation. That is, in the final analysis, we have to assess people's beliefs about the advantages and disadvantages of using the bus and their normative beliefs concerning this behavior.

The point is that the solution of specific problems often requires formulating our questions in terms of a single intention and the corresponding behavior. Once this is done, we can use the theory described in the previous chapters to understand the behavior in question and to suggest ways of changing it. To take another example, if one is interested in increasing the amount of money donated to the church, it will be of little practical significance to investigate how much people donate, or to try to understand why a person donated one amount of money rather than another. What is important is discovering the beliefs people hold about the advantages and disadvantages of *increasing* the amount of money they donate or their normative beliefs concerning this behavior. Formulating the question in this manner allows us to obtain information that is useful in dealing with the problem at hand.

## HYPOTHESES LINKING BELIEFS TO BEHAVIOR

Our argument that behavior is ultimately determined by beliefs should not be taken to mean that there is a direct link between beliefs and behavior. Beliefs influence attitudes and subjective norms; these two components influence intentions; and intentions influence behavior. Although we postulate relations between these variables, the variables are neither identical nor interchangeable. That is, from a theoretical point of view we expect certain relations to hold, but for a variety of reasons they may not obtain in practice.

For example, we have argued that a person's attitude toward a behavior is a function of her beliefs that performing the behavior leads to various outcomes and her evaluations of those outcomes. However, this argument assumes that we have identified and measured all of the person's *salient* beliefs and only her salient beliefs, and that these beliefs correspond to the attitude in target, action, context, and time. Since these assumptions are not always met, the relation between a particular set of beliefs and attitude cannot be taken as a given but must be considered an empirical question. The same is true for the relation between normative beliefs and subjective norm.

The relation between the attitudinal and normative components on the one hand and intentions on the other is also an empirical question. Here again, correspondence is a prerequisite for a strong empirical relation. In addition, the weights of the two components have to be considered. Knowing a person's attitude toward the behavior may tell us little about his intention if the intention is primarily determined by normative considerations. Conversely, knowing his subjective norm permits prediction of his intention only if the intention is not under attitudinal control. Moreover, two individuals with identical attitudes and subjective norms may have different intentions if they place different weights on the two components. For all of these reasons, it is necessary to demonstrate that we can predict intentions from attitudes and subjective norms and not simply assume that there is a strong relationship.

Finally, in chapter 4 we discussed the problem of using intention to predict behavior. Although we view intention as the immediate determinant of behavior, we saw that the strength of the obtained intention-behavior relation depends on correspondence and on the intention's stability.

The theory of reasoned action, then, consists essentially of a series of hypotheses linking beliefs to behavior, with each hypothesis requiring empirical verification. Clearly, if a measure of intention is found to be unrelated to the behavioral criterion, it would be foolish to try to understand the behavior by investigating the determinants of the intention. Similarly, only when a measure of attitude can first be shown to serve as a determinant of intention does it pay to investigate the beliefs that underlie the attitude. Finally, a given set of beliefs is of explanatory value only if it can be shown to be the determinant of the attitude or subjective norm that underlies the intention and ultimately the behavior under investigation.

This discussion should make it clear that it is inappropriate to use beliefs in an attempt to directly predict intentions or behavior. Similarly, it is inappropriate to go directly from attitudes and subjective norms to behavior. Such attempts are meaningful only when the intervening relations have first been empirically demonstrated.[1]

## Implications for Changing Behavior

We are often interested in understanding behavior because we would like to know how we can influence or change it. According to the theory of reasoned action, behavioral change is ultimately the result of changes in beliefs. This implies that in order to influence behavior, we have to expose people to information which will produce changes in their beliefs.

Our preceding discussion suggests, however, that changing a person's beliefs will not always affect his behavior. We saw that a number of links intervene between beliefs and behavior. It follows that when we are trying to change beliefs to influence behavior we are making a number of assumptions. First, we assume that a change in beliefs will produce a change in attitude or subjective norm. It should be recalled, however, that attitudes are based on the total set of salient beliefs about performing a behavior. Changing one or more beliefs may not be sufficient to bring about change in the overall attitude. Similarly, changing one or two normative beliefs may have little effect on the subjective norm (see chapter 6). If neither the attitude nor the subjective norm changes, we cannot expect a change in behavior.

Imagine that by changing beliefs we succeeded in changing attitudes toward the behavior. We then have to make the assumption that such a change in attitudes will lead to a change in intentions. Once again, this assumption will be unwarranted if the attitudinal component carries little or no weight in determining the intention. By the same token, the assumption that a change in subjective norms will influence intentions is also unwarranted if the normative component carries little or no weight. Again, if we do not succeed in changing the intention, we cannot expect a change in behavior.

The final assumption we make is that a change in intention will produce a change in behavior. We have repeatedly noted that the empirical relation between

[1]For a more detailed discussion of this issue, see Fishbein and Ajzen (1976).

intention and behavior cannot be taken for granted. Only if the obtained relation between intention and behavior is strong can we expect a change in intention to produce a change in behavior.

We would like to make it clear, however, that changing behavior is really not as difficult as the preceding discussion may imply. A careful investigator will usually be able to identify an intention that is highly related to the behavior he wants to change. Once the intention is identified, it is quite easy to determine the degree to which it is under attitudinal or normative control. This tells the investigator whether his influence attempt should be directed at the set of beliefs underlying attitude toward the behavior or toward the set of beliefs underlying the subjective norm. The investigator's remaining task is to expose individuals to information which will change a sufficient number of beliefs to produce the desired change in attitude or subjective norm.[2] The question of behavioral change will be considered in greater detail in chapter 15.

## EFFECTS OF EXTERNAL VARIABLES

Our discussion has focused on those concepts or variables that, from our point of view, are central for predicting and understanding human behavior. Note that our approach differs considerably from other attempts to explain behavior. In contrast to most other approaches, we have not attempted to explain behavior by referring to such things as personality traits, attitudes toward people or institutions, or demographic variables. Although we do not deny that "external" variables of this kind may sometimes be related to behavior, from our point of view they can affect behavior only indirectly. That is, external variables will be related to behavior only if they are related to one or more of the variables specified by our theory.

The relation between an external variable and behavior can be mediated in a number of ways. Assume, for example, that education is found to be related to cigarette smoking, such that there are fewer smokers among the more highly educated. One reason for this relation might be that highly educated individuals believe that smoking leads to different outcomes than do individuals with less education. For example, the beliefs that "my smoking leads to chronic bronchitis" and that "my smoking leads to emphysema" may be salient among many more of the better educated individuals than among the less educated ones. These differences in salient beliefs could affect attitudes, such that increased education would be accompanied by a more negative attitude toward one's own smoking. This attitude could be related to the intention to smoke and, ulti-

---

[2]It is beyond the scope of this book to discuss the various strategies that may be used to change beliefs. In chapter 15 we briefly consider one of these strategies, persuasive communication. For a review of other strategies, see Fishbein and Ajzen (1975, chaps. 10 and 11).

mately, to actual smoking behavior. Thus, if education influenced the kinds of salient beliefs individuals hold about the consequences of their smoking, this would account for the obtained relation between education and smoking.

Even if education did not affect the beliefs that are salient for an individual, it might influence the strength with which one or more beliefs are held. For example, the belief that "smoking is hazardous to my health" may be salient irrespective of education. Highly educated individuals, however, may hold this belief more strongly than individuals with less education. Again, this difference in beliefs due to level of education may eventually be reflected in behavior, such that smoking is observed to decrease with education.

A third possibility is that people with different degrees of education may have different evaluations of the same outcome. As an illustration, imagine that people with different degrees of education believe with equal strength that "my smoking increases the chances that my children will smoke." If highly educated individuals had a more negative evaluation of this consequence than individuals with less education, then they could have more negative attitudes toward their smoking than the less educated. This difference in attitudes could again be reflected in behavior, thus accounting for the observed relation between education and smoking.

So far we have considered how the relation between education and smoking might be mediated by the determinants of the attitudinal component. In a similar fashion, the relation could be mediated by the determinants of the normative component. That is, highly educated people may differ from people with less education in terms of 1) their salient referents with respect to their smoking, 2) the normative beliefs attributed to given referents, and 3) the motivation to comply with given referents. For example, highly educated individuals may believe more strongly that their spouses think they should not smoke and they may be more highly motivated to comply with their spouses than individuals with less education. Such differences could lead well educated people to have more negative subjective norms than less educated people, and this difference in subjective norms could in turn influence intentions and behavior. This chain of effects could account for the observed relation between education and smoking.

The relation between education and smoking can thus be mediated by the determinants of the attitudinal and normative components. In addition, an external variable, such as education, may affect the relative weights of the two components in determining intentions to smoke. Imagine, for example, that, irrespective of education, people have slightly favorable attitudes toward their smoking and negative subjective norms. If the intentions of highly educated individuals were primarily determined by their subjective norms and the intentions of less educated individuals were determined by attitudes, fewer of the former than of the latter would intend to smoke. This difference in intentions could account for observed differences in smoking behavior.

Figure 7.1 illustrates how different types of external variables can influence intentions and behavior indirectly by their effects on behavioral beliefs, outcome

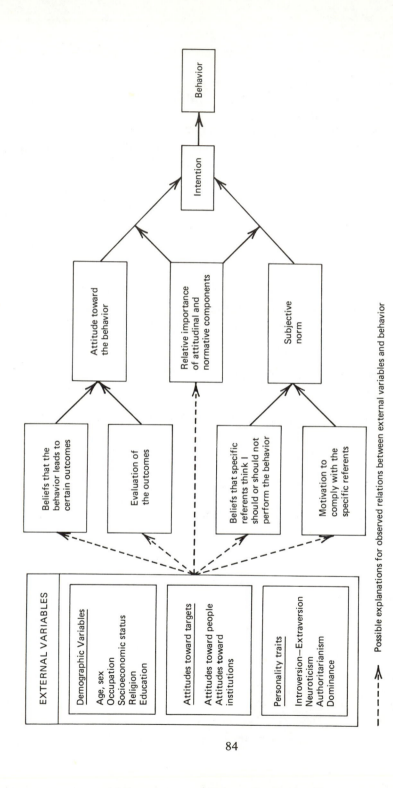

**FIGURE 7.1**

Indirect effects of external variables on behavior.

The figure contains the following labeled boxes and text:

Behavior

Intention

Attitude toward the behavior

Relative importance of attitudinal and normative components

Subjective norm

Beliefs that the behavior leads to certain outcomes

Evaluation of the outcomes

Beliefs that specific referents think I should or should not perform the behavior

Motivation to comply with the specific referents

EXTERNAL VARIABLES

Demographic Variables

Age, sex
Occupation
Socioeconomic status
Religion
Education

Attitudes toward targets

Attitudes toward people
Attitudes toward institutions

Personality traits

Introversion—Extraversion
Neuroticism
Authoritarianism
Dominance

- - - → Possible explanations for observed relations between external variables and behavior

——→ Stable theoretical relations linking beliefs to behavior

84

evaluations, normative beliefs, motivations to comply, or on the relative weights of the attitudinal and normative components.

We have shown how such indirect effects could explain an observed relation between education and smoking. Note, however, that we assumed fewer smokers among highly educated individuals merely for purposes of illustration. It would have been just as easy for us to illustrate our point by assuming that highly educated individuals are *more* likely to be smokers. Alternatively, we could argue that there is no relation at all between education and smoking. First of all, different degrees of education may have none of the effects represented by the broken arrows in Figure 7.1. For example, people differing in level of education need not differ in their normative beliefs or in their motivations to comply. Nor need they differ with respect to their beliefs that performing a behavior will lead to certain consequences or with respect to their evaluations of those consequences.

Equally important, even if education did influence, say, beliefs about the consequences of smoking, there might still be no differences between the attitudes toward smoking of well educated and less well educated individuals. For example, although well educated people may hold more salient beliefs than less well educated people, their additional beliefs may associate smoking with both positive and negative consequences.

Further, as noted earlier, even when the external variable is related to attitude, it will not be related to intention if the intention is primarily under the control of normative considerations. Finally, an external variable may be related to intention, but if the intention-behavior relation is low, it cannot be expected to influence behavior.

The main point to be made is that, for all of these reasons, there is no necessary relation between any external variable and a given behavior. Whereas the relations specified in our theory (unbroken lines in Figure 7.1) are always assumed to hold so long as appropriate measures are obtained, external variables are not expected to have such consistent effects (broken lines in Figure 7.1). If an external variable is found to be related to a given behavior at a given time, it may no longer be related to the behavior at some other time. For example, ten years ago in the United States religious preference was strongly related to the use of contraceptives. Catholics were much less likely to use contraceptives than were Protestants or Jews. These religious differences no longer exist (see chapter 11). From our point of view, one possible explanation is that ten years ago the religious groups differed greatly in their beliefs about the advantages and disadvantages of using contraceptives, whereas there are no such differences today.

Also, just because some external variable is found to be related to one behavior does not mean that it has to be related to another behavior, even if the behaviors appear similar. We have seen that behaviors can vary in action, target, context, and time elements. A change in one or more of these elements can lead to very different beliefs about the *consequences of performing* the behaviors in question.[3] A person's beliefs about smoking cigarettes may be very different from her beliefs about smoking marijuana (change in target element). Similarly, a person's beliefs about smoking cigarettes in an elevator may differ greatly from his beliefs about smoking cigarettes in his office (change in context), and a person's beliefs about smoking before breakfast may differ from his beliefs about smoking later in the day (change in time element). Finally, beliefs about smoking marijuana may be different from beliefs about selling marijuana (change in action element).

Although it is conceivable that a given external variable will be related to one set of beliefs, there is no reason to expect that it will have the same relations to all other sets of beliefs. Differences in education may be related to beliefs about smoking in general, but education may have little to do with beliefs about the advantages or disadvantages of smoking cigarettes in an elevator. Education might thus be related to smoking in general but be unrelated to smoking in an elevator.

We have discussed the effects of external variables in terms of demographic characteristics, such as education and religion, but everything we have said applies to any variable external to our theory. Most attempts to predict and explain behavior have focused on two classes of external variables, namely, personality traits and traditional attitudes toward such targets as individuals, classes of individuals, institutions, and policies.

### Personality Traits and Behavior

Whatever the behavior, we can always name one or more personality traits that appear to underlie or influence the behavior in question. To help explain delinquent behaviors, such as shoplifting or truancy, investigators have considered such personality traits as dominance, aggressiveness, and neuroticism. In marketing research, attempts have been made to explain the purchase of different products by looking at consumers' masculinity-feminity, life style, nurturance, or extraversion-introversion.

Another area of research where personality traits have frequently been invoked is helping behavior. In particular, altruism has been used in attempting to explain such varied actions as donating blood, stopping at the scene of an accident, and contributing money to charity. Although it is possible that altruistic and nonaltruistic individuals differ in their beliefs concerning some helping behaviors, they may hold the same beliefs about other helping behaviors. For example, in comparison to nonaltruistic people, altruistic individuals may believe that donating blood will lead to more favorable outcomes, but people's altruism may be unrelated to their beliefs about the consequences of coming to the aid of a victim of a mugging or a rape.

---

[3]Changes in behavioral elements may also lead to very different evaluations of the consequences, different normative beliefs, etc.

Generally speaking, attempts to relate personality traits to specific actions have been disappointing. More often than not personality traits are unrelated to specific behaviors and, when a relation is found, it is usually not very strong. From our point of view, such findings are to be expected. As in the case of demographic characteristics, we see no reason why people differing on a given personality trait should hold different beliefs with respect to each and every behavior that may appear to be relevant for that trait.

A personality trait is usually viewed as a predisposition to perform a certain class of behaviors (e.g., aggressive behaviors or altruistic behaviors). No particular target, context, and time elements are specified. It is assumed that aggressive individuals, more than nonaggressive ones, are likely to engage in a large variety of aggressive acts irrespective of the target of the aggressive act, the context in which it occurs, or the time of its occurrence. This implies that although an aggressive person is expected to perform a greater number of aggressive behaviors than a nonaggressive person, the aggressive individual need not perform any given aggressive act.

Viewed in this way, it can be seen that the only behavioral criterion that corresponds to a personality trait is one that is based on observation of a set of behaviors representing the trait in question and that generalizes across targets, contexts, and time. That is, personality traits correspond only to *behavioral categories*, not to single actions.

Consider, for example, the following "altruistic" behaviors.

Pushing a handicapped person's wheelchair
Attempting to rescue a rape victim
Donating blood to the Red Cross
Stopping at the scene of an accident
Helping an old lady across the street
Contributing money to charity
Donating a kidney to a relative
Donating a kidney to a stranger
Turning off car headlights that were inadvertently left on
Employing a mentally retarded person

We would not expect a strong relation between any one behavior and a general measure of altruism. However behaviors of this type could be used to construct a behavioral category (see chapter 3), and this index of altruism should be related to personality measures of altruism. That is, measures of altruism should correlate with the total behavioral score, even though they may have little or no relation to any single behavior comprising the index.[4]

[4]Support for this argument can be found in Jaccard (1974).

In chapter 2 we saw that past attempts to predict and explain behavior have most frequently involved attitudes toward individuals; ethnic, religious, and national groups; institutions; and policies. It has usually been assumed that the more favorable a person's attitude is toward some object, the more likely he will be to perform any given positive behavior with respect to that object, and the less likely he will be to perform any negative behavior with respect to the object. For example, people's attitudes toward blacks have been measured in attempts to predict or explain hiring of blacks, selling one's house to a black family, sending one's child to an integrated school, voting for a black candidate, etc. By the same token, attitudes toward "family planning" or "zero population growth" have been assumed to explain the number of children in a completed family, use of the birth control pill, visits to a family planning clinic, signing a petition for (or against) legalized abortion, etc.

As in the case of demographic or personality characteristics, there is no reason to expect that attitudes toward a target will be related to each and every behavior that a person can perform with respect to that target. Like any other external variable, an individual's attitude toward a target may be unrelated to his beliefs about the consequences of performing a specific action toward that target, in a given context, and at a given time. His attitude toward the target may also be unrelated to his evaluations of the behavior's consequences, his normative beliefs concerning performance of the behavior, his motivations to comply with relevant referents, and the relative weights he places on the attitudinal and normative components.

To be sure, the perceived consequences of performing a certain behavior toward a liked target may in some situations differ from those of performing the same behavior toward a disliked target. In such a situation, the attitude toward the target is expected to be related to the attitude toward the behavior, and hence to influence intention and behavior (assuming that the attitude toward the behavior carries a significant weight as a determinant of the intention). In other situations, however, a given behavior will be perceived to lead to the same consequences irrespective of the actor's liking for the target. No influence of the attitude toward the target on the attitude toward the behavior would be expected in this case. Here, liking for the target will be unrelated to the intention and the behavior (unless it influences intentions via subjective norms).

Similarly, there are situations where one is expected to behave differently toward a liked than toward a disliked person; in other situations normative beliefs regarding behavior toward liked and disliked persons are identical. In the former case, some relation between attitude toward the target and behavior might be obtained because of the influence of the attitude on the normative beliefs. Such a relation is unlikely in the latter case.

This discussion suggests that attitudes toward targets will have no consistent relations to specific behaviors with respect to those targets. In fact, as in the case

88

of personality traits, research has usually found no relation between attitudes toward targets and specific behaviors, and whenever relations were obtained they
have typically been of low magnitude.[5]

Another way of explaining the lack of relation between attitudes toward targets and single-action criteria has to do with the correspondence between these
measures. A single-action criterion involves a specific action, a specific target, a
given context, and a given point in time, whereas attitudes toward targets specify
a given target but generalize across the remaining elements. Given this lack of
correspondence, strong relations cannot be expected.

In order to obtain correspondence between behavior and traditional measures
of attitudes toward targets, the behavioral criterion would also have to generalize
across action, context, and time elements. Such a measure would constitute a
behavioral category, where each of the behaviors comprising the category is
scored in terms of its favorableness or unfavorableness with respect to the target
in question. The greater the number of favorable behaviors a person performs
and the fewer unfavorable behaviors he performs, the higher his score will be on
the behavioral index. This index should be related to a measure of attitude toward the target. The more favorable the person's attitude is toward the target,
the greater the number of positive behaviors (and the smaller the number of
negative behaviors) the person will perform with respect to the target, although
there will not necessarily be any relation between his attitude and any given behavior comprising the index.[6]

It is important to note that, over the last 50 years or so, investigators who
have used attitudes to predict and explain behavior have relied on an assumption
which can now be seen to be inappropriate. The assumption was that a person's
attitude toward an object determines his specific behaviors with respect to that
object. However, we have tried to show that the considerations which lead
people to perform a given behavior may have little to do with their attitudes toward the target of the behavior. People do not hire blacks because they like or
dislike them but because they have favorable attitudes toward *hiring* blacks (i.e.,
they have positive beliefs about the consequences of hiring blacks), or because
they believe that important others think they should hire blacks. Similarly,
whether or not a person contributes to the President's campaign fund, watches a
televised presidential address, or accepts a presidential invitation to attend a
party at the White House probably has little to do with how much the person
likes the President. Instead, a person will perform these behaviors if he thinks
that the performance will lead to favorable consequences or if he believes that
most of his important referents think he should do so. Clearly, one may dislike
the President but still believe that there are many advantages to be gained by
attending his party at the White House. The same is true of attitudes toward
various products and people's buying behavior. Although I may have a very

---

[5]For literature reviews, see Wicker (1969) and Ajzen and Fishbein (1977).

[6]Support for this argument was provided by Fishbein and Ajzen (1974).

favorable attitude toward a particular make of car (e.g., a Jaguar or a Cadillac), I may believe that important others think I should not purchase such a car or I may believe that purchasing one of these cars will lead to more disadvantages than advantages. Even for such everyday products as breakfast cereals or toothpaste, my liking for a particular brand may be unrelated to my purchasing behavior. Although I may hate a given breakfast cereal, I may nevertheless buy it if I believe that my children think I should do so.

As we shall see throughout the remainder of this book, this simple shift from attitudes toward targets to attitudes toward behaviors and subjective norms goes a long way in helping us to account for apparently inconsistent human behavior.

## PREDICTION VERSUS UNDERSTANDING

As we move from behavior to intention, from intention to attitude toward the behavior and subjective norm, and from these two components to the underlying beliefs, we can gain increasing understanding of the factors determining the behavior under consideration. However, this gain in understanding is not accompanied by improved prediction. According to the theory of reasoned action, intention is the immediate determinant of behavior and thus allows us to predict behavior. It follows that knowing the intention's determinants will not improve the accuracy of our prediction. A person's intention is assumed to reflect his attitude toward the behavior and his subjective norm; the effects of these two components on behavior are thus mediated by the intention. Measuring the two components in addition to the intention provides for better understanding, but it cannot improve prediction of the behavior.

Similar considerations apply to the prediction of intentions. Measures of attitudes toward the behavior and of subjective norms provide all the information needed to predict the intention. Assessing the beliefs underlying these two components may help us understand the basis for the intention. However, since their effects are mediated by the attitudinal and normative components, they will make no independent contribution to the prediction of the intention.

Within our theory, a behavior is explained once its determinants have been traced to the underlying beliefs. A question can be raised, however, about the origins of these beliefs. Generally speaking, beliefs reflect a person's past experience; exposure to different kinds of information leads to the formation of different beliefs.[7] It may be argued that demographic variables are very global indices of different prior experiences. Thus, Catholics have different experiences from Protestants or Jews, and children of upper-class parents are raised differently from children of lower-class parents. In a similar fashion, personality variables and traditional attitudes are sometimes viewed as residues of past experience

---

[7]For a discussion of belief formation, see Fishbein and Ajzen (1975, chap. 5).

or are assumed to influence the person's interpretation of his environment and thus the beliefs he holds.

It is for this reason that external variables are sometimes related to beliefs underlying a given behavior. If so, they can provide insight into the factors determining these beliefs and thereby ultimately increase our understanding of the behavior in question. Note again, however, that according to our theory the effects of external variables are mediated by beliefs, and therefore, taking external variables into account (in addition to beliefs) is not expected to improve prediction of attitudes and subjective norms. For the same reason, measuring external variables in addition to attitudes and subjective norms is not expected to improve prediction of intentions, nor should measuring them in addition to intentions improve prediction of behavior.[8]

## SUMMARY AND CONCLUSION

In this chapter we have examined the potential effects of variables external to our theory, such as demographic characteristics, personality traits, and traditional measures of attitudes toward persons, institutions, and policies. We argued that such variables have no necessary relation to any particular behavior, since they have no consistent effects on the beliefs underlying these behaviors. More important, we showed that measures of personality and attitudes toward targets do not correspond to any single behavior, but they do correspond to behavioral categories. The behavioral criterion corresponding to a personality trait is a behavioral category defined in terms of a class of actions (e.g., aggressive behaviors) without specification of target, context, or time elements. In the case of attitudes toward targets, the corresponding behavioral criterion specifies the target but generalizes across actions, context, and time.

We also argued that there is a causal chain linking beliefs to behavior. On the basis of different experiences, people may form different beliefs about the consequences of performing a behavior and different normative beliefs. These beliefs in turn determine attitudes and subjective norms which then determine intention and the corresponding behavior. We can gain understanding of a behavior by tracing its determinants back to the underlying beliefs, and we can influence the behavior by changing a sufficient number of these beliefs.

---

[8]One possible exception occurs when the intention changes before the behavior is observed. Taking into account external variables that are related to the change in intention may improve behavioral prediction. For a more complete discussion of this point, see Ajzen and Fishbein (1974) and Fishbein and Ajzen (1975).

# PART 2

# Applications

# CHAPTER
# 8

## Overview

In the introduction to part 1 we emphasized the importance of a systematic theoretical framework for the prediction and understanding of human behavior. Most social scientists have attempted to explain behavior in a single domain, and they have invoked different variables to deal with different kinds of behaviors. In contrast, we have described a theory that involves a limited number of constructs and that can be applied to any behavior under volitional control.

As we saw in chapter 7, attempts to explain behavior have typically relied on such variables as demographic characteristics, personality traits, traditional measures of attitude, and values. That is, most explanations have relied on what we have called external variables. From our point of view external variables cannot provide satisfactory explanation of behavior. Although such external variables are sometimes found to be related to the behavior, no consistent relations are found in other cases. For example, in a large number of presidential elections, attitudes toward candidates were found to be related to voting behavior; people were more likely to vote for the candidate they liked than for the one they disliked. In contrast, the relations between demographic characteristics and voting have changed over time. Social class, religion, and place of residence (rural versus urban) were found to be directly related to voting behavior in the 1940s, but this is no longer the case today. Finally, and perhaps most often, seemingly relevant external variables are found to have no relation to the behavior under investigation. In the family planning area, for example, neither a woman's attitude toward children nor her need to nurture are related to her use of contraceptives.

Such findings are hardly surprising since, as we saw in chapter 7, external variables are at best *indirectly* related to any given behavior. It is possible to devise many different explanations to account for an observed relation between an external variable and a given behavior. Some explanations posit a direct causal effect of the external variable on the behavior (e.g., the individual performed the behavior because he is an introvert). Other explanations assume one or more intervening steps (e.g., an introvert has certain expectations which lead him to perform the behavior). If the relation between external variables and behavior is inconsistent over time, additional explanations are required. Since investigators have invoked many different external variables to explain various behaviors, the number of possible explanations linking external variables and behavior is virtually limitless. In contrast, the theory of reasoned action proposes a single set of constructs that accounts for any observed relations between external variables and behavior.

Obviously, it has taken some time to develop this theory and it has undergone many revisions. The theory has grown out of an initial interest in understanding the determinants of traditional attitudes and their relations to behavior. While early work showed that attitudes toward any object could be predicted from beliefs about the object's attributes and the evaluations of those attributes (see chapter 6), we saw in chapter 2 that the relations between such traditional attitudes and behavior could not be consistently demonstrated. Since the ultimate utility of any attitude theory rests on its ability to predict and explain behavior, we rejected the assumption that traditional measures of attitude predict behavior and looked for an alternative approach. The current status of this continuing process has been described in the first part of this book.

We have long been convinced that it is important to demonstrate the utility of a theory in applied settings as well as in laboratory settings. This has led us to investigate such diverse problems as voting behavior, family planning, consumer behavior, occupational choice, and weight reduction. Each of the following chapters will consider a different behavioral domain. We will begin by summarizing the general conclusions reached by investigators in the area. As indicated earlier, most of these conclusions are statements of a relationship between an external variable and the behavior in question. Where an external variable is consistently found to be related to the behavior under investigation, we will show that its effects are mediated by the predictors in our theory.

In each of the behavioral domains, we will provide examples of the utility of our theory for the prediction and understanding of one or more behaviors. As stated previously, our theory has developed over a number of years, and the data collected throughout this period reflect the changes in the theory that have occurred. For example, the concept of subjective norm is a relatively recent development; prior to the introduction of this construct, the normative component was measured in terms of normative beliefs and motivations to comply.

To provide a complete account of the relationships specified in our theory, it would be necessary to measure 1) behavioral and normative beliefs, outcome evaluations, and motivations to comply underlying the attitudinal and normative components; 2) the attitude toward the behavior and the subjective norm; 3) the intention to perform the behavior; and 4) the behavior itself. In part 1 we described procedures for the measurement of these variables. Appendix A provides a brief outline of the steps involved in constructing a standard questionnaire that can be used to assess all of the variables comprising the theory of reasoned action. For purposes of illustration, appendix B shows the form an actual questionnaire might take if we were interested in predicting and understanding people's voting decisions in a political referendum.

From a practical point of view, however, it is not always necessary to measure all of these variables to answer certain questions. Specifically, in a number of cases we measured the attitudinal and normative components without assessing the underlying beliefs. In other instances we were not concerned with the intention-behavior relation, but merely with the theory's ability to predict intentions. In these cases no measures of behavior were obtained. Taken in combination, however, the data we will present span the whole range of relations from external variables through beliefs, attitudes, subjective norms, and intentions to behavior.

## DATA PRESENTATION AND THE USE OF STATISTICS

In presenting our data, we will need a means of describing the strength of the relationships among the variables of our theory. A useful index for this purpose is known as the *correlation coefficient,* or simply *correlation,* symbolized by the letter $r$. This coefficient can take on values that range from $-1$ through 0 to $+1$. The more the correlation between two measures departs from zero and approaches the value of either $-1$ or $+1$, the stronger the relationship will be between the two measures in question. When $r = 0$, there is absolutely no relation between the two variables.[1] Correlations greater than zero indicate that as the value of one variable increases, so, too, does the value of the other. In contrast, negative correlations indicate that as the value of one variable increases, the value of the other decreases.

Consider, for example, the relation between attitude toward visiting Europe and intention to visit Europe. Imagine that for each person in a sample of respondents we have measures of the attitude and intention in question. By computing the correlation coefficient, we can describe the strength and direction of the relation between these two measures. A positive correlation would support the assumption that a person's intention to visit Europe increases as his attitude toward this behavior becomes more positive. The higher the correlation (i.e., the closer it is to $+1$), the stronger is the relationship, and the better we can predict a person's intention from his attitude.[2] We would also be able to predict intentions from attitudes in the case of a negative correlation between these variables. Again, the closer the correlation is to $-1$, the better our ability is to predict. The negative correlation, however, would indicate that the more favorable a person's attitude is toward his visiting Europe, the weaker is his intention to go.

In addition to reporting the strength of a correlation, we will often indicate

[1]Strictly speaking, a correlation describes only the degree of *linear* relationship between two variables. Two uncorrelated variables may be related in a nonlinear fashion.

[2]Since correlations are simply measures of association and do not imply directionality, we could also predict a person's attitude from his intention.

whether or not it is statistically *significant.* A correlation is significant when the observed relation between two variables is unlikely to be due to chance alone. By tradition, a finding is considered statistically significant if its probability ($p$) of occurrence by chance alone is less than 5 in 100 ($p < .05$). The statistical significance of a correlation coefficient depends not only on its magnitude (the extent to which it deviates from zero in either a positive or a negative direction) but also on the size of the sample on which it is based. For example, whereas a correlation of .20 or greater is statistically significant ($p < .05$) in a sample of 100 respondents, for a sample of 30 the correlation would have to be at least .36 before we could conclude that it was unlikely to be due to chance alone.

Clearly, statistical significance does not necessarily imply a strong relationship. Although it is an arbitrary decision to term a correlation "weak" or "strong," some general guidelines can be suggested. In the social sciences, correlations around .30 have been considered satisfactory and, consistent with this practice, we would suggest that correlations below this level are usually of little practical value even if they are statistically significant. Correlations in the range of .30 to .50 may be considered of moderate magnitude, while correlations exceeding .50 indicate relatively strong relationships between two variables.

Empirical tests of our theory require that we have not only an index of the relationship between two variables, but also an index of the degree to which we can predict one variable (the intention) from a simultaneous consideration of two other variables (attitude toward the behavior and subjective norm). Such an index is provided by the *multiple correlation coefficient* ($R$) which can range from zero (no predictability) to 1.0 (perfect predictability). The multiple correlation indicates the degree of correlation between two or more predictor variables and a given criterion measure. In computing this index, we also obtain a weight for each of the predictor variables which represents the independent contribution of that variable in the prediction of the criterion. When testing our theory, then, weights are obtained for the attitude toward the behavior and the subjective norm. These weights ($W$) can be taken as indicants of the relative importance of each component in the prediction of the intention.

In subsequent chapters, we will often present the relationships among the variables comprising our theory in the form of a diagram such as the one shown in Figure 8.1. Starting on the left, it can be seen that we will describe the relation between an estimate of attitude, based on behavioral beliefs and outcome evaluations, and a direct measure of attitude toward the behavior. Similarly, we will present the correlation between an estimate of subjective norm, based on normative beliefs and motivations to comply, and a direct measure of subjective norm. The direct measures of attitude and subjective norm are then used to predict the intention. We will show not only the correlation of each component with the intention, but also the multiple correlation and the relative weight of each component. Finally, we will show the strength of the relation between intention and behavior. These diagrams will thus provide summaries of the major findings in each of the applied areas.

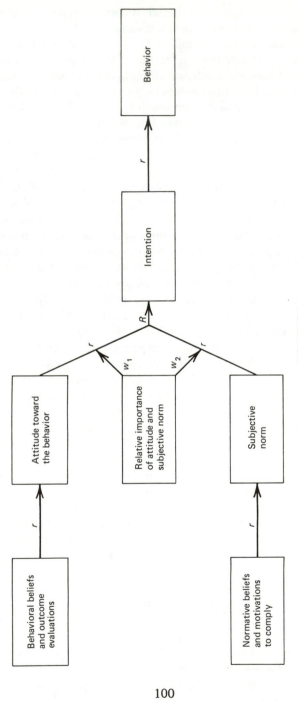

**FIGURE 8.1**
Relations among beliefs, attitude, subjective norm, intention, and behavior.

# CHAPTER 9

## Predicting and Understanding Weight Loss: Intentions, behaviors, and outcomes

Dorothy Sejwacz
Icek Ajzen
Martin Fishbein

This book deals primarily with the predication and understanding of behavior, but in some instances the behavior itself is less important than the outcomes it produces. Conserving energy, succeeding or failing on a test, giving birth to a child, and preventing disease are all examples of outcomes that are of considerable importance to us. In this chapter we look at the effects of behavior on one such outcome, namely, weight loss.

The problem of obesity is widespread and of great concern to a large proportion of the American population. Estimates indicate that there are from 40 to 80 million obese Americans, depending on the criterion used (Stuart & Davis, 1971). Given the magnitude of this problem, it is hardly surprising that various treatment techniques have been proposed by laymen as well as by professionals to assist people in their attempts to control their body weight. Unfortunately, most of these techniques have produced only mediocre results (Stunkard & McLaren-Hume, 1959). Even the most successful techniques, such as behavior modification, have not been equally effective for all individuals, with some patients even gaining weight and many not maintaining weight loss after the program has been terminated (e.g. Jeffrey, 1974).

Attempts to explain the success of a given program with some individuals and the lack of success with others have often focused on personality factors and general attitudes concerning obesity and body image. Yet, Hall and Hall (1974), after reviewing a number of studies that investigated the efficacy of behavioral treatment of obesity, concluded that

> Prediction of individual differences in weight loss has not been at all successful. Clinical intuition, MMPI, MPI, weight prior to treatment, general anxiety, situation specific anxiety, PAS, EPQ, I-E scale, body image measures, attitudinal measures, and the 16 PF questionnaire have all failed to predict success in treatment (p. 362).

This chapter is based on the first author's doctoral dissertation, Department of Psychology, University of Massachusetts at Amherst, 1977.

There can be little doubt that variables of this kind are largely unrelated to weight loss, but it would be inappropriate to conclude that the social psychological approach has failed.

It is generally agreed that "... virtually all obesities have in common an association between an excessive caloric intake and a deficient level of energy expenditure" (Stuart & Davis, 1971, p. 23). Thus, a decrease in caloric intake (i.e., dieting to reduce weight) and/or an increase in energy expenditure (i.e., an increase in physical activity) ought to result in weight loss. Neither dieting nor engaging in physical activity can be directly observed, since both refer to behavioral categories rather than single actions. Many specific behaviors, such as cutting down on sweets, bread, or potatoes; eating lighter meals; not having a second helping; and avoiding snacks between meals may be indicative of dieting to reduce weight. A general measure of dieting is obtained by constructing an index based on the observation of such specific dietary behaviors. Similarly, a general measure of physical activity can be derived by considering the performance of such specific behaviors as jogging, hiking, calisthenics, swimming, and skiing. The procedures for constructing behavioral indices were described in chapter 3.

Once we have obtained indices of dieting and physical activity we must test the assumption that engaging in these categories of behavior will result in weight loss. The effectiveness of dieting or physical activity may depend on the population in question as well as on the nature of the weight reduction program. For example, the effect of dieting may be different for men and women, for young and old, for black and white, and for heavily obese and mildly overweight. Moreover, a dieting program that results in considerable weight loss over a long period of time may be relatively ineffective when it comes to producing a rapid decrease in body weight.

To the extent that dieting and physical activity are effective in producing weight loss, we can turn our attention to the determinants of these behavioral categories. One possible approach would be to assess general intentions to diet and to engage in physical activity. These intentions can further be understood in terms of the antecedent attitudes and subjective norms with respect to performing each class of behaviors. The final link in the causal chain is found by identifying the beliefs that determine these attitudes and subjective norms.

We noted in chapters 3 and 4, however, that respondents may differ in their interpretations of terms like "dieting" or "physical activity," and intentions concerning these behavioral categories may be relatively poor predictors of indices based on a set of single behaviors. We suggested that this problem can be avoided by measuring intentions (as well as attitudes, subjective norms, and beliefs) with respect to each of the single behaviors comprising the behavioral category and then computing indices of intention that parallel the behavioral indices.

We saw that past research has found attitudes and personality factors to be largely unrelated to weight reduction. These negative results are to be expected.

Attitudes toward such concepts as "the fat me" or "the thin me" and personality variables, such as neuroticism or anxiety are what we have called external variables. There is no reason to assume that these attitudes and personality factors will have systematic effects on beliefs concerning the performance of weight-related behaviors. Consequently, these external variables cannot be expected to systematically influence the performance of weight-related behaviors or actual weight loss.

In conclusion, to predict and understand weight loss we have to identify the behaviors or behavioral categories that are effective in reducing weight and investigate the determinants of those behaviors. It must be emphasized, however, that even if dieting and physical activity are found to influence weight reduction, this outcome, like most other outcomes, will be determined only in part by the person's actions. In an attempt to reduce weight, two people may perform identical behaviors but with very different results. Initial body weight, hormonal differences, and other constitutional factors may contribute to the ultimate weight loss. A person's behavior, therefore, will not permit perfect prediction of weight reduction.

## AN EMPIRICAL STUDY OF WEIGHT LOSS

A study conducted at the University of Massachusetts illustrates the points made in the preceding discussion. The study investigated loss of weight among 88 college women over a two-month time period. Most of the women who volunteered to participate considered themselves to be overweight. At the first session, the women completed a questionnaire assessing their diet and weight histories and were individually weighed by the experimenter. Their weight was measured again two months later, and the amount of weight lost (or gained) during the two-month period served as the main dependent variable.[1] The women differed considerably in the amount of weight they lost, and some actually gained weight. For the sample as a whole, the reduction in weight was not significant; the average weight loss was approximately one pound.

In keeping with previous research, the questionnaire administered at the first session also measured attitudes toward eating, "the thin me," "the fat me," "the me right now," and going out on dates. It has been assumed that people who have favorable attitudes toward "the thin me" and dating, and unfavorable attitudes toward eating, "the fat me," and "the me right now" should be more likely to lose weight than people with the opposite pattern of evaluations. In addition, the participants completed Collins's (1974) version of the I-E scale, a personality measure of the generalized expectancy that one's fate is controlled by internal

---

[1]This measure was highly related to the percentage of body weight lost.

or external forces. The assumption here is that people who believe their fate to be internally controlled are better able to lose weight than people who believe that their fate is controlled by external forces. Contrary to these expectations, but consistent with previous findings, neither the I-E scale nor any of the attitude measures were found to predict changes in weight over the two-month period. Clearly, external variables of this kind contribute little to our understanding of weight loss or gain.

## Construction of Dieting and Physical Activity Indices

Our point of departure is the common assumption that weight loss is a function of the extent to which a person engages in dietary behaviors and physical activities. To test this assumption we must first obtain measures of these two behavioral categories. In a pilot study an independent sample of 40 college women were asked to list behaviors they would perform if they wanted to lose weight. As might be expected, most of the behaviors listed appeared to fall within the domains of physical activity or dieting to reduce weight. A content analysis led to the identification of the following seven types of dieting behaviors and five types of physical activities.

### Dieting behaviors
1. Avoid snacking between meals and in the evenings.
2. Cut down on all starchy foods (e.g., sweets, bread, potatoes).
3. Avoid being in places where one might be tempted to eat starchy foods and/ or eat too much (e.g., restaurants, bakeries, coffee shops).
4. Decrease food intake in general by eating lighter meals, not having seconds, and not overeating.
5. Eat on a consistent and regular schedule.
6. Maintain a balanced diet by eating all the essential nutrients.
7. Keep drinking of any alcoholic beverages to a minimum.

### Physical activities
1. Avoid long periods of inactivity (e.g., watching TV, just sitting around).
2. Do exercises, such as jogging or calisthenics, on a regular basis.
3. Participate in sports on a regular basis (e.g., swimming, skiing, tennis, skating, bike riding, basketball).
4. Walk whenever possible instead of riding the bus, driving a car, or riding an elevator.
5. Avoid excessive sleeping or napping during the daytime (especially after meals).

As a first step in constructing a behavioral index, it is necessary to consider whether each of the behaviors is a valid indicant of the category in question.

Examination of the above dieting behaviors suggests that the first five types of activities are clearly indicative of dieting to reduce weight. For example, most observers would agree that a person who is decreasing his or her food intake is probably dieting to lose weight. In contrast, performance of the last two behaviors (6 and 7) does not necessarily imply dieting to reduce weight. A person who avoids drinking alcoholic beverages, for example, may do so for many reasons unrelated to weight loss.

Examination of the physical activities similarly suggests that only the first three types of behaviors are clear indicants of this behavioral category. A person who regularly participates in sports or who avoids long periods of inactivity is expending energy. In contrast, a person who avoids excessive sleeping or napping is not necessarily engaged in physical activity; she may be watching TV or reading a book.

These considerations thus led to the identification of five behaviors that seemed to indicate dieting to reduce weight, and another three that seemed to indicate engaging in physical activity.[2] In the final session, all 88 respondents indicated, on a 7-place scale ranging from *all the time* to *never,* the extent to which they had performed each of the specific dietary behaviors and physical activities in the course of the preceding two months. The responses to the five dieting behaviors were used to derive an index of dieting to reduce weight, and the responses to the three physical activities were used to construct an index of the second behavioral category. The scores of the two indices could thus range from 5 to 35 and from 3 to 21 for dieting and exercising, respectively. The higher a person's score was, the greater was the extent to which she was dieting or performing physical activities.

In addition, 45 of the respondents were asked to complete the same behavior inventory on a weekly basis. Dieting and physical activity indices were computed for each week, and the final measures of behavior were obtained by averaging these weekly scores. These measures of behavior were highly related ($r = .88$) to the measures obtained at the end of the two-month period, suggesting that the retrospective behavioral reports reflected the behaviors performed during the preceding weeks quite accurately. Since the weekly schedules were completed by only part of the sample, the results will be discussed in terms of the retrospective reports of behavior which are available for all respondents. However, an analysis of the weekly reports led to the same conclusions.

At this stage, then, we have measures of the extent to which each respondent dieted and engaged in physical activity during a two-month period, as well as a measure of the actual amount of weight she lost in the course of that period.

### Effects of Dieting and Physical Activity on Weight Loss

To examine the effects of dieting and physical activity on weight loss, the respondents were classified as falling above or below the median in each of the two

[2]Item analyses of the seven dietary behaviors and five physical activities confirmed the intuitive selection procedure.

behavioral categories. Predictably, women who had high scores on the dieting index lost an appreciable amount of weight (2.02 pounds on the average), whereas women who dieted relatively little actually gained a small amount (.31 pounds). In a parallel though less pronounced finding, physically active women lost an average of 1.12 pounds, compared to a loss of only .72 pounds for less active women.

These effects were also reflected in the correlation coefficients. Whereas the dieting index had a significant correlation of .42 with weight loss, the correlation between physical activity and weight reduction was only .14 and not significant. Moreover, the simultaneous consideration of dieting and physical activity did not appreciably improve prediction ($R = .43$) over the level obtained on the basis of the dieting index alone.

## Determinants of Dieting and Physical Activity

The preceding discussion showed that dieting had a moderate relation to weight loss, while physical activity had little effect on this outcome. Nevertheless, it is instructive to examine the factors that determine the extent to which a person will perform these two classes of behavior. The study's main findings are summarized in Figure 9.1 and are discussed below.

**Predicting dieting and physical activity.** According to the theory of reasoned action, the immediate determinants of dieting and physical activity are corresponding intentions. Since we were dealing with behavioral categories, two types of corresponding intentions were assessed. First, respondents directly indicated their general intentions to diet and to engage in physical activity and, second, they stated their intentions to perform each of the single behaviors comprising the two behavioral categories.

Specifically, at the time of the initial interview the women responded to the following items.

1. I intend to adhere to a diet to reduce weight during the next two months.

    likely ____ : ____ : ____ : ____ : ____ : ____ : ____ unlikely

2. I intend to engage in physical activity to reduce weight during the next two months.

    likely ____ : ____ : ____ : ____ : ____ : ____ : ____ unlikely

These two measures corresponded to the behavioral indices in terms of their targets, actions, context, and time elements. For example, the behavioral dieting index specified a general action (dieting) as well as the time element (the two-month period); it generalized across the target element and left context unspecified. The intention to adhere to a diet during the same two-month period

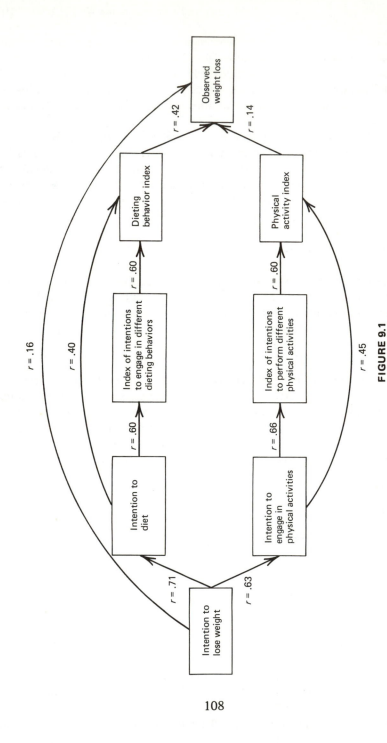

**FIGURE 9.1**

An analysis of intentions and behaviors influencing weight loss.

corresponds exactly to this behavioral criterion. The same arguments can be made for the correspondence with respect to the intentional and behavioral measures of physical activity.

We noted earlier, however, that a concept, such as dieting, may mean different things to different people. A measure of intention to diet or to engage in physical activity may therefore not be the best predictor of the corresponding behavioral category. To avoid these difficulties, respondents indicated their intentions with respect to each of the single behaviors comprising the dieting and physical activity categories. The following examples illustrate the measures obtained.

1. I intend to avoid snacking between meals and in the evenings for the next two months.

   likely ____ : ____ : ____ : ____ : ____ : ____ : ____ unlikely

2. I intend to do exercises, such as jogging or calisthenics, on a regular basis for the next two months.

   likely ____ : ____ : ____ : ____ : ____ : ____ : ____ unlikely

In this case, there is perfect correspondence between a given intention and a single behavior. It follows that the sum of a person's intentions to engage in the five dietary behaviors corresponds to her behavioral index of dieting. This index of intention should be a better predictor of the extent to which a person will perform dietary behaviors than the more general measure of intention to diet described earlier. The same arguments apply in the case of physical activities.

The results of the study support these hypotheses. The direct measures of intention correlated with the intentional indices ($r$ = .60 for dieting and $r$ = .66 for physical activity). More important, both the general measures of intention as well as the intentional indices permitted prediction of the corresponding behaviors. Consistent with expectations, however, the *index* of dieting intention led to more accurate prediction of dieting behavior ($r$ = .60) than did the direct measure of intention to diet ($r$ = .40). In a similar fashion, the *index* of intentions to perform physical activities was a better predictor of the behavioral criterion ($r$ = .60) than was the general intention to engage in physical activity ($r$ = .45).

To summarize briefly, the amount of weight a woman lost was, at least in part, the result of the extent to which she performed dieting behaviors and physical activities. For this sample of women, and under the conditions of the present study, dieting contributed more to this outcome than did physical activity. Performance of the two classes of behavior was found to be related to corresponding intentions. Although general intentions to diet and to engage in physical activity permitted some prediction, *indices* based on intentions to engage in the single dieting behaviors and physical activities led to more accurate prediction. This finding is consistent with our argument that the ambiguities associated with intentions to perform a general class of behaviors are avoided at the level of single actions.

**Predicting single dieting behaviors and physical activities.** Our theory stipulates not only that an intentional index will be related to a corresponding index of behavior, but also that the intention to perform any of the single behaviors will be related to the actual performance of that behavior.[3] The data of the present study provided support for this prediction.

For example, intentions to avoid snacking between meals and in the evenings for the next two months (measured during the initial session) were significantly related to the women's retrospective reports of the extent to which they performed this behavior over the two-month period ($r = .55$). The average intention-behavior correlations for the five dieting behaviors was .49. Similarly, intentions to do certain exercises were related to the retrospective reports of this behavior ($r = .54$), and the average correlation for the three physical activities was .50.

Although all eight intention-behavior correlations were statistically significant, they were of only moderate magnitude, ranging from .34 to .64. Since the behaviors took place over a two-month period, this finding is hardly surprising. It seems reasonable to assume that at least some changes in intentions to perform single behaviors will occur in a two-month period. Indirect evidence to support this argument can be found by considering the weekly records of behavior. Recall that 45 women kept weekly behavioral records throughout the two-month period. Of these women, 24 took part in an additional interview at the end of the first month, at which time they indicated their intentions to perform each of the eight single behaviors during the following month.

Considering only the 24 women who took part in the additional interview, we can first examine the relations between their initial intentions and corresponding behaviors during the subsequent two-month period. These relations can then be compared to the relations between their intentions to perform the behaviors during the final month and their actual behavior in the course of that one-month period. Since intentions are less likely to change in the shorter period of time, the intention-behavior correlations for the one-month period should be stronger than those for the two-month period.

These expectations were borne out by the data. For example, the correlation between intentions to avoid tempting places and performance of this behavior was higher when the time period was one month ($r = .64$) than when it was two months ($r = .46$). Similarly, in the case of avoiding long periods of inactivity, the intention-behavior correlations were .72 for the one-month period and .47 for the two-month period. Considering all eight behaviors, the average correlation increased from .51 for the two-month period to .67 for the one-month period.

---

[3]It is possible to obtain a strong relation between two indices even when there is little relation at the level of the individual intentions and behaviors comprising the indices.

Thus far we have said nothing about the role of a woman's intention to lose weight as a factor underlying her attempts to achieve this outcome. In chapter 4 we pointed out that, for at least two reasons, a person's intention to attain an outcome may be a rather poor predictor of the outcome's actual occurrence. First, the outcome may be only in part a function of the individual's behavior and, second, even when the outcome is under behavioral control, holding an intention to attain the outcome does not guarantee that the individual will perform the appropriate behaviors. Thus, although a woman's intention to lose weight may lead her to form intentions to engage in various behaviors which she believes will attain the desired outcome, her performance of these particular behaviors may have little effect on her weight.

To test these notions, the women in our study were, in the initial interview, asked to indicate their intentions to reduce weight on the following scale:

I intend to reduce weight during the next two months.

likely ____ : ____ : ____ : ____ : ____ : ____ : ____ unlikely

As might be expected, this intention correlated significantly with the general intentions to diet ($r = .71$) and to engage in physical activity ($r = .63$) during the next two months. Although to a lesser extent, the intention to lose weight also correlated with the two intentional indices ($r = .58$ in both cases). Thus, the intention to lose weight did seem to exert a relatively strong directive influence on the women's general intentions to diet and to engage in physical activity, but to have somewhat less effect on intentions to perform any given single action.

We saw earlier, however, that the general intentions to diet and to engage in physical activity had only moderate correlations with actual behavior, as measured by our two behavioral indices. It follows that the correlation between intentions to lose weight and the two behavioral categories will also be relatively low. Consistent with this expectation, intentions to lose weight correlated .43 with the dieting index and .36 with the physical activity index.

Recall also that whereas dieting was moderately related to weight loss ($r = .42$), women who engaged in physical activity lost little if any weight ($r = .14$). Given all of these findings, it is hardly surprising that intentions to lose weight were not significantly related to the actual amount of weight a woman lost ($r = .16$).

## SUMMARY AND CONCLUSION

This chapter has provided an account of the first step in a social-psychological analysis of weight reduction. According to this account, a person who wants to lose weight forms general intentions to diet or engage in physical activity. These general intentions then lead to the formation of intentions to perform various single behaviors within these two domains,[4] and these latter intentions lead to actual performance of the corresponding behaviors. Unfortunately, some of the behaviors that people intend to (and actually do) perform in an effort to lose weight turn out to be unrelated to this outcome.

To design an effective weight reduction program, therefore, we first have to identify a set of behaviors or behavioral categories that have been shown effective in producing weight loss. In the present study, only the behaviors comprising the dieting index would have met this criterion. The program must then attempt to change intentions to perform some of the single behaviors in question. This requires an understanding of the factors that determine a person's intentions to engage in these particular behaviors. Although it is beyond the scope of the present chapter, we may note in passing that in our weight reduction study, attitudes and subjective norms with respect to each of the single behaviors were assessed. Consistent with expectations, these measures permitted highly accurate predications of the corresponding intentions.

Finally, it must again be emphasized that, regardless of a program's success in producing behavioral change, such change cannot guarantee weight loss. The reason for this is that many factors other than a person's behavior may affect his or her weight. The findings reported in the present chapter, however, suggest that in the area of weight reduction there is at least a moderate relation between behavior and outcome. It follows that, by carefully selecting the behaviors that are to be changed, it should be possible to develop effective weight reduction programs.

[4]The intention to lose weight also appears to have some direct effect on intentions to perform single dieting behaviors and physical activities.

# CHAPTER 10

## Predicting and Understanding Women's Occupational Orientations: Factors underlying choice intentions

Brenda M. Sperber
Martin Fishbein
Icek Ajzen

In the preceding chapter we saw that a woman's intention to reduce weight leads her to form intentions to engage in various dieting behaviors and physical activities which, in her opinion, will produce the indended outcome. The intention to lose weight or to attain some other outcome thus exerts a directive influence on a person's behavior. Since our choice of goals profoundly affects our lives, it is important to explore how we arrive at our intentions to strive for one goal rather than another.

Consider, for example, the plight of many young women today. There is growing social concern about the life goals of females and the fulfillments that result from attaining these goals. Until recently, it had been assumed that psychological adjustment and self-fulfillment in females were optimally achieved through being a wife and mother. The calling of "homemaking" was considered the natural goal of a mature woman. Vocational aspirations were seen as a temporary interest that would not completely satisfy the needs of a woman. Her psychological adjustment was in question if she persisted in showing a greater interest in a career than in being a homemaker (Helson, 1972).

More recently, the socialization process that made homemaking a "natural" goal has come under a great deal of criticism. It is seen as limiting the full potential of women and directing them toward a singular life pattern and self-concept based on the notion that anatomy is destiny. Its critics see this conditioning as totally reprehensible, and as something to which today's young women should not be subjected (Friedan, 1970; Weisstein, 1971).

In this conflict-inducing setting, we see today's young women with a variety of life plans they wish to implement—from the very "traditional" to the very "liberated." Women are essentially placed in the position of having to choose

This chapter is based on the first author's master's thesis, Department of Psychology, University of Illinois at Champaign-Urbana, 1974. We would like to thank Donald Holste, Assistant Superintendent, Leslie Randle, Patti Brown, and Edna Cooper of the Urbana, Illinois School System for their assistance in collecting the data.

between becoming a homemaker or having a career. We can conceptualize these two occupational orientations as plans or intentions to attain a certain future lifestyle. The focus of this chapter is to investigate the factors that lead young women to form intentions to pursue one lifestyle rather than another.

## PREVIOUS RESEARCH

The major emphasis of the existing career vs. homemaking literature has been descriptive (Edwards, 1969; Gysbers, Johnston, & Gust, 1968; Hoyt & Kennedy, 1958; Matthews & Tiedeman, 1964; Rand, 1968; Tyler, 1964; Wagman, 1966; Watley & Kaplan, 1971). The basic design is to first classify a group of females as career-oriented or homemaking-oriented. The criterion for inclusion in a particular orientation is usually a pre-selected pattern of responses on a rating scale or questionnaire or a given profile on the Strong Vocational Interest Blank for Women. Then tests are administered to all respondents to determine any psychological or behavioral characteristics (interests, attitudes, personality traits, abilities, achievements) which distinguish between the two orientations.

These studies have often reported that career- and home-oriented women have different patterns of interests and attitudes. It should come as no surprise that home-oriented women tend to place a high value on having children and being a good wife, while career-oriented women emphasize achievement in education and the importance of work. Such findings tell us very little, however, since the obtained differences are similar to the information that is used to define homemaking versus career orientations in the first place.

Of greater interest are differences in general personality characteristics and abilities. For example, Rand (1968) found that in comparison to home-oriented women, career-oriented women viewed themselves as relatively aggressive, independent, and intellectually self-confident. In addition, they had higher estimates of their own scientific and working abilities. Unfortunately, the findings concerning variables of this kind have been rather weak and inconsistent. A study by Tangri (1972), for example, assessed the effects of ten personality characteristics (e.g., competence, independence, intellectualism) as well as need for achievement and motivation to avoid success. The relations of these variables to career orientation were low and for the most part not significant.

Generally speaking, then, previous work in this area has served primarily to describe the two different lifestyles, but it has provided little information as to why women choose to become homemakers or to have a career. This chapter shows how our approach can be used to provide an understanding of the social-psychological factors that determine women's career intentions.

A woman's intention to pursue a career or to become a homemaker reflects a choice between these two possible occupational orientations. To assess this choice intention, we could ask our respondents to place a checkmark on the following scale:

| | | |
|---|---|---|
| | | I intend to |
| I intend to | | become a |
| pursue a career. ___ : ___ : ___ : ___ : ___ : ___ : ___ | | homemaker. |

In chapter 4 we argued that a choice intention of this kind can be explained in terms of the intentions to perform each of the alternatives involved. In the present case, we might use the following scales to assess the two intentions under consideration.

1. I intend to become a homemaker.

   unlikely ___ : ___ : ___ : ___ : ___ : ___ : ___ likely

2. I intend to pursue a career.

   unlikely ___ : ___ : ___ : ___ : ___ : ___ : ___ likely

The numerical difference between these two responses should be related to the choice intention.

Consider, for example, a young woman who indicates a low likelihood of becoming a homemaker and a high likelihood of pursuing a career. When asked to respond to the choice intention measure, she should check a space toward the career end of the scale. By way of contrast, a woman who states that she is likely to become a homemaker and unlikely to pursue a career should express this difference in intention by checking the homemaker side of the choice-intention scale. That is, when dealing with a choice situation, we need to identify the available options and then assess intentions with respect to each option. The relative strength of these intentions should predict the choice.

This discussion implies that we can explain a woman's intention with respect to occupational choice by examining the determinants of her intention to become a homemaker and of her intention to pursue a career. In the framework of our approach, this means that we have to investigate the attitudes and subjective norms that determine each of the two intentions. Finally, for a more thorough account of the factors that influence occupational orientation we can turn to the beliefs that underlie the attitudinal and normative components.

The major sample of respondents in our study consisted of 111 young high school women in the eleventh and twelfth grades. Of the women sampled, 96 were white and 13 were black.

Our first task was to devise an appropriate instrument to measure the occupational choice intentions of these high school students. Simply asking them whether they intended to become homemakers or pursue a career seemed unwise, since young women may differ greatly in their interpretations of the two occupational orientations. To avoid this ambiguity, the women read the following two sketches, one of Jane, a career-oriented woman, and the other of Mary, a woman with a homemaker orientation.

*Career orientation*

Jane is looking forward to having a career. She believes that she will find fulfillment and meaning in her life by being successful in the career she chooses. She may have to stop work for a while in order to have a family, but will return to it as quickly as possible. For her, education is basically a means of obtaining the right training in order to enter into her career.

*Homemaker orientation*

Mary is looking forward to getting married and having a family. She believes that she will find fulfillment and meaning in her life by doing all the things that make up being a wife and mother. She might go to work to supplement the family income, but going to work does not really hold any interest for her. She is also thinking of furthering her education in order to become a more interesting person and to learn more about the world around her.

After reading these two descriptions, the girls were asked to indicate their occupational orientations on the following choice intention scale.

I intend to have a future like

Mary ____ : ____ : ____ : ____ : ____ : ____ : ____ Jane

Consistent with previous research we first examined the relation of various personality and demographic characteristics to this response. The personality measures were self-reports designed to assess ten factors: need for achievement, impulsivity, aggression, self-confidence, need for social recognition, need for succorance, nurturance, need for affiliation, need for change, and need for autonomy. The demographic information was age, grade, religion, racial origin, number of older sisters, marital status of older sisters, whether the respondents

117

were living with parents or guardians, the occupation of older sisters and mother, and the parents' socio-economic status.

None of these 19 variables had a strong effect on intended occupational choice, although the relation was significant for succorance ($r = .23$), need for change ($r = .23$), and mother's occupational status ($r = .24$). Clearly, this approach is of little use in explaining the choice intentions of our respondents.

**Attitudes and subjective norms as predictors of intended lifestyles.** The first step in our analysis is to demonstrate that the choice to have a future like Jane or Mary can be predicted accurately by obtaining independent assessments of intentions to have a future like each of these two women. These separate intentions were measured as follows:

1. I intend to have a future like Jane.

    likely ____ : ____ : ____ : ____ : ____ : ____ : ____ unlikely

2. I intend to have a future like Mary.

    likely ____ : ____ : ____ : ____ : ____ : ____ : ____ unlikely

For each of the young women in our sample, we obtained a *differential intention* by subtracting her response to the first item from her response to the second. Thus, positive scores indicated an intentional preference for a home orientation like Mary's and negative scores indicated an intentional preference for a career orientation like Jane's.

The differential intention was used to predict the respondent's choice intention. Consistent with expectations, the difference between the two separate intentions predicted the choice intention with considerable accuracy ($r = .87$). As might also be expected, this correlation was significantly higher than the correlations between the choice intention and either the intention to be like Jane ($r = .79$) or the intention to be like Mary ($r = .79$). These findings support our argument that in a situation which involves a choice between two alternatives, better prediction can be obtained by considering the *difference* between the intentions concerning each of the two alternatives than by considering either intention individually.

Given that we can accurately predict a woman's intended occupational choice from her differential intention score, we must now try to account for this difference between her intention to become a homemaker and her intention to pursue a career. We therefore obtained measures of attitudes and subjective norms with respect to each alternative.

Attitudes toward attaining the two occupational orientations were assessed in the following manner.

1. Having a future like Jane is

    good ____ : ____ : ____ : ____ : ____ : ____ : ____ bad

2. Having a future like Mary is

    good ____ : ____ : ____ : ____ : ____ : ____ : ____ bad

Single seven-point scales were also used to measure subjective norms.

1. Most people who are important to me think I ought to have a future like Jane.

    likely ____ : ____ : ____ : ____ : ____ : ____ : ____ unlikely

2. Most people who are important to me think I ought to have a future like Mary.

    likely ____ : ____ : ____ : ____ : ____ : ____ : ____ unlikely

Since we were concerned mainly with understanding choice between the two lifestyles rather than with a woman's intention to pursue any single lifestyle, we computed differential attitude scores and differential subjective norms by subtracting responses to the first scale from responses to the second. These two differences were then used together to predict the differential intention. In support of our theory, this prediction was found to be highly accurate ($R = .86$). High school women who preferred Mary's home orientation to Jane's career orientation and who believed that important others thought they should be more like Mary than Jane intended to have a future like Mary. Conversely, women whose differential attitudes and subjective norms favored Jane's lifestyle had stronger intentions to pursue a career than to become a homemaker.

Although both attitudes and subjective norms contributed significantly to the women's choices of a lifestyle, it is interesting to note that the differences in their attitudes toward the two lifestyles were much more important determinants of their ultimate choices than were the differences in their subjective norms.[1] Put differently, the choices our young women made between pursuing a career and becoming homemakers were primarily a function of their personal preferences rather than their perception of the wishes and desires of important others.

[1]As can be seen in Figure 10.1, the regression coefficients or weights which provided these estimates of relative importance were .67 and .29 for the attitudinal and normative components, respectively.

Our discussion up to this point has shown that we can predict choices of occupational orientations by measuring intentions and underlying attitudes and subjective norms. With the possible exception of the finding that for this choice personal (attitudinal) considerations were more important than social (normative) ones, we have really learned nothing unique about this particular problem area; that is, we would expect that any choice will be determined by differences between intentions, and that differences between attitudes and subjective norms will predict the differential intentions. We begin to obtain information uniquely relevant to the choice of an occupational orientation when we explore the cognitive structure or beliefs that, in the final analysis, provide the basis for this choice.

While we can construct appropriate measures of intentions, attitudes, and subjective norms on the basis of a careful theoretical analysis, such a theoretical analysis cannot tell us what beliefs are salient in a given population. To identify the salient beliefs in our subject population, an elicitation questionnaire was given to 27 eleventh grade high school women, The questionnaire included the sketches of Jane and Mary given earlier. After reading each sketch, the respondents were asked to list the advantages and disadvantages of *their* having a future like the girl described by the sketch. They were then asked to list sources or persons from whom they would seek or avoid information regarding their *own* future goals. Following the procedures discussed in chapter 6, 20 salient consequences and 9 relevant referents were identified and used to construct a standard questionnaire. The 20 consequences are listed in Table 10.2 and the 9 referents in Table 10.3 Recall that behavioral beliefs involving consequences are presumed to provide the basis for a person's attitude, whereas normative beliefs concerning the prescriptions of relevant referents should underlie the subjective norm. Since in our study attitudes were found to be the more important determinant of a woman's choice of lifestyle, let us first examine beliefs concerning the consequences of each lifestyle.

The 111 women in the main sample made three judgments with respect to each of the 20 consequences. They were asked to evaluate each consequence and to indicate the likelihood that each of the two lifestyles would lead to that consequence. For example, one of the consequences emitted most frequently was "feeling emotionally secure," and the respondents provided the following judgments.

1. To feel emotionally secure is

        good ____ : ____ : ____ : ____ : ____ : ____ : ____ bad

2. If I had a future like Jane I would feel emotionally secure.

        likely ____ : ____ : ____ : ____ : ____ : ____ : ____ unlikely

3. If I had a future like Mary I would feel emotionally secure.

likely ___ : ___ : ___ : ___ : ___ : ___ : ___ unlikely

Before turning to a detailed examination of these beliefs, we must verify that they can be used to predict the attitudes. Thus, following the procedures discussed in chapter 6, the behavioral beliefs and outcome (or consequence) evaluations were used to compute separate estimates of attitudes toward having a future like Jane's (i.e., pursuing a career) and having a future like Mary's (i.e., becoming a homemaker). In support of our assumption that the salient beliefs elicited provide the basis for attitudes, these estimates were found to predict the direct measures of the corresponding attitudes with a high degree of accuracy. For example, the correlation between the estimate and direct measure of attitude toward becoming a homemaker was .77. More important, in the context of a choice situation, the difference between the two estimates also permitted highly accurate prediction of the differential attitude score ($r = .81$).

Given the high correlations, we can justifiably examine the specific underlying beliefs in an attempt to account for the differences in attitudes toward the two occupational orientations. First, however, let us see whether normative beliefs concerning the prescriptions of specific relevant referents can similarly be used to explain the differences in subjective norms.

As in the case of ratings concerning the consequences of attaining each of the two lifestyles, the respondents were asked to make three judgments with respect to each of the 9 referents shown in Table 10.3. They indicated their motivations to comply with each referent as well as their normative beliefs concerning the referent's prescriptions for each lifestyle. The scales used to measure motivation to comply and normative beliefs concerning the most frequently mentioned referent where the following:

1. With respect to my making future plans, I would

very much                                              very much not
like to        ___ : ___ : ___ : ___ : ___ : ___ : ___ like to
           do what my mother thinks I ought to do.

2. My mother thinks I ought to have a future like Jane.

likely ___ : ___ : ___ : ___ : ___ : ___ : ___ unlikely

3. My mother thinks I ought to have a future like Mary.

likely ___ : ___ : ___ : ___ : ___ : ___ : ___ unlikely

The normative beliefs and motivations to comply were used to compute separate estimates of subjective norms with respect to pursuing a career (like

Jane) and becoming a homemaker (like Mary), as described in chapter 6. These estimates were found to predict the corresponding direct measures of subjective norms ($r = .81$ for the career orientation and $r = .74$ for the homemaker orientation). As in the case of attitudes, we then computed the difference between the two estimates of subjective norm in an attempt to predict the difference between the two direct measures. A high correlation ($r = .83$) attests to the accuracy of this prediction.

Our discussion up to this point is summarized in Figure 10.1 with respect to differential intentions, attitudes, and subjective norms. The figure shows that the intentions of our high school women to pursue careers or to become homemakers depended on the difference between their intentions to attain each of the two alternative lifestyles. The stronger their intentions were to attain one lifestyle (in comparison to the alternative), the more likely they were to select that lifestyle when confronted with the choice. The differential intentions were in turn a function of differential attitudes and subjective norms, with attitudes being the more important of the two determinants, as shown by the two weights ($w$). Finally, estimates based on the respondents' behavioral beliefs concerning each lifestyle and on outcome evaluation predicted the differential attitudes. Similarly, estimates based on normative beliefs concerning the prescriptions of relevant referents with respect to each lifestyle and on motivations to comply with the referents provided accurate prediction of the differential subjective norms.

## Cognitive Foundation of Career Intentions

Having verified our theory's assumptions about the relations among beliefs, attitudes and subjective norms, intentions, and choice, we turn to a more detailed analysis of the beliefs that constitute the underlying cognitive foundation. To examine the effects of beliefs on choice of career- or home-orientation, the sample of 111 high school women was divided into three groups on the basis of their responses to the choice intention scale.

1. *Career-oriented women.* The first group consisted of 44 respondents who had checked one of the three positions on the Jane-side of the intention scale, indicating that they intended to have a career-oriented future like Jane's.
2. *Home-oriented women.* The second group was made up of 42 respondents who had indicated an intention to have a home-oriented future by checking one of the three positions on the other side of the choice intention scale which was labeled "Mary."
3. *Undecided women.* The remaining 25 women had checked the middle position on the choice intention scale. They may thus be considered as undecided in their occupational orientations.

The utility of this classification is evident in Table 10.1 where we present the average differential intentions, attitudes, and subjective norms of the three

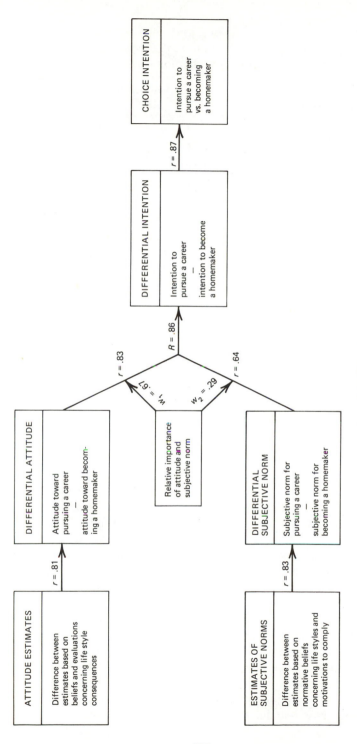

**FIGURE 10.1**

Relationships between attitudes, subjective norms, differential intentions and choice intentions concerning occupational orientations.

123

**TABLE 10.1**

Differential Intentions, Attitudes, and Subjective Norms of
Career-oriented, Undecided, and Home-oriented Women

| | CHOICE INTENTION | | |
| ANTECEDENT VARIABLE | Career-oriented | Undecided | Home-oriented |
|---|---|---|---|
| Differential intention | − 2.90 | .56 | 3.59 |
| Differential attitude | − 1.62 | − .24 | 2.32 |
| Estimate of differential attitude | −53.83 | 11.64 | 80.86 |
| Differential subjective norm | − 1.12 | 1.16 | 3.14 |
| Estimate of differential subjective norm | −19.05 | 21.48 | 83.66 |

groups. Positive scores indicate a preference for the home orientation, while negative scores indicate a preference for the career orientation. It is clear that the differential intentions, attitudes, and subjective norms of career-oriented women favored this lifestyle and that the opposite was true for home-oriented women. The differential intentions, attitudes, and subjective norms of the undecided women were intermediate, indicating no clear preference for either occupational orientation.

We now turn to an examination of the beliefs that lead women to choose one lifestyle rather than another. For purposes of this analysis, we shall consider the beliefs of only those women who chose either to pursue careers or to become homemakers, disregarding the undecided women. We will show first how differences in the perceived consequences of the two lifestyles can account for differences in occupational orientations and then present a similar analysis for normative beliefs.

**Behavioral beliefs underlying attitudes toward alternate lifestyles.** The young women in our sample were asked to state two beliefs with respect to each of 20 consequences (or outcomes): the likelihood that having a career-oriented future like Jane's would lead to the consequence (or outcome) and the likelihood that having a home-orientated future like Mary's would lead to the outcome. In addition, they were asked to evaluate each of the 20 consequences.

It should be clear that a given woman's preference for one of the two lifestyles must be due to differences in the two sets of beliefs. That is, her evaluation of each outcome is assumed to be the same, whether it is attained by pursuing a career or by becoming a homemaker. For example, using one's talents wisely is a positive outcome irrespective of one's lifestyle. In contrast, a woman may believe that pursuing a career is more likely to allow her to use her talents wisely than is becoming a homemaker. Such differences in her behavioral beliefs will determine her preference for one lifestyle over another. Columns 3 and 4 of Table 10.2 present the average differences in beliefs for the career- and home-oriented women in our study. A positive score represents the differential belief

124

**TABLE 10.2**

Average Evaluations and Differential Beliefs of
Home- and Career-oriented Women

| OUTCOMES | OUTCOME EVALUATIONS | | DIFFERENTIAL BELIEFS[a] | |
|---|---|---|---|---|
| | Home-oriented | Career-oriented | Home-oriented | Career-oriented |
| Having work and responsibilities all cut out for me | .19 | − .27 | .36 | .20 |
| Being burdened with a lot of responsibilities | − .45 | − .50 | − .93 | − .06 |
| Not having to worry about working | .81 | 1.25 | .81 | − .43 |
| Being financially secure | 2.02 | 2.14 | − .14 | −2.88* |
| Not having problems finding a job | 2.00 | 2.34 | − .33 | −2.75* |
| Having a glamorous life | .23 | .41 | − .33 | −2.38* |
| Not having problems supporting myself and my family | 2.14 | 2.50 | − .45 | −3.00* |
| Using my talents wisely | 2.64 | 2.68 | .07 | −4.05* |
| Having time to devote to my own goals and plans | 2.45 | 2.75 | .71 | −2.59* |
| Being hard and selfish | −2.86 | −2.50 | −2.16* | .34 |
| Being able to go to school just to keep up on things | .98 | .50 | 1.38* | .80 |
| Not having to worry about grades | 2.21 | 1.80 | 1.79* | 1.69* |
| Being dependent | −1.67 | −1.82 | 1.15* | 1.79* |
| Having time to devote to my family | 2.79 | 2.50 | 3.72* | 1.50* |
| Being constantly exposed to new people, ideas, and situations | 1.90 | 1.91 | −1.34* | −4.21* |
| Enjoying life | 2.98 | 2.77 | 2.86* | −2.39* |
| Feeling emotionally secure | 2.67 | 2.64 | 2.81* | −2.00* |
| Feeling fulfilled | 2.52 | 2.50 | 3.05* | −2.88* |
| Doing what I want | 2.05 | 2.18 | 2.76* | −3.62* |
| Missing out on a lot of things | −1.52 | −1.86 | −1.57 | +2.84 |

[a]Positive scores indicate that home-orientation is more likely to lead to the outcome than career-orientation; negative scores the opposite.
*Significantly different from zero ($p < .01$).

that the outcome in question is more likely to be attained by becoming a home-maker than by pursuing a career. The reverse pattern of beliefs is indicated by a negative score. In addition, Columns 1 and 2 of the table show the average evaluation of each consequence or outcome for the home-oriented and for the career-oriented women.

The first thing to note in Table 10.2 is that home- and career-oriented women had very similar evaluations of the various consequences. Regardless of occupational orientation, outcomes such as enjoying life, feeling emotionally secure, using my talents wisely, having time to devote to my family, and being financially secure were evaluated positively by all women. Similarly, both groups of women had negative evaluations of outcomes such as missing out on a lot of things or being hard and selfish. These findings imply that the differences between career- and home-oriented women must be related to differences in their beliefs, rather than to differences in outcome evaluations.

Table 10.2 in fact reveals considerable differences in the patterns of differential beliefs held by the two groups of women. Consider first the women who intended to become homemakers. As can be seen in Column 3, these women believed that with respect to attaining 9 of the 20 outcomes it would make little difference whether they pursued a career or became homemakers. For example, they believed that the two lifestyles were about equally likely to allow them to use their talents wisely, to give them financial security, and to burden them with a lot of responsibilities.

With respect to attaining the remaining 11 outcomes, however, these women believed that their choice of lifestyle would make a big difference. For the most part, they believed that by becoming homemakers rather than career women they were more likely to attain favorable outcomes and avoid unfavorable ones. To illustrate, they viewed having time to devote to their families, feeling fulfilled, and enjoying life as more likely to result from becoming a homemaker than from pursuing a career. Similarly, they believed that if they became homemakers they were less likely to become hard and selfish or to miss out on a lot of things than if they became career women. On the other hand, these home-oriented women did admit that their preferred lifestyle had certain disadvantages in comparison to pursuing a career. They believed that in contrast to career women, homemakers were less likely to be exposed to new people, ideas, and situations and were more likely to be dependent.

In sum, this group of women believed that there were nine distinct advantages to becoming a homemaker rather than a career woman and only two disadvantages associated with this choice. Clearly, this pattern of beliefs explains their preference for the homemaking orientation.

Turning now to the career-oriented women, we can see by looking at the fourth column in Table 10.2. that these women also believed certain outcomes to be attainable by means of either lifestyle. There were five such outcomes. For example, the women believed that being burdened with a lot of responsibilities, not having to worry about working, and being hard and selfish were about equally likely, regardless of lifestyle.

A consideration of the remaining 15 outcomes shows why these women preferred a career to homemaking. In only two instances did they believe that by becoming a homemaker they would be more likely to achieve a desirable outcome than by pursuing a career: not having to worry about grades and having time to devote to my family. In all other cases, they viewed the career orientation as more advantageous. In comparison to the homemaking orientation, the career orientation was seen as less likely to make women dependent or to miss out on lots of things and more likely to result in such outcomes as exposure to new people, ideas, and situations, allowing them to use their talents wisely, enjoying life, and feeling fulfilled. In sum, when a woman believed that a given life-

( style resulted in more positive and fewer negative outcomes than the alternative ) +
  lifestyle, she preferred the former to the latter.

**Normative beliefs underlying subjective norms with respect to alternate lifestyles.**
An analysis of the cognitive basis of subjective norms parallels the analysis of
beliefs and evaluations described earlier. Table 10.3 presents average motivation-
to-comply scores and differential normative beliefs for home-oriented and career-
oriented women. Columns 1 and 2 of the table show that the two groups did not
differ in their motivations to comply with their parents (mother and father) or
friends (close friends and boyfriends). There was also little difference in their
motivations to comply with the prescriptions of their religious and academic
referents (pastors, teachers, and school counselors). The only significant differences were found with respect to what may be considered occupational role   +
models: career women and housewives. While neither group was particularly
motivated to comply with housewives, the home-oriented high school students
had significantly higher scores than the career-oriented students. As might also
be expected, the reverse pattern was found with respect to motivation to comply
with career women. Interestingly, even the home-oriented women were somewhat more motivated to comply with career women than with housewives.

Columns 3 and 4 show the differences in each referent's prescriptions concerning the two lifestyles. A positive score means that the respondent believed
that the referent wanted her to become a homemaker rather than to pursue a
career. Conversely, a negative score indicates perceived pressure from the referent
to pursue a career more than to become a homemaker.

**TABLE 10.3**
Average Motivations to Comply and Differential Normative Beliefs of
Home- and Career-oriented Women

| REFERENTS | MOTIVATION TO COMPLY | | DIFFERENTIAL NORMATIVE BELIEFS[a] | |
|---|---|---|---|---|
| | Home-oriented | Career-oriented | Home-oriented | Career-oriented |
| Mother | 4.24 | 4.27 | .69 | −2.91* |
| Father | 4.31 | 3.98 | .69 | −3.06* |
| Close friends | 3.52 | 3.57 | .64 | −2.18* |
| Boyfriend | 4.24 | 3.98 | 2.31* | −2.00* |
| Pastor | 3.81 | 3.57 | .47 | −1.32* |
| School counselor | 3.50 | 3.66 | − .85* | −2.64* |
| Teachers | 3.33 | 3.82 | − .92* | −2.30* |
| Career women | 3.50 | 4.27** | −2.28* | −4.00* |
| Housewives | 3.33 | 2.41** | 1.95* | .75 |

[a]Positive scores indicate home-oriented normative prescriptions; negative scores career-
oriented prescriptions.
*Significantly different from zero ($p < .01$).
**Significant difference between home- and career-oriented groups.

Note first that both groups of women recognized that career women, counselors, and teachers support a career orientation, while they viewed housewives as supporting a homemaking orientation. More importantly, when a woman believed that her parents and friends (as well as her pastor) thought she ought to have a future like Jane's, she was likely to choose a career, and when she believed that these referents prescribed a future like Mary's, she was likely to choose the homemaking orientation.

To summarize the results, one group of women believed that eight of the nine referents strongly urged them to pursue careers rather than become homemakers, and these women did in fact choose the prescribed lifestyle. In contrast, the second group of women saw themselves faced with conflicting pressures. While they believed that six of their referents favored a home orientation, only in the case of two was this perceived preference significant. At the same time, they also believed that their remaining three referents strongly urged them to pursue a career. The fact that these women ultimately indicated an intention to become homemakers, despite the conflicting pressures, is consistent with the relatively weak influence of subjective norms on the choice of an occupational orientation.

## SUMMARY AND CONCLUSION

What we have shown in this chapter is that a young woman's decision to pursue a career or become a homemaker is based primarily on her judgments concerning the pros and cons of the alternative lifestyles. The perceived prescriptions of important others seem to play a relatively minor role in this area.

In thinking about their futures, young women (like anybody else) strive to attain some outcomes and avoid others. Most women want to enjoy life, feel emotionally secure and fulfilled, use their talents wisely, have time to devote to their own goals and plans as well as to their families, and be exposed to new people, ideas, and situations without having to worry about work or financial security. At the same time, they don't want to be burdened with a lot of responsibilities, miss out on things, or become hard and selfish. Some women believe that they can achieve more of these goals by becoming homemakers than by pursuing careers, whereas others believe the opposite. Their choice of lifestyles follows directly from these beliefs.

Note that this account differs greatly from conventional explanations of occupational choice. The conventional approach appears to be based on the assumption that the role of a career woman requires very different personality characteristics, abilities, needs, interests, and values than does the role of a homemaker. Consequently, it is assumed that dominant, aggressive, assertive women with intellectual interests, who value achievement and independence, will opt for careers, whereas women who are passive, warm, compliant, empathetic, who are

primarily interested in interpersonal relations with high needs for affiliation and
succorance, and who value security and compassion, are likely to become homemakers. In other words, the conventional approach suggests that as a result of
their different personalities, interests, and needs, home-oriented and career-
oriented women will place very different values on the same outcomes.

The results of our study are inconsistent with this view since we found no
differences between the evaluations of career- and home-oriented women. Although a woman's personality, needs, or interests might influence her beliefs
concerning the outcomes of different lifestyles, and thus affect occupational
choice, external variables of this kind did not provide a satisfactory explanation
of the women's choice intentions in our study.

In fact, there appears little reason to expect that personality characteristics,
needs, or interests will have a strong effect on women's beliefs as to consequences
that will follow from certain lifestyles. Such beliefs are more likely to reflect the
prevailing views of a woman's social environment. As these views change, or as
the woman moves from one social environment to another, her beliefs about the
different lifestyles will also undergo change. Not too long ago, the prevailing
view in American society was that women could achieve fulfillment and happiness only in the role of homemaker. Recent changes in sex-role stereotypes have
led many women to realize that there are alternative paths to the same goals and
that the pursuit of a career may further rather than hinder the attainment of
valued outcomes.

# CHAPTER 11

Predicting
and Understanding
Family Planning
Behaviors:
Beliefs,
attitudes, and
intentions

Martin Fishbein
James J. Jaccard
Andrew R. Davidson
Icek Ajzen
Barbara Loken

Many serious problems of modern life have been blamed on the rapid growth in the world's population. It is generally agreed that continued population growth is partly responsible for, among other things, the energy crisis, depletion of other national resources, food shortages, and pollution of the environment. Moreover, the rapid increase in the world population has been viewed as contributing indirectly to such problems as poverty, unemployment, illiteracy, disease, and crime (cf., McKee & Robertson, 1975).

Although it may be an oversimplification to blame all of society's ills on the "population explosion," the potential dangers of continued rapid expansion can hardly be denied. As Fawcett and Arnold (1973) have noted, "growth must eventually cease, and the only legitimate questions are how and when" (p. 24). Generally speaking, the increasingly rapid growth in population is due to a widening of the gap between birth rate and death rate. This is not to say that women are giving birth to more children today than in the past. Rather, the population explosion is due largely to advances in medicine and agriculture which have reduced infant mortality and raised life expectancies. Since it is obviously desirable to maintain the lowest possible death rate, the only practical way of controlling population growth is through a reduction in the birth rate.

Extensive data are available that estimate birth rates in different countries and among different segments of the populations within those countries. By comparing these birth rates and examining their changes over time, we can gain some insights into the factors related to variations in fertility. For example, it has been found that developing countries have higher birth rates than developed countries. Perhaps more important, while the birth rate has shown a consistent decline in the industrialized nations, it has remained relatively stable in most third world nations. The major body of research conducted in the United States, however, has focused not on such aggregate statistics but rather on the factors that determine how many children a woman (or family) desires, expects, or plans to have.

Four major large-scale field studies of fertility and family planning behaviors have been conducted in the United States: The Indianapolis Study (Kiser & Whelpton, 1958); the Growth of American Families studies (Freedman, Whelpton, & Campbell, 1959; Whelpton, Campbell, & Patterson, 1966); the Family Growth in Metropolitan America or Princeton Studies (Westoff, Potter, Sagi, & Mishler, 1961; Westoff, Potter, & Sagi, 1963) and the National Fertility Study (Westoff & Ryder, 1977). The major family planning variables investigated in these studies have been 1) actual family size at time of interview, or "fertility rate," 2) expected, desired, or ideal family size, 3) birth intervals, 4) use and knowledge of contraceptive techniques, and 5) fecundity or ability to reproduce. Since there is considerable evidence that contraception is used almost universally by fecund couples in the United States (Freedman, 1962; Westoff et al., 1961; Westoff, 1972), it has also been argued that "the patterns of family planning followed are successful in enabling most couples to have the number of children they want" (Freedman, 1962, p. 219).

Consequently, the major portion of research to date has attempted to account for the number of children a person or couple intends to have, that is, the expected, desired, or planned family size.[1] This research into the determinants of family size has primarily centered around situational and demographic variables. Most major studies have dealt with such independent variables as place of residence, social mobility, religion, socio-economic status, and education. Consistent with the aggregate data mentioned above, desired and actual family size are often found to vary among different demographic segments of the population. For example, Catholics are typically found to desire and to actually have larger families than Protestants or Jews.

However, these studies have also attempted to account for family size preferences by reference to purely social psychological factors. Consider the first major survey of fertility in the United States. Conducted in 1941, the study was based on a random sample of 1000 couples residing in Indianapolis who had virtually completed their families (see Kiser & Whelpton, 1958). Among the social psychological variables considered in this study were liking for children, fear of pregnancy, tendency to plan, beliefs about religion, conformity to group patterns, marital adjustment, and husband-wife dominance. Unlike the demographic characteristics, none of these variable was found to influence a couple's actual or desired family size.

These findings were generally corroborated in the subsequent investigations. For example, in the third major study of fertility, Westoff et al. (1961, 1963)

---

[1]Strictly speaking, intentions are not equivalent to expectations, desires, or plans, but most previous research has not obtained direct measures of intentions.

considered the relationships between desired family size and social relations within the family, as well as a number of personality characteristics. Social relations within the family refers to such variables as adjustment to marriage, adjustment to mother role, liking for children, and dominance in running the house. The correlations between variables of this type and family size preferences were very low, and the authors concluded that, "so far research has failed to uncover substantially important correlations between fertility variables and specific aspects of the nature and tenor of social relationships within the family" (Westoff et al., 1961, p. 182).

The main personality variables included in this study were generalized manifest anxiety, need for nurturance, compulsiveness, tolerance of ambiguity, cooperativeness, and need achievement. Once again, the findings were negative, and the authors concluded that "there is little evidence . . . that the area of personality has produced fruitful results" (p. 184).

Generally speaking, then, the major result of this line of research has been the identification of existing differences in fertility rates and in certain family planning behaviors among various demographically defined segments of the population. Note however that these differences are culture- and time-bound. For example, previously observed differences between Catholics and Protestants in the use of contraceptives are no longer found to exist (see Davidson & Jaccard, 1975). More importantly, as numerous investigators have pointed out, demographic differences provide little information of an explanatory nature (Pohlman, 1969; Rainwater, 1965; Wyatt, 1967). Although "we probably know more about the fertility and family planning of the American population than about that of any other country in the world . . . our large-scale field surveys have been much more successful in measuring and describing variations in fertility and family planning than in finding the causes of these variations" (Freedman, 1962, p. 211). If we are to truly understand fertility-related behavior, we must not only describe variations in fertility but also determine the probable causes of these variations. Addressing this point, Pohlman (1969) argued

> To say that a man wants a larger or smaller family "because" he is lower class or belongs to a certain church is not a satisfactory psychological explanation; we must ask what factors associated with class or church influence his desires for children (p. 149).

It is therefore unfortunate that the previous research in the family planning area has been unable to identify nondemographic factors influencing fertility-related behaviors and that attempts to predict family size intentions from social psychological variables have for the most part been unsuccessful. In fact, many family planners have come to agree with Mauldin (1965) that "significant relationships between psychological factors and fertility simply have not been found" and that "perhaps such relationships do not exist" (p. 9). Some investigators of family planning have suggested that these negative findings may be due in part to the fact that research in this area has not been based on any underlying or organizing theory but has instead tended to test large numbers of relatively unrelated hypotheses. Indeed, although the members of the steering committee of the Family Growth in Metropolitan America Study "made a special effort to . . . formulate an 'organizing principle' or 'body of theory' to guide their work, they found this task 'rather frustrating' and this effort 'was finally abandoned'" (Kiser, 1962, pp. 163-164).

## APPLICATION OF THE THEORY
## OF REASONED ACTION TO FAMILY PLANNING

In contrast to these pessimistic conclusions, it is our contention that social psychology can contribute substantially to an understanding of the variations in fertility and family planning. After reviewing the family planning literature we see no a priori reasons why the pyschological processes underlying the formation of family planning intentions should differ from the processes underlying the formation of any other behavioral or outcome intention. Consistent with this argument, several studies conducted in recent years have provided strong evidence for the utility of the theory of reasoned action in the family planning area. The theory has been used to predict, among other things, intentions to engage in premarital sexual intercourse (Fishbein, 1966), intentions to practice family planning behaviors, such as the use of birth control pills (Jaccard & Davidson, 1972), and intentions concerning family size, such as intentions to have two children in the completed family (Davidson & Jaccard, 1975) and intentions to have a child in the next two years (Davidson & Jaccard, 1975; Vinokur-Kaplan, 1978).

## DETERMINANTS OF FAMILY SIZE

We saw earlier that family size has constituted the major focus of research in the area of family planning. In many ways there is really nothing mysterious about the factors that determine the number of children in a completed family. If a woman wants to increase the size of her family, she has two options. She can engage in those kinds of activities that will maximize the likelihood of giving live birth to a child, including sexual intercourse during the appropriate phase of her menstrual cycle and following her doctor's advice with respect to prenatal care. Alternatively, she can try to adopt a child. On the other hand, couples who want to maintain the present size of their families can abort unwanted pregnancies or practice abstinence or contraception.

Clearly, the number of children in a completed family must be considered an *outcome* of certain behaviors rather than a behavior as such. It would appear that in contrast to many other outcomes, a couple can exercise considerable control over the size of their family by performing appropriate behaviors. This is not to say, however, that activities designed to increase or maintain family size will always result in the desired outcome. Attempts to increase family size may be thwarted by lack of fecundity, miscarriage, stillbirth, or failure to adopt a child. Thus, even if a couple behaves in an appropriate manner, they may not be able to have as many children as they intended to have.

In contrast, by exercising all of their options, a couple can (in principle) ensure that they have no more than their intended number of children. Although few couples go to the extreme of celibacy, and improper use of contraceptive methods can result in unwanted pregnancies, the couple still has the option of terminating the pregnancy by means of abortion or of bearing the child and putting it up for adoption. The reason families sometimes have a greater number of children than intended is that many people are reluctant to exercise options of this kind.

## Child-bearing Intentions and Family Size

This discussion implies that we cannot expect strong correspondence between the number of children a couple intends to have and the actual size of their family; some couples will have fewer children than intended while others will have more. Unfortunately, we could find only two studies that measured family-size intentions and that later reinterviewed the same respondents to determine the actual size of their completed families. Both studies provide strong support for our analysis. Westoff, Mishler, and Kelley (1957) interviewed 145 couples immediately after their engagement had been announced in the newspaper. Each member of the couple was asked to indicate the number of children he or she desired in their completed families. Twenty years later they were again contacted to find out how many children they actually had. Although no data were presented concerning the extent to which couples had fewer or more children than they had originally desired, correlations between intended and actual family size were found to be quite low ($r = .27$ for wives and $.26$ for husbands).

The second study (Bumpass & Westoff, 1969) presented the data of interest. The women respondents were initially interviewed six months after the birth of their second child and were asked how many children they wanted altogether, counting the two they had at the time. Somewhere between 6 and 10 years later (near the end of their reproductive periods) they were reinterviewed to obtain information about the number of children in their completed families. The correlation between intended and actual family size was substantially higher in this study ($r$ = .56), but since the women already had two children at the time of the first interview, the size of this correlation is undoubtedly inflated.[2]

Despite the relatively high correlation and the fact that all respondents already had two children, only 41% of the women achieved exactly the number of children they desired. Approximately 30% had more children than intended, and the same percentage had fewer than intended. Although in the majority of cases the discrepancy between intended and actual family size involved only one child, 14% of the women missed their goals by two or more children.[3]

**Aggregate predictions.** If we ignore the individual and consider the population as a whole, a very different picture emerges. Bumpass and Westoff (1969) reported that, on the average, the women in their sample desired and ultimately had 3.3 children. In the study by Westoff, Mishler, and Kelley (1957), an analysis at the aggregate level also showed high correspondence between intended and actual family size. On the average, 2.6 children were born per couple. This number was identical to the average number of children desired by males, and only slightly lower than the average of 2.8 children desired by females.

These results obviously reflect the fact that in both studies the number of children exceeding the intended was counterbalanced by an approximately equal number of children below the intended. Recall that in the Bumpass and Westoff study, equal percentages of women had more and fewer children than they desired. In contrast to the individual level, therefore, intended family size was a very accurate predictor of actual family size at the aggregate level.

This conclusion is supported by various other studies that have analyzed average or aggregate data of intended and actual family size. To take just one example, Whelpton, Campbell, and Patterson (1966) reported the findings of two separate interviews taken in 1955 and 1960. Although different women were interviewed, the two samples were comparable on almost all social and demographic variables, except that the women in the second sample were five years older than those in the first. The 1955 sample was asked to indicate the number of children they expected to have during the subsequent five years. On the average, women in 1955 expected to give birth to at least .90 but no more than .93 children in the next five years. These expectations were found to be remarkably accurate predictors of the average number of births during that five-year time period. The 1960 sample reported an average of .92 births per woman.

There is considerable evidence, then, that at least in the United States, actual family size corresponds closely to intended family size at the aggregate level. It

---

[2]The shorter time span may also have contributed to the higher correlation.

[3]In a more recent study, Westoff & Ryder (1977) did not measure family size intentions, but they did assess intentions to have additional children. These intentions (measured in 1970) were found to have a correlation of .56 with actual fertility (observed between 1971 and 1975).

may be tempting to conclude on the basis of this finding that the birth rate in the American population can be reduced by persuading people to lower the number of children they intend to have. Although this might have little effect on the size of any given family, the aggregate data seem to suggest that, on the average, such a strategy might succeed. Unfortunately, there is reason to believe that lowering family-size intentions may be quite ineffective precisely in those segments of the population that have the highest birth rates.

Available evidence shows that in populations with relatively high birth rates, people, on the average, intend to have fewer children than they actually have. For example, in the United States, segments of the population low in socio-economic status (i.e., the poorer, less educated, or blue-collar workers) are found to have more children than people relatively high on this dimension. There are, however, no corresponding differences in intentions. The differential birth rate has been attributed to the fact that low socio-economic populations are less successful in having as few children as they intend to have (cf., Pohlman, 1969; Ryder & Westoff, 1971). Related to these findings, Jaffe and Guttmacher (1968) reported that nonwhites intend to have slightly fewer children than whites, although they actually have somewhat larger families.

Since most populations with high birth rates already intend to have fewer children than they eventually will have, lowering these intentions any further is unlikely to have much impact on the birth rate. The lack of correspondence between intended and actual family size at the aggregate level is even more apparent in countries whose birth rates are higher than that found in the United States. For example, in the 1960s, surveys conducted in Sri-Lanka (formerly Ceylon) showed that the average family had 4.3 children, whereas the intended number of children was only 3.2 on the average. Similarly, at about the same time in Taiwan, the average intention was to have 3.8 children, but the actual number of children per family was 5.0.[4]

Findings of this kind have been viewed as support for the argument that family size intentions determine actual family size only where people have knowledge about, and access to, effective means of birth control. We would argue, however, that irrespective of such knowledge or access, intended family size has little direct effect on the size of the completed family. From our point of view, intentions to have a certain number of children can influence attainment of that outcome only to the extent that they direct people to take appropriate actions. Clearly, information about, and access to, effective contraceptive methods are no guarantee that people will use those methods. We have seen that even in the United States the majority of couples do not have the number of children they originally intended. The finding of accurate prediction at the aggregate level

---

[4]Data concerning present intentions are not available for Taiwan, although recent surveys show that actual family size has declined to about 2.6 children in the average family. Interested readers can find population statistics for various countries in the United Nations *Demographic Yearbook* and in the *Population Index*.

merely reflects a rather unique and fortuitous situation that exists in the United States. Although far from completely successful, the actions taken by the American public have reduced the number of unintended births in the United States to the exact point where it matches the number of failures to bear intended children.[5]

Clearly then, in order to understand why people have as many children as they do, we have to examine not their intentions to have a certain number of children but rather the fertility-related behaviors they perform. To be sure, the intention to have or not have a child is important since it directs people to perform certain behaviors they consider appropriate for attaining the desired outcome. For example, people who do not want to have a child tend to have stronger intentions to use contraceptives than those who do want to have a child. This is not true for everybody, however, and even if we know that a person intends to use contraceptives, we do not know which method will be used or whether the chosen method will be used effectively. The actions taken by a person to prevent birth of a child are often not effective, and it is for this reason that our approach attempts to identify the appropriate behaviors and explore their determinants. Nevertheless, since child-bearing intentions may direct people's family planning behavior, it is of interest to examine the factors that influence intentions to have or to not have children.

### Predicting Child-bearing Intentions

In chapter 10 we saw how our approach has been applied in the case of intentions to attain career goals. The theory of reasoned action has also been used to explore the factors that underlie intentions to attain outcomes such as having a two-child family and having a child in the next two years (Davidson & Jaccard, 1975) or the next three years (Loken & Fishbein, 1978). As expected, women's intentions to attain these outcomes were predicted with a high degree of accuracy from their attitudes and subjective norms with respect to the outcomes in question. In each case, the attitude was a somewhat more important factor than the subjective norm, although both components contributed significantly to the prediction. The attitudes and subjective norms were in turn predictable from estimates of those components based on the underlying behavioral and normative beliefs.

Given these findings, it was possible to compare the beliefs of women who intended to attain a given outcome with the beliefs of women who did not. These analyses provided some interesting insights into the underlying causes of child-bearing intentions. To illustrate, among the considerations that determined a woman's intention to have a child in the next three years were the following:

---

[5]Recent evidence (e.g., Westoff & Ryder, 1977) suggests that even in the United States, aggregate prediction may no longer be accurate; women were found to have 15% fewer children than they intended.

whether the family could afford a child; whether the woman was at a good age for child-bearing; whether the addition of a child would make the marriage stronger, fulfill family life, or reduce time for the woman's own goals and plans (Loken & Fishbein, 1978). At the time of the interview, the women in this study were without children. As might be expected, women who believed that they could afford to have a child in the next three years and that this would fulfill their family lives without creating emotional strain intended to have a child, while women holding the opposite beliefs did not. In addition, while all women agreed that having a child would add responsibility and reduce their time for their own goals and plans, women who evaluated both consequence negatively were much less likely to intend having a child within the next three years.

Interestingly, the same kinds of considerations were salient for women who already had children (Davidson & Jaccard, 1975). Two differences are worth noting, however. The belief as to whether adding a child would mean having less time for one's own goals and plans was not salient in this population. On the other hand, for many of the women with children, a salient concern was family size, namely, whether an additional child would mean having more children than they wanted in their completed families.

An interesting difference also emerged with respect to normative beliefs. Not surprisingly, women without children reported greater pressure from their parents to have a child than did women who already had children. In addition, some of the women in each sample believed that their husbands thought they should not have a child. Many of the childless women, therefore, perceived conflicting social pressures: they believed that their parents were in favor while their husbands were against their having a child. Since most women are more highly motivated to comply with their husbands than with their parents, the conflict was usually resolved by forming the intention to not have a child.

Although we did not go into much detail, the preceding discussion suggests that people's intentions to have or to not have a child are based largely on reasonable considerations concerning the various consequences that would follow. By influencing some of these beliefs, it should be possible to lower child-bearing intentions. As we noted earlier, however, even if we were successful, the lower intentions would in many cases have little or no effect on the birth rate, since they are unlikely to be translated into appropriate action. A more promising stragety is to first identify the appropriate behaviors and then attempt to understand their determinants.

## EMPIRICAL STUDIES OF CONTRACEPTIVE BEHAVIOR

Among the more important of these behaviors are sexual intercourse, prenatal care, use of contraceptive methods, and abortion. Contraception is by far the major focus of most family planning programs, and millions of dollars are spent each year to promote the use of contraceptive methods around the world. Unfortunately, these efforts have often been surprisingly unsuccessful. Before we consider possible reasons for these failures, it may be instructive to look at the results of two studies dealing with women's use of a popular contraceptive method, namely the birth control pill.

The two studies used similar methods, except that the respondents in one study were unmarried college women in their freshman year (Jaccard & Davidson, 1972), while in the second study (Davidson & Jaccard, 1975) they were married women almost all of whom had children. In both studies, the major objective was to understand the factors that underlie a woman's intention to use or to not use birth control pills. A prior question that must be answered, however, is the extent to which an intention of this kind can accurately predict the woman's behavior. In one part of the second study, married women indicated their intentions on the following scale:

I intend to use birth control pills within the next year.

likely ___ : ___ : ___ : ___ : ___ : ___ : ___ unlikely

Approximately one year later they were re-interviewed and asked to report their use or nonuse of the pill during the past year. Consistent with expectations, a strong intention-behavior relation was observed ($r = .85$), reflecting the fact that most women (93%) behaved in accordance with their intentions.

The central focus of the two studies, however, were the women's general intentions to use birth control pills (without a specified time period). As a first step in each study, small samples of respondents from the respective populations were interviewed in order to identify the salient beliefs and referents for this behavior. It is interesting to note that the salient beliefs emitted by the two samples were virtually identical, despite the fact that one sample was comprised of unmarried women and the other of married women with children. Similarly, the six most frequently mentioned referents were the same in both samples.

Using the procedures described in part 1 of this book and outlined in appendix A, standard questionnaires were constructed. These questionnaires contained the usual measures of behavioral beliefs, evaluations of outcomes, normative beliefs, and motivations to comply with each referent.[6] Also included were measures of intentions to use birth control pills, attitudes toward personal use of birth control pills, and subjective norms[7] with respect to this behavior.

Analyses of these data showed that both attitudes and subjective norms were important determinants of the women's intentions to use the pill, although college women placed somewhat greater weight on the attitudinal component

[6]The example discussed in chapter 6, illustrating the construction of a set of modal salient beliefs, in fact dealt with beliefs about using the pill.

[7]A direct measure of subjective norms was obtained only with the college sample.

while married women placed somewhat more weight on the normative component. Knowledge of the two components led to highly accurate predictions of intentions in both samples ($R$ = .89 for the college women and $R$ = .86 for the married women with children). Attitudes and subjective norms were in turn accurately predicted from beliefs based on salient outcomes and referents. The correlations among beliefs, attitude, subjective norm, and intention for the college sample are shown in Figure 11.1.

Given the findings in Figure 11.1, examination of beliefs should help explain why some women intended to use the pill while others did not. To illustrate, Table 11.1 (see p. 146) shows average belief strength and outcome evaluations for college women who did intend to use the pill and those who did not. Note first that all women were in essential agreement that using the pill was inexpensive, convenient, and would enable them to regulate birth intervals and family size. Women who intended to use the pill, however, did so in part because they placed somewhat more values on convenience and regulation of family size.

The major considerations that entered into the women's decisions to use or to not use the pill revolved around questions of physiological side effects, morality, and effectiveness. Although all women believed that using the pill leads to minor side effects (such as weight gain), they differed in their beliefs about severe consequences. The more certain a woman was that using the pill would not lead to such negative outcomes as blood clots and birth defects, the more likely she was to intend using the pill. Also associated with intentions to use the pill were beliefs that this was the best available method for preventing pregnancy.

Although clearly a reasonable basis for making a decision, questions of safety and effectiveness constituted only part of the picture; considerations of im-

**FIGURE 11.1**

Relationships among beliefs, attitude, subjective norm, and intention with respect to using birth control pills among college women.

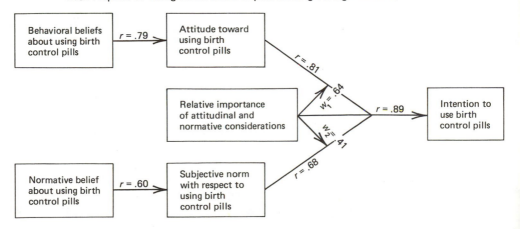

morality and guilt also played a major role. Women intended to use the pill only if they had no strong moral reservations. In retrospect, this finding is perhaps not really surprising since, for the unmarried women in this sample, use of birth control pills is obviously associated with the issue of premarital sexual intercourse. Consistent with this argument, beliefs concerning morality did not affect intentions to use birth control pills in the sample of married women with children (see Davidson & Jaccard, 1975). All married women were in essential agreement that using the pill was neither immoral nor would it give them guilt feelings. The beliefs that did influence their intentions (in addition to questions of safety and effectiveness) were beliefs concerning sexual pleasure and regulation of family size. Given safety and effectiveness, the more a married women believed that using the pill would regulate her family size and increase her sexual pleasure, the more likely she was to intend using the pill.

On the normative side, the women's major concerns centered on the prescriptions of their husbands or boyfriends and doctors. They were highly motivated to comply with these referents and women who believed that their husbands or boyfriends and doctors thought they should use the pill intended to do so. By the same token, women who believed that these two referents opposed their use of birth control pills formed intentions to not use them.

With respect to the remaining referents (mother, father, friends, and "religion in which I was raised"), the women reported only moderate motivations to comply. Thus, although all women generally believed that their religions were opposed to their using birth control pills, and the college women also saw their parents as being opposed to it, those beliefs had little effect on the women's intentions. While it may seem surprising that religious prescriptions had little effect, this finding is quite consistent with other observations. Even among Catholics, conformity to Catholic directive on birth control has been steadily declining. Westoff and Ryder (1970) reported that the percentage of fecund white Catholic women conforming to their church's directive was 70% in 1955, 62% in 1960, 47% in 1965, and only 36% by 1970.

In sum, the results of these studies make it clear that a woman's intention to use a certain method of contraception, such as birth control pills, is ultimately determined by her beliefs concerning the advantages and disadvantages of using the method in question and by her beliefs that relevant referents think she should or should not use that method.

## IMPLICATIONS FOR FAMILY PLANNING PROGRAMS

We can now turn to the question of why many family planning programs have been unsuccessful. It must first be recognized that not all family planning programs are designed with the same goal in mind. Some programs, particularly those in underdeveloped countries, are established in response to problems of malnutrition, disease, and overcrowding which are attributed to the excessive population growth in those countries. Consequently, the major aim of these programs is to reduce the birth rate in the target population. Other family planning programs are concerned with the problem of unwanted pregnancies. Among married couples, these programs attempt to help families achieve their desired number of children and to control birth intervals. Another major effort has been directed at preventing pregnancies among teenagers and other unwed women. Programs of this kind may be in part motivated by the desire to enhance the individual's right to control her own fertility and to prevent or reduce the need for abortions.

Despite their different goals, all of these programs are designed to motivate people to practice contraception. Once people are so motivated, the programs provide information about birth control techniques and in many cases make these techniques available to the target population. Each program's particular goal, however, often guides the strategy that is adopted to increase people's motivation to use contraceptive methods. Generally speaking, family planning programs are based on the assumption that people will be motivated or will intend to practice contraception if 1) they are made aware of the problem toward which the program is directed and 2) they are informed that the problem can be avoided by proper use of birth control techniques. In order to overcome resistance to innovation which often accompanies the introduction of new technologies, many programs attempt to enlist the aid of respected members of the community in disseminating information and serving as role models, thus putting social pressure on other community members.

From our point of view, this strategy is unlikely to result in the adoption of the recommended methods of birth control. We saw earlier that intentions to use a given contraceptive technique are based on many different attitudinal and normative considerations. Changing one or two of these considerations will seldom be sufficient to increase such intentions. Yet, in the final analysis, a change in one or two beliefs is all that is usually accomplished in most family planning programs.

For example, consider a program designed to reduce population growth. Suppose the program succeeded in making people aware of the dangers of overpopulation and in showing them the disadvantages of large families and the advantages of having fewer children. As a result, individuals may form (more) negative attitudes toward overpopulation and large families and (more) positive attitudes toward smaller families. Further, these changes may produce intentions to have fewer children. Unfortunately, as we saw earlier, such intentions are not necessarily related to effective use of contraceptives and they may have little effect on the birth rate.

However, such a family planning program will also lead people to believe that their use of contraceptives will reduce the danger of overpopulation by enabling them to have smaller families. Although this may be one of the salient beliefs on which attitudes toward use of contraceptives are based, such attitudes will also be affected by considerations of safety, effectiveness, convenience, morality, etc. Unless the program addresses these additional salient beliefs, little change in attitudes—and hence in intentions to use specific contraceptive methods—can be expected. Clearly, people who come to believe that using a certain birth control method can help reduce family size may continue to believe that using the method is inconvenient, immoral, and would reduce their own or their spouse's sexual enjoyment. They would thus maintain their negative attitudes toward this behavior.

Enlisting the help of respected members of the community will often also be an ineffective means of increasing intentions to practice contraception. From our point of view, this strategy may lead to the formation of beliefs that these members of their community approve of using some recommended method of birth control. At the same time, people may continue to believe that other referents (spouse, parents, religious leaders) think they should not use the method in question and they may be more highly motivated to comply with these referents. Consequently, changing normative beliefs concerning the prescriptions of the referents enlisted in the family planning program may have little effect on subjective norms and hence on intentions.

Similar arguments apply to family planning programs that have been developed in response to other problems. To be sure, it may be important for people to realize the potentially harmful effects of allowing insufficient time between births and the many negative consequences of unwanted pregnancies, including abortions and child neglect. From our point of view, providing information about these problems will serve primarily to influence people's attitudes toward unwanted pregnancies and the regulation of birth intervals. However, like attitudes toward overpopulation, small families, or family planning, attitudes toward unwanted pregnancies and birth spacing are unlikely to influence people's intentions to use any one of the available contraceptive methods. Although the family planning programs may again emphasize that contraception allows regulation of birth intervals and prevents unwanted pregnancies, these are only two of the many beliefs that underlie intentions to use some method of birth control.

Our analysis thus suggests that making people aware of the existence of a problem and then persuading them that contraception provides the best solution is insufficient to influence intentions concerning the use of contraceptive techniques. What is needed is an approach that systematically explores the determinants of these intentions. We must first identify the extent to which, within our target population, intentions to use a recommended method are under attitudinal or normative control. Clearly, the outcomes and referents that are salient, and the particular beliefs that lead to the formation of different intentions, may vary from one target population to another and from one contraceptive method to another. The information gained in this fashion can be used to design a family planning program that is directed at a set of beliefs underlying the intention in question.

Earlier, we discussed women's intentions to use birth control pills. Our findings suggest that women who do not intend to use the pill might do so if, among other things, they could be persuaded that using the pill is safe, effective, and increases sexual pleasure, and that their husbands and doctors think they should use birth control pills. In addition, it might be effective to lead college women to believe that using the pill is not immoral and that they should not feel guilty about its use. Raising this issue with married women, however, would accomplish very little, since, irrespective of their intentions, those women already believe that using the pill is not immoral. Along the same lines, providing information that the pill is convenient could be effective in the case of married women, but it would have little effect on the intentions of the unmarried college women, since most of them already hold this belief.

It should be obvious that an effective family planning program would have to deal with very different issues and referents in an underdeveloped country or in the case of a birth control technique such as the rhythm method or vasectomy. Again, however, we should be able to identify a set of attitudinal and normative considerations that determine intentions to use a given method within the target population. These beliefs should then serve as the focus of the family planning program.[8]

Many people in the family planning area might object to our analysis and argue that their programs deal with more than the single belief that use of contraceptives will resolve a particular problem. In fact, many family planning programs have an extensive educational component whose major thrust is to provide information about the reproductive process and the ways in which different methods of birth control prevent fertilization and conception. Although such sex education may be worthwhile and may in the long run help people practice contraception more effectively, from our point of view, descriptive accounts of the menstrual cycle and the reproductive system will have little effect on intentions to practice contraception in general or to use a particular method of birth control. As we saw, to influence such intentions, the program must be directed at various beliefs concerning the advantages and disadvantages of using a certain method as well as at normative beliefs concerning the prescriptions of relevant referents.

To be sure, some educational programs touch upon questions of safety, effectiveness, and convenience, and some may even raise issues of morality, sexual pleasure, and likely reactions of parents, spouses, or religious leaders. Being educational in nature, however, these programs are likely to provide both sides of these issues, and the resulting changes in beliefs will not necessarily favor adop-

---

[8]For a discussion of ways to produce change and an illustration in a different behavioral domain, see chapter 15.

**TABLE 11.1**
Mean Beliefs and Outcome Evaluations for Women Who Intend and
Do Not Intend to Use Birth Control Pills

| USING BIRTH CONTROL PILLS | BELIEFS | | OUTCOME EVALUATIONS | |
|---|---|---|---|---|
| | *Intend to Use* | *Intend Not to Use* | *Intend to Use* | *Intend Not to Use* |
| Leads to major side effects | − .35* | 1.19 | −2.54 | −2.50 |
| Leads to minor side effects | 1.35 | 1.25 | −1.05 | −1.81 |
| Produces children who are born with something wrong with them | −2.42* | − .37 | −2.54 | −2.50 |
| Is using a method of birth control that is unreliable | −2.26* | −1.06 | −2.53 | −2.00 |
| Is using the best method available | 2.04* | .88 | 2.67 | 2.06 |
| Would remove the worry of becoming pregnant | 2.37* | 1.13 | 2.75 | 2.19 |
| Would affect my sexual morals | −1.89* | − .44 | −1.40 | −1.62 |
| Is immoral | −2.74* | − .69 | −1.81 | −1.81 |
| Would give me guilt feelings | −2.25* | .06 | −2.40 | −2.44 |
| Is using a method of birth control that is expensive | − .88 | − .81 | −1.12 | −1.56 |
| Is using a method of birth control that is convenient | 2.56 | 1.75 | 2.65* | 1.69 |
| Would enable me to regulate the size of my family | 2.70 | 2.19 | 2.67* | 1.81 |
| Would enable me to regulate time intervals between pregnancies | 2.70 | 2.19 | 2.65 | 1.88 |
| Would regulate my menstrual cycle | 2.35* | .81 | 2.14 | 1.38 |
| Would increase my sexual pleasure | .51 | − .12 | 2.21* | 1.06 |

*Significant difference between intend-not intend ($p < .05$).

tion of a birth control method. For example, a woman may become aware of the negative side effects of one method and the reduction of sexual pleasure inherent in the use of another.

More important, this educational effort—and especially the information concerning advantages and disadvantages of different birth control techniques—is typically not part of the initial appeal of most family planning programs. We saw that, instead, they attempt to motivate people to practice family planning by arguing that contraception will prevent a particular domestic or social problem. The educational part of the program is designed to provide additional information to those individuals who, as a result of the initial appeal, have been motivated to find out about contraception or adopt a given method. Thus, a person will learn about the safety, effectiveness, and convenience of using a given birth control technique if she has become motivated enough to participate in the educational program. The problem with this approach is that, as we have noted repeatedly, the initial appeal focuses only on one belief and is thus unlikely to motivate people (i.e., to change people's intentions) to practice contraception. According to our approach, information about the advantages of recommended birth control practices and about normative prescriptions of relevant referents should be part of the initial appeal.

We have discussed the effectiveness of family planning programs without any attention to ethical considerations. It should be clear that certain potentially effective strategies would be quite unacceptable from an ethical standpoint. For example, we indicated that an effective method of changing women's intentions to use birth control pills might be to provide information that this method is safe and effective. While the pill's proven effectiveness can hardly be contested, the question of safety is more controversial. Clearly, an ethical program could not simply argue that it is safe to use the pill, but would have to provide information about its potentially harmful side effects. At a more general level, ethical objections could be raised with respect to any program of persuasion. However, persuasion is inherent whenever people are exposed to new information. The more important ethical concern is that the information presented be accurate and that all relevant information be provided.

# CHAPTER 12

# Predicting and Understanding Consumer Behavior: Attitude-behavior correspondence

Martin Fishbein
Icek Ajzen

In recent years scholars in the area of marketing have increasingly turned their attention to the behavior of the consumer. The mounting interest in consumer behavior can be attributed in part to the desire of business firms to obtain a competitive advantage by basing their marketing decisions on information about the factors that determine the consumers' preferences among products. At the same time, consumers have organized to express their dissatisfaction and demand political action to ensure, among other things, higher standards of quality and safety, lower prices, and better service. The consumer movement further underscores the need to gain a better understanding of the factors that determine the behavior of individuals who consume the products of our economy.

The result has been the rapid emergence of consumer behavior as a distinct area of investigation. Research in this area deals largely with the processes that underlie the decision to purchase or use economic goods and services. Needless to say, many of our day-to-day activities fall within the realm of consumer behavior. Whether we buy toothpaste or an automobile, go to a restaurant, or fly across the ocean, we are consumers of goods and services. On the face of it, we are dealing with a form of behavior that is both distinct and of broad social significance.

The ubiquity of acts falling within this category, however, makes it clear that there is really nothing particularly unusual about consumer behavior. It is human action involving a choice among various alternatives, and there is little reason to assume that novel and unique processes will have to be invoked in order to account for such action.

A review of theoretical efforts in the area of consumer behavior supports this argument. The major theories designed to explain consumer behavior are highly eclectic, borrowing extensively from psychology and other behavioral sciences (e.g., Engel, Kollat, & Blackwell, 1975; Howard & Sheth, 1969; Nicosia, 1966). Among the explanatory concepts proposed are motive, need, personality, habit,

We would like to thank James J. Jaccard and Jean Chung for their assistance in collecting and analyzing the data presented in this chapter.

149

attitude, intention and satisfaction. In their efforts to provide a comprehensive description of the processes whereby consumers choose a given product, theorists have attempted to incorporate virtually every feature of human information processing, attitude formation and change, and decision making within their models of consumer behavior.

Current theories can be viewed as attempts to specify the factors and psychological processes that influence or underlie people's needs, on the one hand, and their perceptions of various products, on the other. The complexity of the theories derives in large part from the desire to incorporate interactions between needs and perceptions. Needs, motives, or desires are assumed to influence the information a person seeks about a product, as well as her attention to, and perception of, the product's attributes. At the same time, however, these needs, motives, or desires may themselves be aroused or modified by exposure to the product, to advertising, or to other social and cultural forces. The product attributes or functions are assumed to be judged in relation to the person's needs by means of certain evaluative criteria, and this process presumably results in the formation of an attitude which ultimately influences intention and purchase behavior. To add to this complexity, once the product has been purchased, the resulting satisfaction or dissatisfaction is assumed to feed back into the system, influencing needs, perceptions, attitudes, etc. In other words, every factor in these elaborate theories directly or indirectly influences (and is influenced by) every other factor.

As an illustration, Figure 12.1 presents a simplified description of the Howard-Sheth model. In addition to the variables shown in this diagram, Howard and Sheth (1969) also considered exogenous factors, such as importance of purchase, personality traits, culture, financial status, and time pressure, as well as additional output factors, such as product class comprehension, routinized response behavior, and limited and extensive problem solving.

While models of this type have been criticized on many grounds (see e.g., Ehrenberg, 1972; Tuck, 1976), the major objection has been that they "suffer from untestibility and lack of specificity of variables" (Tuck, 1976, p. 37). Theories that incorporate virtually every known social psychological construct and process not only lack in parsimony but, more important, they are likely to generate confusion rather than real understanding.

In many ways, these rather complex theories are attempts to elaborate and refine the widely accepted proposition that the more a particular product satisfies certain needs or fulfills certain functions, the more the product or brand will be liked, purchased, and used. Consumers' needs are assumed to influence the criteria they use in arriving at their purchase decisions. For example, in deciding upon a brand of detergent, the consumer may look for a brand that smells good, has no phosphates, gets her clothes clean, makes her feel more feminine, raises her status in the eyes of her friends and neighbors, or reduces her unconscious fear of being a lesbian. Criteria such as these presumably serve as the basis for comparing and evaluating the available alternatives. Consumers are said to

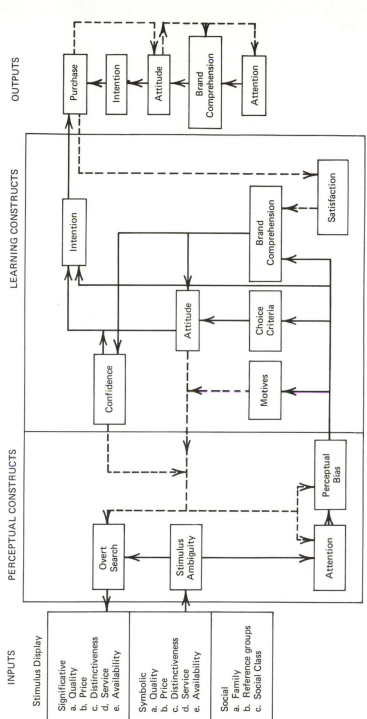

**FIGURE 12.1**

A simplified description of the theory of buyer behavior.
(John A. Howard and Jagdish N. Sheth, *The theory of buyer behavior*
(New York: John Wiley, 1969). Reprinted by permission of the publisher.)

*Note:* Solid lines indicate flow of information; dashed lines, feedback effects.

which the different brands are satisfactory with respect to each criterion and to choose the brand they believe best meets their criteria.

A major focus of marketing research is the attempt to identify the "evaluative criteria" consumers employ in their purchase decisions. Techniques used for this purpose have varied, depending on the investigator's theoretical orientation. Those who believe that consumers are aware of the criteria they use in their purchase decisions have typically taken the direct approach of asking respondents to state their reasons for buying or not buying a given product. This is frequently done in the context of group discussions, and the views exchanged during those discussions provide the basis for constructing a set of attributes that seem to serve as evaluative criteria. In contrast, investigators who believe that buying behavior is motivated primarily by unconscious needs and desires have tended to rely on depth interviews and projective techniques to identify the "true" decision criteria. Another common procedure is to use a technique, known as the Kelly repertory grid, in which consumers are essentially asked to identify attributes that distinguish one brand from another. It is also not uncommon for marketing researchers to generate lists of attributes on the basis of their own knowledge of the brand or product class.[1]

These procedures often result in long lists of attributes associated with the brands or product class under consideration. In order to identify a small number of attributes that serve as the most important evaluative criteria, investigators often rely on sophisticated quantitative techniques. Some of these techniques attempt to derive the basic dimensions underlying the attributes, while others attempt to identify the attributes that best discriminate between buyers and nonbuyers.[2] One advantage of such an approach is that, by having respondents rate several brands with respect to each attribute dimension, information about the relative strengths and weaknesses of various brands within a product class can be obtained, and this information can then be used to develop marketing strategies.

In conclusion, most market researchers assume that consumer decisions are guided by the extent to which alternative brands or products meet certain evaluative criteria. What remains to be explained is exactly how such comparisons are translated into buying decisions.

[1]Still other investigators use more sophisticated quantitative methods to identify the decision criteria. For example, one method relies on consumers' ratings of similarity or dissimilarity among a set of brands and identifies the dimensions or criteria underlying these judgments by means of multidimensional scaling procedures. These methods are usually associated with the use of decomposition models (see footnote 3).

[2]These techniques require that a sample of respondents rate the extent to which each brand possesses each attribute. One type of technique, usually some form of factor or cluster analysis, uses intercorrelations among these ratings to infer underlying dimensions. The second type essentially relies on the relations between each attribute and a criterion such as buying intention or choice; the methods include simple correlation, multiple regression, and discriminative function analysis.

## USE OF ATTITUDE THEORY IN MARKETING RESEARCH

To account for this process and to develop a comprehensive theory of consumer behavior, many investigators turned to social psychological research in the attitude area. A class of theories commonly referred to as *expectancy-value models*[3] (e.g., Fishbein, 1963; Rosenberg, 1956) appeared to be of particular relevance. As we saw in chapter 6, according to these models a person's attitude toward an object is a function of his salient beliefs that the object has certain attributes and his evaluations of these attributes. In the context of consumer behavior the object is typically a product or a brand within a product class. An estimate of attitude toward a product or brand is obtained by multiplying, for each attribute, belief strength and attribute evaluation and then summing these products across all salient attributes.

The popularity this approach enjoys in the marketing field can be traced in part to the fact that it seems to provide a theoretical link between evaluative criteria and the concept of attitude. In addition, it formalizes the widely held view that the consumer's satisfaction with a product (and hence purchase of that product) is determined by her beliefs that the product fulfills certain functions and that it satisfies some of her needs. Moreover, expectancy-value models are compatible with different theoretical orientations, since investigators are free to focus on product characteristics, such as cost, durability, or fragrance; on functions, such as decay prevention, cleaning power, or pain relief; or on psychodynamic and largely unconscious motives, such as the need for femininity, power, or security.

In their attempts to apply the expectancy-value model to consumer behavior, investigators developed measuring instruments they considered to be appropriate in the context of consumer decision making. Rather than assessing the consumer's beliefs that a given product has each of several salient attributes, investigators in the marketing area typically measure the extent to which the consumer views the product as satisfactory, with respect to each attribute that serves as an evaluative criterion. Further, instead of measuring the consumer's positive or negative evaluations of the attributes, they obtain ratings of each attribute's importance in the eyes of the consumer.

To illustrate, suppose an investigator, using one of the methods described earlier, has identified "natural colors, price, reliability, and appearance" to be crucial evaluative criteria in the context of buying a color television set. Any

---

[3]These models are often described as linear composition models. An alternative class of models developed largely by psychometricians and typically called decomposition models are also used by many market researchers. These models rely on sophisticated multidimensional scaling methods and are beyond the scope of the present chapter. For a comparison of composition and decomposition models, see Day (1972) or Green and Wind (1975).

brand within the product class, say Sony, can now be rated on importance and satisfaction scales, such as the following:

1. When considering the purchase of a color television set, natural color is

not at all                                                               extremely
important ____ : ____ : ____ : ____ : ____ : ____ : ____ important
                0       1       2       3       4       5       6

2. With respect to natural colors, Sony color television sets are

extremely                                                               extremely
unsatisfactory ____ : ____ : ____ : ____ : ____ : ____ : ____ satisfactory
                    −3      −2      −1      0      +1      +2      +3

The same scales are used for the remaining evaluative criteria and the satisfaction score for each is multiplied by its importance rating. Table 12.1 shows that these weighted satisfaction scores are summed to provide an overall measure of satisfaction with, or attitude toward, the product (cf., Engel, Kollat, & Blackwell, 1973).

It can be seen that the attitude model implied by these measurement procedures differs greatly from the original expectancy-value model. In the marketing adaptation, salient attributes are replaced by evaluative criteria, and beliefs and attribute evaluations are replaced by measures of attribute satisfaction and importance. Interestingly, however, the measure of satisfaction with respect to a given attribute appears to tap much the same information as the belief strength and attribute evaluation measures within an expectancy-value model. The relation between attribute satisfaction, on one hand, and the product of belief strength and attribute evaluation, on the other, is illustrated in Table 12.2. The table shows four consumers' beliefs, attribute evaluations, and attribute satisfactions with respect to fluoride in toothpaste. It can be seen that a person is likely to judge a toothpaste as inadequate with respect to fluoride either because he believes that the toothpaste has fluoride and he values this attribute

**TABLE 12.1**
Computation of Overall Satisfaction With a Product—Hypothetical Examples

| EVALUATIVE CRITERION | SATISFACTION WITH SONY VIS-A-VIS CRITERION | IMPORTANCE OF CRITERION | SATISFACTION × IMPORTANCE |
|---|---|---|---|
| Natural colors | +2 | 6 | 12 |
| Price | −3 | 3 | − 9 |
| Reliability | +1 | 2 | 2 |
| Appearance | +1 | 1 | 1 |
| | | Overall satisfaction | + 6 |

negatively (Consumer A) or because he believes it does not have fluoride and he values this attribute positively (Consumer B). Conversely, the remaining two consumers are likely to be satisfied with the fluoride content of the toothpaste, since one evaluates fluoride positively and believes that the toothpaste has fluoride (Consumer C) while the other evaluates fluoride negatively and believes the toothpaste does not possess this attribute (Consumer D). This example illustrates that attribute satisfaction is a relatively direct, albeit confounded, measure of belief strength multiplied by attribute evaluation.

Our discussion also suggests that the measure of attribute importance is extraneous to an expectancy-value model. Although it may appear reasonable to take into account the importance of each attribute, we noted in chapter 6 that the inclusion of an important measure, in addition to measures of belief strength and attribute evaluation, actually lowers rather than improves the predictive validity of the expectancy-value model.[4] Research on consumer behavior has also shown that weighting attribute satisfaction by importance often reduces the model's predictive power (see, for example, Sheth & Talarzyk, 1972). As a result, some investigators in the marketing area have decided to omit the attribute importance construct from their theories.[5]

In conclusion, the typical approach to consumer behavior has attempted to identify product or brand attributes that serve as the evaluative criteria for purchase decisions and has used ratings of satisfaction and importance with respect to these attributes to derive measures of overall satisfaction with, or attitude toward, the product or brand. In most studies, these measures are obtained with respect to two or more brands in a product class and are used to predict preferences among the different brands. Generally speaking, the studies have shown

**TABLE 12.2**
Illustration of the Relation Between Attribute Satisfaction,
Belief Strength, and Attribute Evaluation

| CONSUMERS | BELIEF THAT TOOTHPASTE HAS FLUORIDE | EVALUATION OF FLUORIDE | BELIEF-EVALUATION PRODUCT | SATISFACTION VIS-A-VIS FLUORIDE |
|---|---|---|---|---|
| A | +1 | −1 | −1 | No |
| B | −1 | +1 | −1 | No |
| C | +1 | +1 | +1 | Yes |
| D | −1 | −1 | +1 | Yes |

[4]For a more detailed discussion of these issues, see Cohen, Fishbein, and Ahtola (1972).

[5]Recognizing that the attribute satisfaction-importance model differs from the expectancy-value model, marketing researchers have in recent years proposed numerous variations on these models, and much research has tested and compared these different formulations (see Wilkie and Pessemier, 1973; Mazis, Ahtola, and Klippel, 1975).

that measures of "brand attitudes" typically lead to significant prediction of consumer preferences, although the accuracy of these predictions has been found to vary across brands and across product classes (see e.g., Bass & Talarzyk, 1972; Mazis, Ahtola, & Klippel, 1975). Let us now consider this approach within the framework of our theory.

## EVALUATION OF ATTITUDE RESEARCH IN MARKETING

From our point of view, two major problems are associated with the preceding approach. The first concerns the assessment of satisfaction with, or attitudes toward, a given brand or product. The second problem is related to the assumption that these attitudes can explain and predict various aspects of consumer behavior.

### Assessment of Brand Attitudes

Our approach suggests that attitudes toward a brand or product are determined by salient beliefs about that brand or product. Recall that salient beliefs can be obtained by asking respondents to list the characteristics, qualities, and attributes of the brand or product under consideration. The most frequently mentioned attributes can then be used to construct a list of modal salient beliefs (see chapter 6 and appendix A). In contrast, market research has focused largely on identifying evaluative criteria that discriminate between buyers of different brands within a given product class. For several reasons, these evaluative criteria need not correspond to salient beliefs.

First, when investigators generate lists of evaluative criteria on the basis of depth interviews, projective techniques, or psychoanalytically oriented group discussions, they are unlikely to obtain salient beliefs, since the very purpose of these techniques is to discover "unconscious" or "hidden" reasons for a purchase decision.

Second, the techniques used to reduce a large number of attributes to a relatively small and manageable set of evaluative criteria will often eliminate salient beliefs (see Fishbein, 1971). Not all salient beliefs discriminate between people who perform a given behavior and people who do not. Consider, for example, an investigator interested in identifying the evaluative criteria people use in their decisions of whether or not to purchase a Rolls Royce. Clearly, two of the most salient beliefs about the Rolls Royce are that the car is both expensive and prestigious. However, those attributes would not distinguish between buyers and nonbuyers, since both groups of consumers would agree that the Rolls Royce is expensive and prestigious. The same is true when the investigator attempts to identify evaluative criteria that discriminate between buyers of different brands of luxury cars. It follows that elimination of attributes that fail to discriminate between buyers of different brands may result in the elimination of salient beliefs about those brands.[6]

Finally, it must be realized that evaluative criteria are usually of a general nature, applicable to all brands within a product class. In contrast, different attributes may be salient with respect to competing brands within a given product class. To illustrate this point, we elicited salient beliefs concerning two brands of automobiles: Mercedes and Chevrolet. A sample of students was asked to respond to the following question with respect to each brand: "Suppose you are thinking about buying a car,[7] what do you see as the characteristics, qualities, and attributes of a Chevrolet (Mercedes)?" Following the procedures described in chapter 6, we used the most frequently mentioned attributes to construct the lists of modal salient beliefs shown below.

| *Chevrolet* | *Mercedes* |
|---|---|
| moderately priced | very expensive |
| ordinary car | good looking |
| well built | well built |
| dependable | status symbol |
| easily serviced | safe |
| American made | good reputation |
| | handles well |
| | luxurious |
| | German made |

It can be seen that our sample of respondents had more salient beliefs about the Mercedes than about the Chevrolet. Further, although the three most frequently mentioned attributes for both cars concerned price, styling, and the quality of construction, the particular attributes emitted were not always the same. Both cars were viewed as well built, but the Chevrolet was seen as moderately priced and ordinary while the Mercedes was seen as very expensive and good looking. Other differences between the two brands revolved around the view that the Mercedes is prestigious, luxurious, and safe while the Chevrolet is dependable and easily serviced. Finally, the countries of origin also entered the lists of salient beliefs.

Clearly, if salient beliefs were elicited with respect to the product class (automobiles) rather than particular brands within that class, still other types of attri-

---

[6]Note also that an attribute which *does* discriminate between buyers and nonbuyers is not necessarily salient. Further, it need not even serve as a decision criterion since its correlation with preference or buying behavior is not evidence for a causal link. For a more detailed discussion of these issues, see Fishbein (1971, pp. 306-310).

[7]This preamble need not be used to obtain salient beliefs about a particular brand. This clause was included however, since recent research in the consumer behavior area has tended to focus on brand or product attributes in the context of a buying situation.

butes might emerge. Specifically, beliefs concerning a product class are likely to be of a relatively general nature, applicable to all brands within the class, rather than dealing with attributes particular to specific brands. In fact, when asked to list the characteristics, qualities, and attributes they would consider in buying a car, consumers tend to give such responses as gas mileage, styling, quality of workmanship, price, and safety (see Mazis, Ahtola, & Klippel, 1975). Although these more general characteristics correspond to some of the attributes associated with the particular brands considered earlier (e.g., price, styling, quality of construction), eliciting beliefs about the product class fails to tap many brand-specific attributes (e.g., status symbol, good reputation, American made).

The difference between salient beliefs about particular brands and about the general product class can be seen even more clearly in a study on detergents conducted in Great Britain.[8] A salient belief about Brand A was that it causes scum and a salient belief about Brand B was that it was good for woolens. Yet neither of these attributes was emitted with respect to detergents in general.

To summarize briefly, the methods used in market research attempt to identify a small number of attributes that correlate with consumer preferences or behaviors, such as buying a given brand or choosing between competing brands. We have tried to show that the evaluative criteria thus identified need not correspond to the salient beliefs about the product class nor to the salient beliefs about particular brands within that class. This should not be taken as a criticism of marketing methods, since the stated objective of those methods is to identify evaluative criteria in the purchase decision rather than salient beliefs that underlie consumer attitudes, Nevertheless, since evaluative criteria need not correspond to salient beliefs, it is inappropriate to assume that evaluative criteria provide us with information about the factors that determine consumers' attitudes toward brands or products.

As we saw earlier, market researchers have used evaluative criteria as a basis for their measures of satisfaction with, or attitude toward, a given product or brand. To be sure, it is possible to obtain valid attitude measures on the basis of nonsalient beliefs.[9] In our earlier discussion, however, we noted some of the problems associated with using an attribute satisfaction-importance model to assess attitudes toward brands or products. One problem is that the inclusion of importance ratings tends to reduce the validity of the attitude score. Moreover, although summing a person's satisfactions with various attributes of a brand can result in a valid attitude score, the validity of such a measure cannot be taken for granted.[10] In previous chapters we have argued that even when the estimate of

[8]Unpublished proprietary research conducted by Mary Tuck for the British Market Research Bureau in 1970.

[9]In fact, standard attitude measurement by means of Guttman, Likert, Thurstone, or semantic differential scales, is based on largely nonsalient beliefs. For a more detailed discussion of salient and nonsalient beliefs in attitude measurement, see Fishbein (1967c) and Fishbein and Ajzen (1975).

[10]This is particularly true if only a very small number of attributes (perhaps 3 or 4) is considered.

attitude is based on salient beliefs, it must be validated by showing that it correlates with an independent measure of the same attitude. Unfortunately, this is rarely done in marketing research.

## Brand Attitudes and Consumer Behavior

In the marketing field, attitudes toward brands and products are typically used to predict preferences among brands, buying intentions, or actual choice behavior. Note first that a measure of brand preferences is not the same as measures of intended or actual choice. While brand preference refers to the relative attractiveness of competing brands (i.e., brand attitudes), intended or actual choice reflects the relative strength of behavioral tendencies. To illustrate the difference between these measures, college students were asked to rank five brands of automobiles, first in the order of overall preference and then again in the order of likelihood that they would buy each brand. The two most preferred brands, Mercedes and Jaguar, were ranked as least likely to be purchased. In contrast, the Chevrolet was ranked as most likely to be purchased but was ranked only third in terms of overall preference. Very similar results were reported by Machnik (1976) with respect to automobiles and soaps. These findings suggest that market researchers may arrive at very different evaluative criteria when these criteria are selected for their ability to discriminate between consumers with 1) different brand preferences or 2) different buying intentions or actual buying behaviors.

Disregarding questions concerning the validity of attitude measures based on attribute satisfaction and importance ratings, let us examine the assumption that attitudes toward brands and products are directly related to buying behavior. According to the theory of reasoned action, consumer behavior is no different from any other kind of behavior. A person's purchase or use of a product is determined by her intention to purchase or use it, and choice among different brands is a function of the relative strength of her intentions with respect to each brand. Her intention to buy or use a given product is in turn determined by her attitude toward buying or using it and by her subjective norm with respect to the behavior in question. Finally, her salient behavioral and normative beliefs account for her attitude and subjective norm, respectively. To gain a more complete understanding of the factors that ultimately determine behavior in this domain, we must examine the cognitive foundation which underlies the consumer's decision.

In contrast to the assumption in most market research, our approach suggests that to predict and understand consumer behavior we have to consider attitudes toward the act of buying or using a product rather than attitudes toward the product itself. It is true of course that, in many instances, the more positive a person's attitude is toward a given brand, the more favorable will be his attitude toward buying that brand. From the point of view of our theory, however, brand attitude is an external variable with no necessary relation to attitudes toward buying the brand or, for that matter, to subjective norms concerning this behavior. Only if brand attitudes are found to affect one or both of these components would we expect them to influence the intentions and behaviors of consumers. The reason that brand attitudes need not predict consumer behavior can perhaps best be understood by considering the question of correspondence between measures of attitude and behavior.

**Correspondence between attitudes and behavior.** In chapter 3 we pointed out that a measure of behavior involves four distinct elements: the action, the target at which it is directed, the context in which it occurs, and the time of its occurrance. Later chapters stressed the importance of maintaining correspondence between the behavioral criterion and measures of intention (chapter 4), attitudes and subjective norms (chapter 5), and beliefs (chapter 6). We argued that the correlation between any two variables depends on the extent to which they correspond in their action, target, context, and time elements; the correlation will decrease as the number of elements on which they fail to correspond increases.

Viewed in this context, it can be seen that brand attitudes specify a target (the brand), but leave action, context, and time elements unspecified. In contrast, consumer behavior involves at least target and action elements (e.g., buying or using a brand or product) and often also context and time elements. For example, in some situations we may want to predict buying of a given product, such as flowers, for another person, say your fiancé. This contextual element would be included in our measure of attitude toward the behavior, since we would assess attitudes toward "buying flowers for my fiancé." A measure of attitude toward the product (flowers) would correspond to the behavior only in its target element. Similarly, attitudes toward products cannot take into account variations in the time element. Thus, attitudes toward "buying a sweater in the next two months" may differ greatly from attitudes toward "sweaters."

To illustrate the difference between brand attitudes and attitudes toward behavior, we assessed both types of attitude with respect to five brands in each of two product classes: automobiles and large chain stores. A sample of 37 college students rated each brand as well as various behaviors with respect to those brands on evaluative semantic differential scales. Table 12.3 shows the correlations between the attitude toward each of five kinds of cars and 1) the attitude toward buying each car and 2) the attitude toward buying each car in the next three years. It should first be noted that brand attitudes were highly related to attitudes toward buying some of the five brands but not others. Not surprisingly, attitudes toward buying relatively expensive foreign cars, such as the Mercedes or Jaguar, had little to do with overall evaluations of these cars. Table 12.3 also shows that the time perspective can have a strong effect on this relationship. For example, although college students' attitudes toward Chevrolets strongly correlated with their attitudes toward buying this brand of car (in general), it was only moderately related to their attitudes toward buying a Chevrolet in the next three years.

**TABLE 12.3**

Effects of Variations in Time Element on Correlation Between
Attitudes Toward Brands *X* and Attitudes Toward Buying

| BRAND *X* | ATTITUDE TOWARD BUYING BRAND *X* | ATTITUDE TOWARD BUYING BRAND *X* IN NEXT 3 YEARS |
|---|---|---|
| Ford | .82* | .58* |
| V.W. | .78* | .59* |
| Chevrolet | .75* | .30* |
| Mercedes | .28* | −.01 |
| Jaguar | −.04 | −.31* |

*Significant correlation ($p < .05$)

Similar conclusions can be derived from Table 12.4 which shows the correlations between attitudes toward five chains of stores and 1) attitudes toward shopping at each chain, 2) attitudes toward shopping at each chain in the next two weeks, and 3) attitudes toward buying toothpaste at each chain in the next two weeks. It can be seen that attitudes toward shopping at a given chain had moderate to low correlations with attitudes toward that chain. The addition of a time perspective further reduced the correlations, and with lack of correspondence in several elements (Column 3), the correlations virtually disappeared. Clearly, then, there is no necessary relation between attitudes toward a given brand or product and attitudes toward performing a particular behavior with respect to the brand or product in question.

That attitudes toward a brand can be unrelated to attitudes toward buying the brand should come as no surprise, since the salient beliefs underlying these two attitudes may differ greatly. Although beliefs about buying a certain product may involve some of the product's attributes, other consequences may also be salient. For example, a person may believe that "the Mercedes is a luxurious car" and that "buying a Mercedes is buying a luxurious car." However, he may also believe that "buying a Mercedes will raise my insurance premium."

The difference between beliefs about a product and beliefs about *buying* that product is particularly obvious whenever some time or contextual element is involved. Clearly, my beliefs about "buying a diamond ring for my lover" are apt to be very different from my beliefs about "diamond rings" as such. Or, to give another example, beliefs about "whiskey" will differ from beliefs about "drinking whiskey in the morning," and these beliefs will in turn differ from beliefs about "drinking whiskey at night."

To illustrate this point, consider the differences between beliefs about Chevrolets and beliefs about buying a Chevrolet in the next three years. Earlier in this chapter we saw that college students associate the following attributes with Chevrolets: moderately priced, ordinary car, well built, dependable, easily serviced, and American made. A new sample of students were asked to indicate what they believed to be the advantages and disadvantages of buying a Chevrolet

**TABLE 12.4**

Effects of Variations in Several Behavioral Elements on Correlation
Between Attitudes Toward Brand X and Attitudes Toward Buying

| BRAND X | ATTITUDE TOWARD SHOPPING AT CHAIN X | ATTITUDE TOWARD SHOPPING AT CHAIN X IN NEXT 2 WEEKS | ATTITUDE TOWARD BUYING TOOTHPASTE AT CHAIN X IN NEXT 2 WEEKS |
|---|---|---|---|
| Osco | .58* | .38* | .16 |
| Eisner | .55* | .44* | .10 |
| IGA | .52* | .30* | −.13 |
| A & P | .44* | .26 | −.14 |
| Kroger | .26 | .16 | .14 |

*Significant correlation ($p < .05$)

in the next three years. The five most salient beliefs that emerged were that "Buying a Chevrolet in the next three years" would

> give me a mode of transportation,
> put me in financial difficulty,
> lead to high upkeep costs,
> cost less now than later, and
> lead to my paying high insurance rates.

Thus, while college students realize that Chevrolets are moderately priced, they also believe that such a purchase within the next three years would have negative financial consequences. This may account for the relatively low correlation between their attitudes toward Chevrolets and toward buying a Chevrolet in the next three years.

The preceding discussion has focused on factors that can reduce the relationship between attitudes toward brands and toward buying or using those brands. It is important to realize, however, that for many consumer decisions these two attitudes will tend to be highly correlated. As we saw, this is most likely to be the case when we are dealing with such a behavior as buying or using a product in general. In this case, brand attitudes and attitudes toward the behavior differ only in one element, the action, and the consumer's beliefs about buying a product may refer primarily to the acquisition of attributes he associates with the product.

An example may clarify this point. Consider a consumer who believes that Coca Cola is carbonated, refreshing, and stimulating. If his only beliefs about buying Coca Cola were that he was buying a carbonated, refreshing, and stimulating drink, his attitude toward Coca Cola would be identical to his attitude toward buying this product.

It seems reasonable to speculate that such strong overlaps in beliefs are most likely to occur in the case of low-cost, nondurable household products, such as toothpaste or detergent. At least with respect to certain product classes, therefore, attitudes toward a given brand may predict purchase intentions and behavior as well as attitudes toward buying that brand. Nevertheless, our theory suggests that even under these circumstances the appropriate measure of attitude is one that corresponds directly to the behavior in question. We would expect such a measure to consistently yield predictions that are as good as or better than the predictions that can be obtained on the basis of brand attitudes.

As an illustration, we can return to the study mentioned earlier (see Table 12.3). Recall that the respondents in this study provided, among other things, ratings of their attitudes toward each of five brands of automobiles as well as ratings of their attitudes toward buying each brand and toward buying each brand in the next three years. In addition, the 37 college students also indicated their intentions to buy each brand of car (in general) and their intentions to buy them in the next three years. Table 12.5 shows the attitude-intention correlations.

**TABLE 12.5**
Prediction of Buying Intentions from Attitudes Toward
Brand X and Attitudes Toward Behaviors

| BRAND X | INTENTION TO BUY BRAND X | | INTENTION TO BUY BRAND X IN NEXT 3 YEARS | |
|---|---|---|---|---|
| | *Attitude toward Brand X* | *Attitude toward buying Brand X* | *Attitude toward Brand X* | *Attitude toward buying Brand X in next 3 years* |
| Ford | .58 | .65 | .45 | .73* |
| V.W. | .62 | .74 | .58 | .44 |
| Chevrolet | .46 | .72* | .29 | .73* |
| Mercedes | .09 | .53* | .01 | .51* |
| Jaguar | .00 | .45* | -.11 | .44* |

*Note:* Correlations greater than .28 are statistically significant (*p* < .05).
*Significant difference between prediction based on brand attitude and on attitude toward behavior (*p* < .05).

Note first that attitudes toward buying and toward buying in the next three years were highly related to the corresponding intentions, although the predictions were somewhat better for moderately priced cars (Ford, V.W., Chevrolet) than for expensive models (Mercedes, Jaguar). In contrast, brand attitudes were unable to predict intentions to buy the expensive models either in general or in the next three years, and in the case of the moderately priced models, they were consistently poorer predictors of the latter intention than of the former. This illustrates the importance of correspondence since brand attitudes correspond more closely to general buying intentions than to intentions to buy in the next three years.

Most important, and consistent with our preceding discussion, in seven of the ten cases attitudes that corresponded to the buying intention produced significantly better prediction of that intention than did the brand attitudes. In only one case was the pattern reversed, but the difference was not significant.[11]

The inconsistent relations between brand attitudes and buying intentions can be explained by returning to Table 12.3. It can be seen that brand attitudes were related to buying intentions whenever they correlated with attitudes toward buying in general or toward buying in the next three years. These findings are consistent with the argument that brand attitudes will predict buying intentions only to the extent that they correlate with a measure of attitude which corresponds to the criterion in question.

Clearly then, reliance on attitudes toward brands or products is inadequate as a basis for understanding and predicting consumer behavior. Our theory suggests that intentions to buy a given product, and actual buying behavior, are determined not by attitudes toward the brand per se but by attitudes toward buying the brand and by subjective norms with respect to this behavior. In the remainder of this chapter we will discuss the application of the theory of reasoned action to consumer behavior.

## PREDICTION OF CONSUMER BEHAVIOR

### Purchase Intentions and Actual Behavior

It is important to distinguish between two levels of analysis in research on consumer behavior. The focus of this chapter is the individual consumer and the factors that influence his purchase decisions. A different level of analysis deals with consumer behavior in the aggregate and is primarily concerned with the forecasting of economic trends. Whereas early attempts to predict buying trends at the aggregate level focused largely on economic and demographic factors, the work of George Katona (1947, 1951) at the University of Michigan Survey Research Center called attention to the importance of psychological variables. Since performance of the economy is reflected in the sale of durable products,

---

[11]Similar results were obtained with respect to the other products and brands considered in this study.

Katona focused on the purchase of such products, especially the automobile. It soon became apparent that, of the psychological variables considered, purchase intentions exhibited a marked relationship to actual purchases and permitted accurate forecasts of future trends (Ferber, 1954). Indeed, for many years the ability of buying intentions to predict economic trends went largely unchallenged.

Following more than a decade of successful prediction, the utility of purchase intentions was called into question when they failed to anticipate the economic recession of the late 1960s and early 1970s. During the 1950s and early 1960s increases and decreases in aggregate intentions to buy a car were followed closely by the number of cars actually sold. In the late 1960s, however, new car sales slumped markedly while intentions at the aggregate level remained relatively stable.

Findings of this kind have not only dampened enthusiasm for the use of purchase intentions as indicants of future economic activity (see McNeil, 1974), but have also led some investigators to question the relationship between buying intentions and behavior at the individual level. It must be noted, however, that it is possible to obtain low correlations between aggregate measures of intention and behavior over time and still have a strong intention-behavior relation across individuals at a given point in time. Consistent with this argument, the economic surveys already mentioned have found that relations between intentions and behavior at the individual level have been strong throughout the years.[12] That is, within a given sample of respondents, the stronger a consumer's intention is to purchase a given product, the greater the likelihood is that he will in fact purchase it. These findings support our contention that buying intention is the best single predictor of actual buying behavior.

The strength of the relation between buying intentions and behavior is also illustrated in a study by Wilson, Mathews, and Harvey (1975). In this study 162 housewives shopping in a mall indicated their intentions to buy each of six brands of toothpaste. Later they were given the opportunity to choose one family-sized tube of toothpaste from a display containing all six brands. Eighty-five percent of the respondents actually selected the brand consistent with their strongest purchase intention. As Wilson et al. pointed out, "This high association is noteworthy when one considers that this study provided the opportunity for the subjects to try a lesser preferred brand with no out-of-pocket cost" (p. 43).

Perhaps the most convincing evidence for a strong intention-behavior relation concerns cigarette smoking, which is often assumed to be beyond the individual's control. Although not a buying behavior, smoking is relevant to consumer behavior since it involves the consumption of a commercial product. We all know of people who have stated intentions to quit or cut down smoking but who have

---

[12]In the language of economic research, intentions are highly accurate predictors of purchase behavior in cross-sectional but not in time-series analyses.

failed to do so. It may therefore come as something of a surprise to learn that the best single predictor of smoking behavior is the person's smoking intention.

For example, in a study of smoking among college women, 192 respondents indicated their intentions to smoke in the next week, the next month, and the next four months (Fishbein et al., 1978). Self-reports of the number of cigarettes smoked were obtained one week, one month, and four months after the initial interview, with a different third of the sample being re-interviewed at each of the three delayed dates. Correlations were computed between a measure of whether or not the woman had smoked during the time since her initial interview and her corresponding intention to smoke during that time period. These correlations were high and significant, ranging from .71 for the four-month period to .96 for the one-week interval. Clearly, respondents' intentions predicted their smoking behavior extremely well over the short run and, despite the fact that smoking intentions can obviously change over time, the correlation remained high even for the four-month period. Further support for a strong relation between smoking intentions and behavior has been provided by Horn (1971) and Salber and Abelin (1967).

In sum, consumer behavior is typically found to be accurately predicted from measures of intention that correspond to the behavioral criteria. Economic surveys have reported strong relations between intentions to buy durable goods and actual purchase of those goods. Other studies have shown that when confronted with a choice between competing brands, consumers choose the brand with respect to which they have the strongest buying intention. Finally, even in the case of a behavior, such as smoking, over which we are assumed to have only limited control, intentions are found to permit highly accurate prediction. In the following section we will present some evidence to show that our theory can be used to predict and explain these purchase intentions.

Prediction of Buying Intentions

In previous chapters we have seen how intentions to perform various behaviors can be predicted from corresponding measures of attitudes and subjective norms with respect to the behavior in question. As noted earlier, there is no reason to assume that the psychological determinants of intentions to buy or use a product differ in any way from the determinants of intentions to perform other types of behavior. It follows that appropriate measures of attitudes and subjective norms should allow us to predict the corresponding purchase intentions.

To demonstrate the ability of our theory to predict purchase intentions, we asked 37 college students to indicate their intentions to perform two or three different behaviors with respect to each of five brands in three product classes.[13] Table 12.6 shows the various intentions, product classes, and brands that were

[13]Much of the data discussed earlier in this chapter were collected as part of this study.

TABLE 12.6
Intentions, Brands, and Product Classes Used in Study of Buying Intentions

| | PRODUCT CLASS | | |
| | *Automobile* | *Toothpaste* | *Beer* |
| --- | --- | --- | --- |
| Brands | 1. Chevrolet<br>2. Ford<br>3. Volkswagen<br>4. Jaguar<br>5. Mercedes | 1. Crest<br>2. Colgate<br>3. Gleem<br>4. Pepsodent<br>5. Ultra-Brite | 1. Michelob<br>2. Budweiser<br>3. Busch<br>4. Miller<br>5. Drewry |
| Intentions | 1. Buy<br>2. Buy in next<br>   3 years | 1. Buy<br>2. Buy in next<br>   2 weeks | 1. Buy<br>2. Buy for my own<br>   use in the next<br>   week<br>3. Buy to serve to<br>   my friends at<br>   a party |

involved. In addition to the measures of intention, we also assessed, among other things, attitudes and subjective norms corresponding to each of the intentions. The following are examples of the scales used to measure these variables.

1. *Purchase intention*
   I intend to buy Miller beer for my own use in the next week.

   likely ____ : ____ : ____ : ____ : ____ : ____ : ____ unlikely

2. *Attitude toward the behavior*
   Buying Miller beer for my own use in the next week would

   be wise ____ : ____ : ____ : ____ : ____ : ____ : ____ be foolish.

   have good
   consequences ____ : ____ : ____ : ____ : ____ : ____ : ____ consequences.
   have bad

3. *Subjective norm*
   Most people who are important to me think I

   should ____ : ____ : ____ : ____ : ____ : ____ : ____ should not
   buy Miller beer for my own use in the next week.

By varying the product class, brand, context, and time of the behavior, a total of 35 intentions and corresponding attitudes and subjective norms were assessed (see Table 12.6). It was found that in each case, a person's buying intention could be predicted with considerable accuracy from knowledge of his corresponding attitude and subjective norm.

Consider, for example, the three intentions measured with respect to buying Miller beer: buying Miller beer (in general), buying Miller beer for own use in the next week, buying Miller beer to serve to friends at a party. Figure 12.2 shows that each of the three intentions was predicted with a high degree of accuracy and that all three intentions were more under attitudinal than normative control. Note, however, that normative considerations played a more important role in determining intentions to buy Miller beer to serve to friends at a party and to buy it in general than to buy the same brand for one's personal use. Not surprisingly, when the behavior was explicitly restricted to personal consumption, the intention was dominated by attitudinal considerations and virtually no weight was given to the subjective norm.

The results for the remaining intentions also supported our theory. Overall 35 intentions, attitudes and subjective norms had an average multiple correlation of .63 with the corresponding intention. The average attitude-intention correlation was .61,[14] and its relative weight in the prediction was .56. The average correlation between the subjective norm and intention was lower ($r = .37$), and its average weight was only .10.

Overall, then, there is little doubt that buying intentions can be accurately predicted from corresponding measures of attitude toward the behavior and subjective norm. With respect to the products and behaviors considered in this study, the attitude toward the behavior seemed to be the more important determinant of buying intention.

In presenting the results of this study we have taken care to maintain high correspondence between our measures of attitudes and subjective norms on the one hand and intentions on the other. We have noted repeatedly that when correspondence is not maintained, predictive accuracy will decline. Support for this argument in the consumer behavior area was reported by Schlegel, Crawford, and Sanborn (1977). These investigators measured intentions to drink each of three types of alcoholic beverages (beer, hard liquor, wine) in each of three social settings (at home with parents, at a party with friends, at a pub). The respondents, 196 male Canadian high school students, also supplied measures of attitudes and subjective norms with respect to each of the nine behaviors.

As in our study, attitudes and subjective norms were found to be highly accurate predictors of intentions, so long as correspondence was maintained. For example, attitudes and subjective norms with respect to "drinking wine at home with parents" correlated highly with intentions "to drink wine at home with parents." The nine multiple correlations under such conditions of correspondence ranged from .71 to .82 with a mean of .75.

In marked contrast, when correspondence was not maintained, predictions were considerably less accurate. As an example of lack of correspondence in target elements (the type of alcoholic beverage), consider attitudes and sub-

---

[14]By way of comparison, the average correlation between brand attitudes and buying intentions was .41.

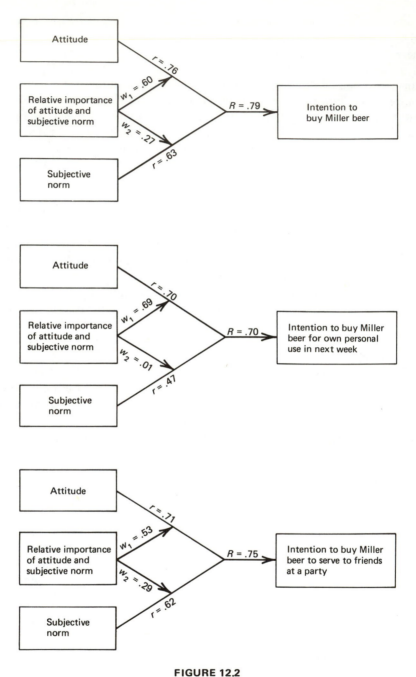

**FIGURE 12.2**
Relationships among attitudes, subjective norms, and
intentions to buy Miller beer.

jective norms with respect to "drinking hard liquor in a pub" and intention "to drink beer in a pub." In cases such as these, the average multiple correlation was only .46. Lack of correspondence in context reduced the predictive accuracy by about the same amount. To illustrate, attitudes and subjective norms with respect to "drinking beer at a party with friends" might be used to predict intentions "to drink beer at home with parents." In cases such as this, the average multiple correlation was found to be .48. Finally, lack of correspondence in target as well as contextual elements reduced the average multiple correlation to .43. An example of lack of correspondence in both elements would be the use of attitudes and subjective norms with regard to "drinking wine at home with parents" to predict intentions "to drink hard liquor at a party with friends."

Viewed in light of these studies, the importance of correspondence becomes so obvious as to appear almost trivial. Recall, however, that most attempts to predict consumer behavior from attitudinal variables have largely ignored the question of correspondence, since they have assumed that, irrespective of context or time, any purchase intention or behavior with respect to a given brand can be predicted from the attitude toward that brand. Throughout this chapter we have tried to show that we cannot ignore the question of correspondence if we want to understand the factors that determine consumer behavior.

## SUMMARY AND CONCLUSION

Much of the research in the area of consumer behavior has focused on what we consider to be a target element: brands and products. The major effort has gone into identifying attributes of the brands or products that serve as evaluative criteria which distinguish between people who buy or prefer different brands within a given product class. Estimates of attitudes based on these evaluative criteria are often used to explain and predict consumer preference and choice.

In this chapter we have tried to show that this approach cannot provide a satisfactory explanation of consumer behavior. First, we noted that evaluative criteria need not correspond to salient beliefs about a brand and, hence, should not be considered the determinants of a consumer's liking or disliking for the brand in question. Second, even if we fully understood the determinants of brand attitudes, we would still be unable to explain the consumer's decision to purchase or use the brand. The reasons for buying or not buying a given product are not the same as the reasons for liking or not liking it. Many parents who detest breakfast cereals buy them regularly, and we suspect that very few readers of this book (or its authors) will purchase a Jaguar or Mercedes in the next year or so.

Like any other behavior, the purchase of a given product is ultimately determined by beliefs concerning the positive and negative consequences of making the purchase and the normative prescriptions of important referents. We have stressed the importance of identifying the four elements involved in any consumer behavior: target (brand, product), action (buying, using, borrowing), context (for own use, in a given store, to give to others), and time (next week, within a year). While one or more elements may be left unspecified (e.g., buying a car for my wife) variations in any element may greatly influence beliefs about performing the behavior in question. Thus, the perceived consequences of buying a car for my wife may be very different from those of buying a car for my daughter, and the consequences of both of these behaviors may be very different from those associated with leasing or renting a car. Variations in the elements of consumer behaviors will similarly affect the consumer's normative beliefs.

Beliefs concerning the likely outcomes of a given consumer behavior and the normative prescriptions of others determine attitudes and subjective norms with respect to the behavior. Together, these two factors then influence the consumer's intention and actual behavior.

Brand attitudes, however, correspond to various consumer behaviors only in the target element, that is, the brand or product. Variations in the behavior's action, context, and time elements are not reflected in measures of brand attitudes. It is for this reason that brand attitudes, although related to some purchase decisions, often have little predictive validity. In terms of our theoretical framework, attitudes toward brands or products are external variables that need not have any systematic relation to consumer intentions or behaviors. Like other external variables, brand attitudes are related to purchase intentions only when they are related to attitudes toward the behavior or to the subjective norm. That is, their effects on intentions and behavior are indirect, being mediated by the attitudinal and normative components. The following chapter considers the issue of mediation in greater detail.

# CHAPTER
# 13

## Predicting and Understanding Voting in American Elections: Effects of external variables

Martin Fishbein
Icek Ajzen
Ron Hinkle

Systematic research on voting behavior began with the pioneering work of Lazarsfeld, Berelson, and Gaudet (1944) at Columbia University's Bureau of Applied Social Research. In their attempt to explain voting decisions in the 1940 presidential election, these investigators interviewed a panel of respondents in Erie County, Ohio. Coming from a sociological tradition, they concentrated their efforts on demographic variables, the role of the mass media, and processes of interpersonal communication.

One of their main conclusions was that "social characteristics determine political preference" (p. 27). This conclusion was based on the finding that a small number of demographic variables permitted fairly accurate prediction of voting behavior. Specifically, they argued that high socio-economic status (SES), affiliation with the Protestant religion, and rural residence predisposed a person to vote for the Republican Party, whereas the opposites of these factors (low SES, Catholic affiliation, urban residence) made for Democratic predispositions.

A subsequent study of the 1948 presidential election (Berelson, Lazarsfeld, & McPhee, 1954) again found demographic characteristics to be related to voting decisions, but Berelson et al. attributed their importance to the role they play in determining the people with whom an individual associates. The investigators found that a person tends to interact primarily with people who are demographically similar to him. This relatively closed system of interpersonal contacts and communications was assumed to produce mutual reinforcement of opinions and thus to maintain demographically determined voting patterns.

In the 1950s a group of scholars working at the University of Michigan's Survey Research Center examined the research discussed above and found it wanting. They argued persuasively that the sociological approach favored by Lazarsfeld, Berelson, McPhee, and Gaudet at Columbia had produced low-level, time bound generalizations and pointed to a number of cases "in which earlier sociological propositions, *as formulated*, had become period pieces in the span of a few years" (Campbell, Converse, Miller, & Stokes, 1960). They challenged as

We would like to thank David Brinberg for his assistance in the collection and analysis of data reported in this chapter.

174

inadequate one of the basic conclusions of the Columbia group—that social characteristics determine political preference—by pointing out that "the distribution of social characteristics in a population varies but slowly over a period of time, yet crucial fluctuations in the national vote occur from election to election" (Campbell et al., 1960, p. 17).

As an alternative, they proposed that psychological factors serve as the immediate determinants of voting behavior. They identified several "psychological forces" or "motivating factors" which were assumed to mediate the effects of social characteristics. The first major study by the Michigan group was a nationwide survey of potential voters in the 1952 presidential election (Campbell, Gurin, & Miller, 1954). In this study, voting choice was found to be determined primarily by three partisan motivational orientations:

*Party identification*—the individual's sense of personal attachment to one party or the other.

*Issue partisanship*—a person's pro-Democratic or pro-Republican orientation as reflected in his responses to a series of questions about the issues of the campaign.

*Candidate partisanship*—the difference between the person's attitudes toward the two candidates.

In *The American Voter,* which is generally regarded as the most important single contribution to the study of voting behavior, Campbell et al. (1960) reaffirmed their position that voting choice depends in an immediate sense on a system of psychological forces. In contrast to the earlier research, however, these forces were conceptualized as a set of six partisan attitudes: 1) toward the Democratic candidate; 2) toward the Republican candidate; 3) toward the parties as managers of government; 4) toward the parties and candidates in relation to foreign issues; 5) toward the parties and candidates in relation to domestic issues; and 6) toward the parties and candidates in relation to reference group interests. Each of these partisan attitudes locates the respondent on a bipolar dimension from pro-Democratic to pro-Republican. Consistent with the position taken by Campbell et al., the six partisan attitudes were highly related to voting choice.

Note that party identification is no longer considered to be one of the forces that serve as an *immediate* determinant of voting behavior but rather as an antecedent of these forces. The stability of electoral behavior is attributed to the long-term influence of party identification, and changes in voting patterns from one election to another are explained by short-term variations in the six partisan attitudes.

In sum, both the Columbia and Michigan schools have focused on what we have called *external* variables, such as demographic characteristics, party identification, and attitudes toward candidates and parties. According to the theory of reasoned action, these types of variables can have only indirect effects on voting behavior and they cannot provide an adequate explanation of the process where-by voters reach their decisions. While there is evidence that people with similar demographic characteristics tend to vote for the same candidate in a given election, we do not know *why* they vote for that candidate or why they may vote for the opposition candidate in another election. Campbell et al. (1960) tell us that people vote for a given candidate because of the direction and intensity of their partisan attitudes, and they state that these attitudes are influenced by party identification. They do not tell us, however, how voters who identify with the same party can have different attitudes or whether and how their attitudes can be changed. In fact, despite the tremendous amount of research that has been conducted on the American voter, "our ability to predict how voters will vote is far more solidly based than our ability to explain why they vote as they do" (Kelley & Mirer, 1974, p. 572).

## APPLICATION OF THE THEORY
## OF REASONED ACTION TO VOTING BEHAVIOR

Although the Michigan school has been remarkably successful in using their measures of partisan attitudes to predict voting behavior in American presidential elections, there is no way these variables could account for the voting process in other types of elections or electoral systems. Clearly, partisan attitudes and party identification are irrelevant in nonpartisan elections such as within-party primaries, some municipal elections, and referenda on various issues. Similarly, partisan attitudes and party identification are largely irrelevant in a one-party electoral system.

In this chapter we will try to show how our theory can be applied to the study of voting behavior in an American presidential election. The next chapter will apply our theory to very different kinds of voting situations, namely, the 1974 general parliamentary election in Great Britain and the Oregon nuclear power referendum of 1976. Within our approach, voting is treated like any other behavior and it makes little difference whether the election is partisan or nonpartisan and whether the vote is cast for a candidate or for an issue.

## PREDICTION OF VOTING IN AMERICAN ELECTIONS

We have seen in previous chapters that a person's choice can be predicted either from her choice intention or by considering her intention to perform each of the available action alternatives. In the context of an election involving two or more candidates, a person can be asked for whom she intends to cast her vote (choice intention) or to separately indicate her intention to vote for each of the candidates (behavioral intentions). Although both measures of intention should permit accurate prediction, we saw that in order to *understand* why a person votes for one candidate rather than for another, we have to consider her intentions to vote for each of the candidates.

The intention to vote for a given candidate is, according to our theory, determined by the person's attitude toward voting for that candidate and by his subjective norm. Attitudes toward voting for a given candidate are in turn determined by beliefs that voting for the candidate will lead to certain consequences and the evaluations of these consequences. Similarly, beliefs that specific referents think one should or should not vote for the candidate in question, and motivations to comply with the specific referents, are viewed as determining the subjective norms. Other (external) variables, such as partisan attitudes, party identification, and demographic characteristics, can influence voting behavior only indirectly as a result of their effects on one or more of the determinants of voting behavior.

It is interesting to note that our theory is quite compatible with the general approach of the Columbia school, which emphasizes the role of interpersonal influence. Consistent with this view, the normative component is a function of a person's beliefs about the prescriptions of relevant referents and of his motivations to comply with those referents. Further, the Columbia school's argument that demographic characteristics influence voting by determining the people with whom an individual interacts is also compatible with our theory. It seems reasonable that people with different social backgrounds may have different salient referents with different normative prescriptions.

Contrary to the Columbia school, we view social influence as only one factor determining voting intentions and behavior. Attitudes toward voting for a given candidate must also be taken into consideration. Just as demographic characteristics may influence the determinants of the subjective norm, they may also be related to the beliefs underlying the attitudinal component. Our theory allows us to investigate the indirect effects of demographic characteristics as well as permitting us to assess the relative importance of social influence (i.e., subjective norm) as a determinant of voting intention and behavior.

The theory of reasoned action also differs from the approach taken by the Michigan school. Although attitudes play an important role in both approaches, our theory deals with attitude toward a behavior (voting for a candidate) whereas the Michigan school has essentially focused on attitudes toward candidates and parties, that is, on attitudes toward targets. However, our approach is not incompatible with the findings of the Michigan school. Attitudes toward candidates and parties will, at least in the American system, be related to the attitude toward voting for a given candidate. This is because attitudes toward a candidate are likely to influence beliefs about the consequences of voting for the candidate, while attitudes toward the candidate's party will often affect evaluation of those consequences.

The effect of a voter's party identification—the other major variable introduced by the Michigan school—is also assumed to be indirect. In this case, it is likely that the relation is mediated by both the attitudinal and the normative components. For example, like attitudes toward the party, party identification may influence evaluations of consequences associated with voting for a given candidate. In addition, the salient referents of voters identifying with the Democratic Party will tend to have different normative expectations than the salient referents of voters identifying with the Republican Party. As a result, subjective norms with respect to voting for a given candidate may be quite different among Democrats and Republicans.

## A STUDY OF THE 1976 PRESIDENTIAL ELECTION

The study reported in this section is the latest in a series of investigations of American voting behavior based on interviews with voting-age residents of Champaign County, Illinois.[1] Most of the early studies in this series focused on such traditional variables as attitudes toward candidates and parties in a number of congressional, senatorial, and presidential elections (e.g., Fishbein & Coombs, 1974). The present investigation is the first complete test of the theory of reasoned action in the context of an American election.

As a first step, a small sample of respondents was used to identify salient outcomes and referents associated with voting for each of the two major candidates, Jimmy Carter and Gerald Ford. Using the standard procedures that apply to any behavioral domain (see appendix A), a questionnaire was constructed and administered to a different sample of respondents one month, and again one week, prior to the 1976 presidential election. The questionnaire contained, among other things, measures of intentions to vote for each candidate and attitudes and subjective norms with respect to voting for each candidate. In addition, it assessed behavioral beliefs that voting for each candidate will lead to certain outcomes, evaluations of these outcomes, normative beliefs, and motivations to comply. In the week following the election, the respondents were contacted again and were asked to reveal for whom they had voted.

### Prediction of Voting Behavior

Analysis of the data showed that voting for Carter or Ford followed directly from intentions to vote for the two candidates. In our sample, 43% were found to have voted for Carter, 43% for Ford, and the remaining 14% either did not

[1]Like the Columbia school, we chose to concentrate our efforts on a single county. Although Champaign-Urbana is a college community, our samples were drawn to represent different levels of various demographic characteristics (e.g., socio-economic status and education).

vote or refused to reveal their choices. Disregarding the latter group of respondents, Table 13.1 shows the relation between voting intentions one week prior to the election and self-reports of actual voting behavior. Respondents whose intentions to vote for Carter were stronger than their intentions to vote for Ford were classified as intending to vote for Carter, and the opposite pattern was viewed as an intention to vote for Ford. A respondent whose intentions to vote for Carter and for Ford were equally strong was classified as undecided. It can be seen that of the eight undecided respondents, four eventually voted for Carter and four for Ford. Of the remaining 68 respondents, 62 voted in accordance with their intentions and only six voted for the opposition candidate.

As in the case of occupational orientation (see chapter 10), voting in an election constitutes a choice among different alternatives. Although other candidates' names also appeared on the ballot (e.g., Eugene McCarthy and Lester Maddox), we will focus our discussion on the choice between the two major candidates. In considering the determinants of this choice, we will be concerned with the extent to which a respondent's beliefs, attitudes, and intentions are different with respect to voting for Carter and voting for Ford. As we showed in chapter 10, such *differential* beliefs, attitudes, and intentions are more appropriate in a choice situation than are separate measures of these variables with respect to each candidate.

We saw earlier that measures of the two intentions permitted accurate prediction of voting choice. In fact, the correlation between differential intention and voting was .80. Consistent with expectations, these differential intentions were accurately predicted from differential attitudes toward voting for the candidates and from the differential subjective norm ($R = .83$). Our discussion of the Columbia and Michigan schools suggests two points of view with respect to the relative importance of the attitudinal and normative components. The Columbia school's conclusion that people vote the way trusted others vote seems to imply that normative considerations will be predominant. In contrast, the Michigan school de-emphasized the role of interpersonal influence while stressing the importance of "partisan attitudes." Despite the difference between these partisan attitudes and attitudes toward voting for a given candidate, the Michigan approach can be viewed as implying that the attitudinal component is a more im-

**TABLE 13.1**
Relation Between Voting Intentions and Voting Behavior
in 1976 Presidential Election

|  |  | VOTING BEHAVIOR | |
|  |  | Carter | Ford |
|---|---|---|---|
| VOTING INTENTION | Carter | 31 | 3 |
|  | Undecided | 4 | 4 |
|  | Ford | 3 | 31 |

portant determinant of voting intentions than is the normative component. Our results suggest that there is some merit in both positions. Each of the two components made a significant contribution to the prediction of voting intentions, although in the context of this presidential election the differential attitude was found to be a more important determinant of the differential intention.[2]

Beliefs that voting for Carter and Ford will lead to certain outcomes and evaluations of these outcomes were used to estimate attitudes toward voting for each candidate. The difference between these estimates was found to permit accurate prediction of the differential attitude scores ($r = .79$). Thus, a person who believed that, on balance, the consequences of voting for Carter would be preferable to those that would follow from voting for Ford formed a more favorable (or less unfavorable) attitude toward voting for Carter. Similarly, differences between estimates of subjective norms, based on normative beliefs and motivations to comply, were found to correlate with differential subjective norms ($r = .73$). The relations among differential beliefs, attitudes, intentions, and actual voting choice are summarized in Figure 13.1. These relations are also reflected in Table 13.2 which presents the average differential intentions, attitudes, and subjective norms of Ford and Carter voters. Positive scores indicate a preference for voting for Carter. Clearly, these differential measures are consistent with the ultimate choice.

Having demonstrated that the salient beliefs considered in this study can provide an explanation of voting choice, we now turn to a more detailed discussion of these beliefs. Since the attitudinal component carried more weight in the prediction of intentions than did the normative component, we will consider first the beliefs that provide the basis for the differential attitudes toward voting for the two candidates.

**Beliefs underlying differential attitudes toward voting.** Table 13.3 presents differential behavioral beliefs and outcome evaluations for Ford and Carter voters. A positive differential belief indicates that a vote for Carter is viewed as more likely to attain the outcome in question than is a vote for Ford. The opposite is true for negative differential beliefs. It can be seen that there were considerable differences between Ford and Carter voters. Generally speaking, the salient issues of the campaign seemed to influence voting behavior in two different ways. With respect to certain issues, voters agreed in their evaluations of the outcomes, but some voters believed that voting for Ford was more likely to lead to the outcomes, while others believed that voting for Carter was more likely to lead to the outcomes. For example, all voters favored a reduction in unemploy-

---

[2]This discussion illustrates how our approach can be used to test hypotheses concerning the relative importance of attitudinal and normative considerations. For example, it has been argued that interpersonal influence plays a greater role at lower levels of election. Consistent with this idea, we have some evidence that the normative component was more important than the attitudinal component in the context of a 1966 senatorial election. However, this finding may reflect changes in the American electorate over the 10-year period, rather than differences in electoral levels.

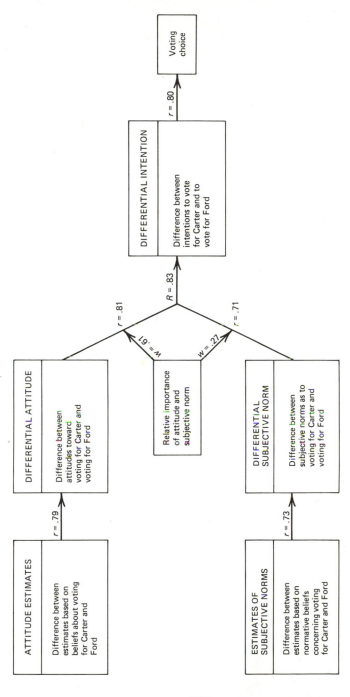

**FIGURE 13.1**

Relationships among differential beliefs, attitudes, intentions, and voting choice in the 1976 presidential election.

**TABLE 13.2**
Differential Intentions, Attitudes, and Subjective
Norms of Ford and Carter Voters

| ANTECEDENT VARIABLES | FORD VOTERS | CARTER VOTERS |
|---|---|---|
| Differential intention | − 4.47 | + 3.79 |
| Differential attitude | − 8.26 | + 5.89 |
| Estimate of differential attitude | −20.10 | +35.74 |
| Differential subjective norm | − 2.58 | + 1.73 |
| Estimate of differential subjective norm | −25.04 | +15.42 |

ment and a major reform in the tax system. Predictably, respondents who believed that these outcomes were more likely to be attained by voting for Ford (rather than Carter) tended to vote for Ford, whereas respondents with positive differential beliefs tended to vote for Carter.

With respect to other issues there was general consensus that voting for one candidate was more likely to produce the outcome than was voting for the other candidate, but there was disagreement as to the evaluation of the outcome. For

**TABLE 13.3**
Mean Differential Beliefs and Outcome Evaluations for Ford and Carter Voters
One Week Prior to the 1976 Presidential Election

| OUTCOME | DIFFERENTIAL BELIEFS | | OUTCOME EVALUATIONS | |
|---|---|---|---|---|
| | Ford Voters | Carter Voters | Ford Voters | Carter Voters |
| 5 to 7 billion dollar cut in defense budget | 1.53 | 2.89* | − .24 | 1.03* |
| National health care system | 1.26 | 3.18* | .24 | 1.24* |
| Reduction in unemployment | −1.02 | 2.29* | 2.26 | 2.37 |
| Amnesty for Viet Nam deserters | 1.29 | 2.97 | − .53 | 1.26* |
| Major reform in the tax system | − .47 | 2.82* | 2.00 | 2.03 |
| Increased price supports for farm products | .47 | .97 | .05 | − .11 |
| Increased presidential control of foreign policy | − .31 | .92 | .26 | .03 |
| Good working relationship between the President and Congress | − .06 | 2.52* | 2.39 | 1.95 |
| Increased federal spending for welfare programs | 2.50 | 3.02 | −1.61 | − .21* |
| Reduction in U.S. troops stationed abroad | 1.27 | 1.89 | .13 | .86* |

*Significant difference between Ford and Carter voters.

instance, all respondents tended to agree that a five to seven billion dollar cut in the defense budget and amnesty for Viet Nam deserters were more likely to be attained by voting for Carter than for Ford. As might be expected, however, voters who favored these outcomes tended to vote for Carter while those who opposed them tended to vote for Ford.

These findings demonstrate that voters in an election favor certain policies and oppose others, and that they consider the likelihood that voting for one candidate rather than the other will further or hinder the implementation of the policies in question. People will tend to vote for the candidate they believe is more likely to promote the outcomes they favor and less likely to promote the outcomes they oppose. In our study, for example, respondents who ultimately voted for Carter believed that with respect to seven of the ten issues there was a distinct advantage in voting for Carter. In the case of two of the remaining three issues, these respondents believed that voting for Ford would be more advantageous than voting for Carter.

In fact, not reflected in the average data of Table 13.2 are many instances of respondents who vote for a given candidate despite their beliefs that with respect to some issues there would be a distinct advantage in voting for the opposition candidate. For example, many respondents who were strongly in favor of a national health care system and who believed that voting for Carter was more likely to lead to the implementation of such a system nevertheless voted for Ford, because, on balance, they saw this choice as having more advantages than disadvantages. Similarly, many respondents were strongly opposed to increased price supports for farm products, and they believed that this policy was more likely to result if they voted for Carter. However, because this negative outcome was outweighed by what they perceived to be the many advantages of voting for Carter, these respondents ultimately cast their vote for Carter. In other words, virtually every voter sees some advantages and some disadvantages in voting for the different candidates; the ultimate voting preferences (i.e., differential attitudes) are determined by the balance of advantages and disadvantages that voters associate with each candidate.

**Beliefs underlying differential subjective norms.** We have seen that differential subjective norms also served as significant determinants of voting choice. We therefore turn next to an examination of the beliefs that provided the basis for the subjective norms. Table 13.4 presents differential normative beliefs and motivations to comply for Ford and Carter voters. Again, positive scores indicate normative beliefs in favor of voting for Carter while negative scores indicate normative beliefs in favor of voting for Ford. It can be seen that differences in perceived social pressure (i.e., differential subjective norms) were due almost entirely to differential normative beliefs; there were virtually no differences in the degree to which Ford and Carter voters were motivated to comply with any given referent (see Columns 3 and 4). With respect to the differential normative beliefs,

Ford voters believed that each referent thought they should vote for Ford and not for Carter, while the opposite was true for Carter voters. In other words, an individual tended to vote for a given candidate if he believed that his relevant referents thought he should vote for that candidate (rather than for the opposition candidate).

To summarize briefly, we have seen that people form behavioral beliefs about the likely consequences of voting for one candidate or another in a political contest, as well as normative beliefs concerning the prescriptions of relevant referents. Generally speaking, these beliefs tend to be quite reasonable in light of the information available to the voters. Differential behavioral beliefs and outcome evaluations were shown to serve as the determinants of differential attitudes toward voting for the candidates. Consistent with common sense, the more a person believed that casting her vote for one candidate rather than his opponent would lead to outcomes she desired, the more positive was her differential attitude toward voting for that candidate. Similarly, differential normative beliefs and motivations to comply were found to determine differential subjective norms. In further support of our theory, these attitudinal and normative components predicted differential voting intentions with a high degree of accuracy, and these intentions were found to determine actual voting choice.

### Effects of External Variables

Note that in applying our theory to voting behavior we have not found it necessary to consider such traditional variables as attitudes toward the parties or candidates, party identification, interest or involvement in the election campaign, liberalism-conservatism, or any of the numerous demographic characteristics (religious affiliation, income, socio-economic status, education, etc.) that have been assumed to influence voting behavior. From our point of view, these variables, external to our theory, influence voting only indirectly by influencing one or more of the underlying determinants of this behavior. An external variable

**TABLE 13.4**

Mean Differential Normative Beliefs and Motivations to Comply
for Ford and Carter Voters One Week Prior
to the 1976 Presidential Election

| REFERENT | DIFFERENTIAL NORMATIVE BELIEFS | | MOTIVATION TO COMPLY | |
|---|---|---|---|---|
| | *Ford Voters* | *Carter Voters* | *Ford Voters* | *Carter Voters* |
| Spouse (date) | −3.21 | 1.98* | 2.82 | 2.89 |
| Parents | −2.36 | 1.16* | 2.74 | 2.74 |
| Three closest friends | −2.42 | 1.42* | 2.53 | 2.82 |
| Co-workers | −2.16 | 1.07* | 2.34 | 2.72 |

*Significant difference between Ford and Carter voters.

may be related to voting in one election, but it may be found to be unrelated to voting in another election. For example, one of the candidates in a given election may be viewed as an intellectual, and highly educated people might have more favorable attitudes toward voting for that candidate than people with less education. In another election, the candidates may be perceived as intellectual equals and there might be no relation between the voters' educational level and attitudes toward voting for either candidate. Thus, in the former election, level of education is more likely to be related to voting choice than in the latter.

In our study of the 1976 presidential election, a wide variety of external variables were assessed. Within our sample of respondents, the majority of these variables were unrelated to voting choice. For example, religiosity, income, socio-economic status, age, interest and involvement in the election, and marital status seemed to have little effect on people's voting choices.

Several other variables, however, were found to correlate significantly with voting behavior, as can be seen in the first column of Table 13.5. The correlations presented in this table are based only on the 76 respondents who reported their voting choices. As in other studies of American elections, partisan attitudes toward candidates and parties (candidate differential and party differential) were found to be strongly related to voting choice, with the differential attitude toward the two candidates being a somewhat better predictor of voting behavior than was the party differential. Consistent with our theory however, differential attitudes toward *voting* for the two candidates provided significantly better prediction of voting behavior ($r = .74$) than either or both the candidate and party differentials.[3] This finding supports our argument that the attitude toward an action is more highly related to that action than is the attitude toward the target at which the action is directed. (See also chapter 12.)

Also consistent with findings in other American elections, voting choice was found to be highly related to party identification and history of voting for the Republican or Democratic candidates in past elections. In addition, the voters' self-reports of their liberalism-conservatism and of their educational levels were found to correlate significantly with voting behavior; liberals and to some extent the more educated voters were more likely to cast their votes for Carter than were conservatives and voters of lower educational achievement.

**Effects of external variables on voting intentions.** From our point of view, the immediate and most important determinants of voting choice are the person's intentions to vote for each of the candidates. As we saw earlier, for the present sample of respondents (excluding the 12 respondents who either did not vote or refused to reveal their choices), the differences between intentions to vote for Ford and Carter correlated .80 with actual voting choice. Our theory implies that when external variables are found to influence voting behavior this influence

[3]The multiple correlation between the two partisan attitudes on one hand and voting choice on the other was .66.

**TABLE 13.5**

Relations of External Variables to Voting Choice and the Determinants of Voting Choice
One Week Prior to the 1976 Presidential Election

| EXTERNAL VARIABLES[a] | VOTING CHOICE | DIFFERENTIAL VOTING INTENTION | MULTIPLE CORRELATION[b] WITH BEHAVIOR | DIFFERENTIAL VOTING ATTITUDE | DIFFERENTIAL SUBJECTIVE NORM |
|---|---|---|---|---|---|
| Candidate differential | .66 | .58 | .84 | .68 | .64 |
| Party differential | .60 | .56 | .82 | .74 | .65 |
| Party identification | .69 | .62 | .84 | .65 | .65 |
| Prior voting history | .50 | .40 | .82 | .28 | .31 |
| Liberalism-conservatism | .62 | .55 | .83 | .55 | .52 |
| Educational level | .26 | .32 | .80 | .17* | .27 |

[a]Descriptions of the external variables are provided in the text.
[b]Prediction of behavior from intention and external variable; effect of the external variable is indicated by the increment above .80, the intention-behavior correlation.
*Not significant; all other correlations are significant ($p < .05$).

is due to their effects on voting intentions. In Column 2 of Table 13.5 it can be seen that each of the external variables that were found to correlate with voting choice was also highly related to the differential intention. In fact, considering these external variables in addition to intentions did little to improve the prediction of behavior. This is evidenced by the fact that the multiple correlations (Column 3) were the same as or only slightly higher than the correlations based on the intentions alone. For example, consideration of party identification in addition to differential voting intentions raised the correlation with behavior from .80 to .84.

**Effects of external variables on attitudes and subjective norms.** Our theory further implies that since intentions are determined by attitudes and subjective norms, the effects of external variables on intentions must be due to their effects on one or both of these components. The correlations in the last two columns of Table 13.5 support this argument. Except for educational level which correlated significantly only with the differential subjective norm, the other external variables correlated significantly with both components. As expected, consideration of the external variables in addition to the two components did little to improve prediction of intentions. In the case of party identification, it can be seen that this external variable was highly related to both the differential attitudes toward voting for the two candidates ($r = .65$) and the differential subjective norms ($r = .65$). Once these differential attitudes and subjective norms were known, however, little improvement in prediction of voting intentions and behavior could be gained by also considering party identification, since its influence was already reflected in the two components. In fact, despite its high correlation with differential intentions, the added consideration of party identification was found to produce only a minimal increment in the predictability of these intentions (from .72 to .74).

**Effects of external variables on the underlying cognitive structure.** As a final step, our approach allows us to explain why the external variables influenced the attitudinal and normative components. Generally speaking, such influence must be due to the effects of the external variables on the determinants of these components, that is, on behavioral beliefs, outcome evaluations, normative beliefs, and motivations to comply. It seems reasonable to assume that people who hold different attitudes toward the candidates or parties will also hold different beliefs about the consequences of voting for the candidates. Similar hypotheses can be formulated about the likely effects of other external variables on the determinants of the attitudinal and normative components. One of the important implications of our approach is that unless the investigator can link the external variable of interest to one or more of these determinants, there is little justification for predicting that the external variable will have an effect on voting behavior.

Consider, for example, the question of the voter's interest in the election campaign. There seems to be no reason to assume that interested and uninterested voters will differ systematically in their outcome evaluations or in their beliefs that voting for one candidate will lead to more positive outcomes than voting for the other candidate. Further, interested and uninterested voters are unlikely to differ in their perceptions that relevant referents think they should vote for one candidate rather than the other or in their motivations to comply with the referents. Consequently, there is no basis for assuming that interest in the campaign will be related to voting choice and, consistent with this argument, voters' interest in the 1976 presidential campaign had only a low and nonsignificant correlation ($r = .11$) with voting behavior.

In contrast, let us again consider the effects of party identification in the 1976 presidential election. It is easy to see that a person's identification with one party or the other may influence some of the determinants of attitudes toward voting for the candidates or of the subjective norms with respect to this behavior. First, and foremost, it is very likely that Democrats and Republicans will differ in their evaluations of certain policies. Since these policies constitute the possible outcomes of voting for the two candidates, Democrats and Republicans are likely to hold different attitudes toward voting for the candidates. Moreover, they are likely to differ in their beliefs that the two candidates will be able to implement these policies. For example, Republicans may believe that voting for Ford is more likely to lead to a reduction in unemployment than is voting for Carter, while Democrats may hold the opposite differential belief. All of these possible effects could explain the obtained relation between party identification and attitudes toward voting for the candidates.

In our study of the 1976 presidential election, respondents were classified into three categories:[4] Democratic identifiers and leaners ($N = 35$), Independents with no leanings toward either party ($N = 12$), and Republican identifiers and leaners ($N = 41$). Table 13.6 shows the effects of party identification on differential beliefs about voting for the two candidates and on outcome evaluations. Positive differential beliefs indicate that voting for Carter is viewed as more likely to lead to the outcome than is voting for Ford, while negative differential beliefs indicate the opposite.

With respect to 5 of the 10 beliefs, Republicans differed qualitatively from Independents and Democrats, and three of these differences were statistically significant. Democrats and Independents believed that voting for Carter (rather than Ford) would be more likely to result in a reduction in unemployment, a major reform in the tax system, increased price supports for farm products, increased presidential control of foreign policy, and a good working relationship between the President and Congress. In contrast, Republicans believed that a reduction in unemployment was more likely to occur if they cast their votes

---

[4]This classification was based on responses to a series of questions developed to measure party identification (see Campbell et al., 1960).

**TABLE 13.6**

Mean Behavioral Beliefs and Outcome Evaluations for Republicans, Independents, and Democrats One Week Prior to the 1976 Presidential Election ($N = 76$)

| OUTCOME | DIFFERENTIAL BEHAVIORAL BELIEFS | | | OUTCOME EVALUATIONS | | |
|---|---|---|---|---|---|---|
| | *Republicans* | *Independents* | *Democrats* | *Republicans* | *Independents* | *Democrats* |
| 5 to 7 billion dollar cut in defense budget | 1.46 | 3.00 | 2.99 | −.22 | .08 | .94* |
| National health care system | 1.53 | 2.42 | 3.09* | .07 | 1.17 | 1.40* |
| Reduction in unemployment | −.70 | 1.75 | 1.97* | 2.22 | 2.42 | 2.46 |
| Amnesty for Viet Nam deserters | 1.39 | 2.08 | 2.85 | −.44 | .00 | 1.03* |
| Major reform in the tax system | −.03 | 1.25 | 2.80* | 2.00 | 2.17 | 1.86 |
| Increased price supports for farm products | .39 | .75 | 1.20 | −.17 | 1.00 | −.14 |
| Increased presidential control of foreign policy | −.10 | 1.08 | .85 | .46 | .25 | .03* |
| Good working relationship between the President and Congress | .43 | 1.84 | 2.20* | 2.17 | 2.75 | 2.00 |
| Increased federal spending for welfare programs | 2.48 | 2.00 | 3.20 | −1.46 | −.58 | −.34* |
| Reduction in U.S. troops stationed abroad | 1.02 | 2.00 | 1.94 | −.02 | .58 | .80* |

*Difference between Republicans, Independents, and Democrats is significant ($p < .05$).

for Ford rather than for Carter, and they tended to see little difference with respect to the remaining four outcomes. Since prior to the election the two candidates had been in basic agreement as to the merits of these five outcomes, and since there was no objective basis for assuming that one or the other candidate was more likely to attain the outcomes, the voters' party identifications were free to influence their judgments.

Turning to the remaining five outcomes, it can be seen that irrespective of party identification, there was general agreement that voting for Carter was more likely to lead to each outcome than was voting for Ford. For example, all respondents believed that voting for Carter was more likely to result in increased federal spending for welfare programs and a reduction in U.S. troops stationed abroad, although for the first of these outcomes the differential beliefs were stronger among Democrats than among Republicans. These overall agreements seem to reflect relatively accurate perceptions of the candidate's positions on the issues in question. It can thus be seen that while party identification does influence some beliefs about voting for the candidates, its potential impact is limited by the fact that beliefs are responsive to reality.

At the same time, party identification is expected to have a substantial impact on outcome evaluations, particularly those involving policy. The last three columns of Table 13.6 show that, in comparison to Republicans, Democrats had more favorable evaluations of a cut in the defense budget, a national health care system, amnesty for Viet Nam deserters, and a reduction in U.S. troops stationed abroad. In most cases, evaluations of Independents fell between those of the Democrats and Republicans.

It is also important to note that party identification did not significantly affect evaluations of all issues. Irrespective of party identification, all respondents had strong positive evaluations of a reduction in unemployment, major reforms in the tax system, and a good working relationship between the President and the Congress.

By looking at the differences in behavioral beliefs and outcome evaluations, we can understand why Democrats, Republicans, and Independents held different attitudes toward voting for the two candidates. To illustrate, consider the outcome "a reduction in U.S. troops stationed abroad." While Republicans were relatively neutral with respect to this policy, Democrats evaluated it favorably. Since both Democrats and Republicans believed that a vote for Carter was more likely to lead to this outcome than was a vote for Ford, these beliefs had relatively little effect on Republicans' differential attitudes, but they made the differential attitudes of Democrats more favorable toward voting for Carter.

In fact, inspection of Table 13.6 shows that, on balance, Democrats and Independents saw more advantages than disadvantages in voting for Carter, whereas the reverse pattern was true for Republicans. The differential attitudes of Democrats and Independents therefore favored voting for Carter, while those of Republicans favored voting for Ford (see Table 13.2).

The same approach can be used to explain the effects of party identification on differential subjective norms. It stands to reason that Democrats, Republicans, and Independents will not differ greatly in their motivations to comply with such referents as their spouses, parents, or their three best friends. Consistent with this argument, party identification was found to be unrelated to respondents' motivations to comply with any of the four referents considered in our study of the 1976 presidential election.[5]

In contrast, we can expect that the families and friends of Democrats will have different political philosophies from the families and friends of Republicans or Independents. As a result, it is reasonable to expect that Democrats will believe their referents think they should vote for the Democratic candidate while Republicans will tend to believe that their referents think they should vote for the Republican candidate.

Table 13.7 provides strong support for these expectations with respect to all four referents. It is interesting to note that in our sample of respondents, Independents reported more normative pressure to vote for Ford than for Carter. These differences in normative beliefs among Democrats, Independents, and Republicans explain the finding that the differential subjective norms of Republicans and Independents favored voting for Ford while those of Democrats favored voting for Carter (see Table 13.2).

Similar analyses could be performed in an attempt to explain the effects of other external variables. Recall that in our study attitudes toward candidates and toward parties, voting history, educational level, and liberalism-conservation were also found to be related to voting choice. As in the case of party identification, an analysis would show that these variables had systematic effects on the cognitive structures underlying differential attitudes and subjective norms.

**TABLE 13.7**
Mean Differential Normative Beliefs for Republicans,
Democrats, and Independets One Week
Prior to the 1976 Presidential Election ($N$ = 76)

| REFERENTS | DIFFERENTIAL NORMATIVE BELIEFS | | |
| --- | --- | --- | --- |
| | *Republicans* | *Independents* | *Democrats* |
| Spouse (date) | −2.54 | −1.16 | 1.79 |
| Parents | −1.90 | .08 | .97 |
| Three closest friends | −1.79 | −1.25 | 1.57 |
| Co-workers | −1.97 | − .67 | 1.18 |

*Note:* The differences between Republicans, Independents, and Democrats are significant with respect to each referent.

[5]Had the set of salient referents included the Democratic or Republican parties, we probably would have found that Democrats and Republicans differed in their motivations to comply with each party.

Perhaps more important, many other external variables were measured and were found to be unrelated to voting choice. An analysis of these variables would reveal no systematic effects on the beliefs that ultimately determine the voting decision. Moreover, some of the external variables that were found to influence voting in our study may have little effect on voting choice in other elections or in other populations. Conversely, the external variables that were found to be unrelated to voting in our study may influence, and in fact have sometimes influenced, voting decisions in other elections. It follows that external variables cannot provide an adequate explanation of voting behavior. Their effects on voting, if any, are indirect and depend on the extent to which they influence the cognitive structure that underlies this behavior.

## SUMMARY AND CONCLUSION

In this chapter we have tried to show how the theory of reasoned action can be used to understand voting decisions in American elections. This analysis has led to the following view of the processes underlying the decision to vote for a given candidate. As a result of their interactions with others and their exposure to the mass media and other sources of information, people acquire various beliefs about our political institutions, prominent political figures, and numerous issues and policies. At any given time, therefore, people associate various attributes with the political parties and public figures, they hold beliefs as to the positions of the political parties and public figures with respect to some of the issues of the day, and they assume that the implementation of certain policies would lead to desirable or undesirable outcomes. On the basis of these beliefs, they form attitudes toward the public figures, the parties, and the policies.

Whenever a new political figure attracts our attention, we tend to form beliefs about him even if we have only very limited information. For example, on the basis of his party affiliation or geographic origin we may infer that he favors certain policies and opposes others or that he is liberal or conservative. Often, these inferences, although based on very little information, turn out to be quite accurate.

When the time of an election draws near, there is a rapid increase in the amount of information available concerning the political parties, the potential candidates, and the issues of the day. This information re-inforces some beliefs and contradicts others, producing changes in existing beliefs; or it may provide the basis for the formation of new beliefs.

By the time of the election, most voters hold quite accurate beliefs about the political candidates and parties (see Colldeweih, 1968; Fishbein & Coombs, 1974). Perhaps more important, the campaign induces people to consider the likely consequences of *voting* for the different candidates. Such beliefs about voting for a given candidate are based in part on the information the person has about the candidate and the party to which he belongs. For example, the belief that voting for a candidate will lead to the implementation of a certain policy depends partly on the belief that the candidate in question favors that policy.

On the basis of these beliefs, the voter forms an attitude toward the act of voting for each candidate. The process whereby these attitudes are formed is eminently reasonable. A person who believes that voting for a candidate will lead to mainly positive outcomes will form a favorable attitude toward voting for that candidate; a person who believes that voting for the candidate will lead to mostly negative outcomes will form a negative attitude. When confronted with different candidates, a person will feel most positive toward voting for the candidate whom she believes can do the most for her. In support of this position, we have shown that people's attitudes toward voting for a candidate can be predicted with considerable accuracy from a knowledge of their beliefs that voting for the candidate will lead to certain outcomes and their evaluations of these outcomes.

In the course of interacting with other people, we often discuss not only the political candidates, parties, and issues but also the likely consequences of voting for a given candidate. As a result of these discussions we may infer that our friends, families, co-workers, or other referents think we should vote for one candidate rather than another. In conjunction with the individual's motivations to comply with each referent, these normative beliefs determine his subjective norm, that is, his belief that most important others think he should vote for one candidate or the other. Even though a person may believe that a specific referent thinks he should vote for a certain candidate, this belief will influence his subjective norm only to the extent that he is motivated to comply with the referent. We presented data showing a strong relation between normative beliefs and motivations to comply, on one hand, and subjective norms, on the other.

We also showed that attitudes and subjective norms with respect to voting for a given candidate provide the basis for intentions to vote for that candidate. From our point of view, the attitudinal and normative components serve as the only direct determinants of voting intentions. We realize, of course, that people hold attitudes toward the parties, candidates, and issues in a campaign and that these attitudes as well as such other external variables as party identification, liberalism-conservatism, or any of a number of demographic variables may influence the beliefs on which the two determinants of intentions are based. However, all of these effects are incorporated within and are taken into account by the measures of the attitudinal and normative components. Although consideration of external variables may help explain the origin of certain beliefs, we saw that the two components of our theory are sufficient to predict voting intentions.

In arriving at his voting intention, a person may place more weight on his attitude toward voting for the candidates or on his subjective norm. We have at present little information about the factors that determine these relative weights. Generally speaking, they are likely to be influenced by individual differences and by the particular election under consideration. For example, it has been suggested that the relative weight of normative considerations may increase as the importance of the voting decision declines. That is, normative considerations may be more important in congressional elections than in presidential elections.

Finally, we demonstrated that a person's choice among the candidates is determined by his intentions to vote for them. The best prediction is afforded when the intentions are measured immediately prior to the election. The reason is that voting intentions often change over time. It must be stressed, however, that these changes in intentions are not arbitrary, but rather they follow systematically from changes in beliefs brought about by exposure to new information. If the new information produces changes in one or more beliefs about the consequences of voting for a candidate, these changes may affect attitudes toward voting for the candidate and, hence, voting intentions. Similarly, new information may influence beliefs about the normative prescription of a relevant referent; this change in normative belief may affect subjective norms and ultimately the voting intention.

Note that even relatively large changes in a person's intentions to vote for each candidate may not be sufficient to shift his choice intention from one candidate to another. Imagine a person who initially thought it quite likely that he would vote for Carter and quite unlikely that he would vote for Ford. This person could lower his intention to vote for Carter and raise his intention to vote for Ford, but the differential intention could still favor Carter. Moreover, changes in intention may often serve to increase, rather than decrease, the initial difference. The absence of reversals in differential intentions, therefore, cannot be taken as evidence that intentions did not change or that the campaign had no effects on the voters. Indeed, it is our contention that political campaigns have large and significant effects on the beliefs of the electorate.

In contrast to this view, other attempts to explain voting behavior have focused on demographic variables, such as social class, religion, income, age, and education; attitudes toward parties, candidates, and issues; and party identification and political ideology (e.g., liberalism-conservatism). Although the prediction of voting choice from variables of this kind has usually been quite successful, we have tried to show that this approach does not provide an acceptable description or explanation of the process whereby people arrive at their voting decisions. In part, this is due to the fact that the traditional approach has focused on what we have called external variables, that is, variables which from our point of view can have only an indirect effect on voting behavior. To be sure, if you assess a large enough number of demographic variables; other individual difference variables, such as party identification, previous voting record, personality traits, or political ideology; and attitudes toward candidates, issues, parties, or other institutions, you will find that many of these variables are in fact related to voting decisions in a given election. Unfortunately, the relations obtained in one election are often not found in other elections and it is thus impossible to arrive at a clear and systematic understanding of the factors that determine voting decisions.

Even the six "partisan attitudes" and party identification which, according to the Michigan school represent the basic determinants of voting choice, cannot provide an adequate explanation of the process whereby voters reach their decisions. First, like other external variables, the relative importance of these "attitudes" varies considerably from election to election, although it is often possible to provide interesting and quite reasonable post-hoc explanations for these shifts. More important, these particular variables are not expected to account for the voting process in certain types of elections or electoral systems.

In marked contrast, the theory of reasoned action can be applied to the prediction and understanding of voting behavior in any kind of election and, for that matter, to any other political or nonpolitical behavior that is under volitional control. Moreover, we have seen how the small set of constructs in our conceptual framework can incorporate any external variable of interest and explain its consistent or inconsistent effects in different elections. Using this approach, we have obtained evidence for a rather complimentary view of the American voter: a person who uses the information available to him and who arrives at his voting decisions in a rational and reasonable manner. One implication of this view is that the American voter would arrive at more informed voting decisions if political candidates addressed the important issues instead of concentrating on personalities. The tendency to avoid controversial issues may explain the American public's current disenchantment with politicians and the political process in general.

# CHAPTER 14

Predicting
and Understanding
Voting
in British Elections
and American Referenda:
Illustrations of
the theory's generality

Martin Fishbein
Carol H. Bowman
Kerry Thomas
James J. Jaccard
Icek Ajzen

In the previous chapter we showed how the theory of reasoned action can be used to predict and explain voting behavior in American presidential elections. We saw that, like any other behavior, voting choice follows directly from the voter's intentions to vote for each candidate and that these intentions can in turn be understood by considering the underlying attitudes and subjective norms with respect to voting for the candidates. Under the American electoral system, a voter who identifies with, say, the Republican Party will tend to have a favorable attitude toward that party. Since the Republican candidate is likely to be viewed as taking the party position on many issues, the voter will also tend to have a favorable attitude toward her party's candidate. The voter will further tend to believe that the Republican candidate is more likely to implement the party's policies (which she herself favors) and she will therefore have a positive attitude toward voting for that candidate.[1] Moreover, since many of her relatives and friends will also identify with the Republican party, she will usually recognize that her important referents think she should vote for the candidate of that party. In support of these arguments, party identification and attitudes toward the parties and candidates have been found consistently to have strong relations to voting decisions.

By way of contrast, the many other external variables that have been considered in studies of American voting behavior have often been unrelated to voting choice or have had inconsistent effects. This is hardly surprising since there is no reason to expect that in every presidential election Catholics, liberals, or members of the middle class will favor voting for one party's candidate while Protestants, conservatives, or members of the working class will have more favorable attitudes toward voting for the candidate of the other party.

Perhaps because of these kinds of findings many investigators have used partisan attitudes and party identification as the major explanatory concepts in their theories of voting behavior, although they often consider demographic and other

[1]It is, of course, possible for a voter to hold very different attitudes toward candidate and party, particularly if the candidate adopts positions discrepant from his party. Attitudes toward voting for the candidate in this case would be more strongly related to the attitude toward the candidate than toward the party or to party identification.

external variables as well. From our point of view, however, there is no necessary relation between any of these variables and voting choice. Partisan attitudes and party identification have been found to predict voting choice in American presidential elections because, as we saw in Chapter 13, these variables were consistently related to attitudes and subjective norms with respect to voting for the candidates. Indeed, the role of party identification, and hence party attitudes, is likely to diminish in future presidential elections if the recent trend for more and more voters to consider themselves independents continues.

More important, attitudes toward, or identification with, the different parties cannot explain voting decisions in other types of elections even within the United States. For example, the candidates in primary elections are all members of the same party and there are many nonpartisan contests, such as elections to the school board and to various municipal and county offices. In such elections, attempts to explain voting choice by means of external variables would tend to focus on attitudes toward the candidates—whether based on considerations of the candidates' personal attributes or their stands on the issues— although demographic characteristics of the voters might also be taken into account.

There is reason to believe, then, that within the American electoral system, where the vote constitutes a choice between candidates, attitudes toward the candidates (because of their systematic relations to attitudes toward voting for those candidates) will be related to voting choice. In contrast, attitudes toward the parties and party identification will tend to be related to voting choice in partisan elections but not in nonpartisan elections.

A very different pattern of relations between these external variables and voting decisions is likely to emerge under the electoral systems of other countries. In some countries, such as Israel, the names of the candidates do not even appear on the ballot; instead, the voter is confronted with a choice among the political parties. Although each party publishes a list of candidates, ordered in terms of their priority to become members of parliament (the Knesset), the actual composition of the parliament depends on the proportion of votes received by each party. Thus, if a party wins seven seats, the first seven candidates on its list will represent the party in the Knesset. Typically, the leader of the party with the largest number of seats in the Knesset will be appointed Prime Minister and will be given the responsibility of forming the government.

If we were to apply our theory in this type of electoral system, we would expect voting choice among parties to follow directly from the voters' choice intentions. These choice intentions should in turn be predictable from intentions to vote for each of the parties. To gain an understanding of the factors that determine intentions to vote for a given party, we would consider the voters' attitudes and subjective norms with respect to voting for that party, and we would ultimately explore the cognitive structure underlying these attitudinal and normative components. In the final analysis, therefore, our explanation of voting choice in an electoral system such as Israel's would involve a description of the voters' behavioral beliefs concerning the relative advantages and disadvantages of voting for the different parties and their normative beliefs concerning the voting prescriptions of relevant referents.

In contrast, a conventional approach would focus on partisan attitudes and party identification. To be sure, in a system where voters make a choice among parties, identification with a party or party attitudes can be expected to be related to attitudes toward voting for the party and hence to voting choice. With respect to attitudes toward the candidates, the situation is more ambiguous. While one would probably assess attitudes toward the leaders of each party, it might also be reasonable to measure attitudes toward other prominent party members or, indeed, toward all candidates on a party's list. However, it is not clear whether attitudes toward any of these candidates will be consistently related to voting for the party in question.

To illustrate, a voter may like the leader of a party but have a negative attitude toward voting for that party because of the party's policies. Conversely, a person may have neutral or even negative feelings toward the party leader yet still see many advantages and few disadvantages in voting for the party. For example, despite their neutral or negative attitudes toward Begin, the leader of the Likud party, many voters cast their ballots for the Likud party in the 1977 general elections in Israel because they believed that such a vote would strengthen Israel's negotiating position in the Middle East conflict.

In sum, we have argued that attitudes toward candidates are likely to predict voting choice in elections in which the vote represents a choice among candidates, while attitudes toward or identification with parties are likely to predict voting decisions when the voter is confronted with a choice among parties. Thus, in the American electoral system, attitudes toward candidates are found to be better predictors of voting choice than are attitudes toward parties or party identification, while we would expect the opposite to be true in a system such as Israel's. Even these limited generalizations concerning the effects of partisan attitudes and party identification, however, cannot be expected to hold in still other electoral systems.

Consider, for example, the election process in Great Britain. Here the voter chooses among the candidates in his constituency who represent the different parties, and the candidate with most votes is elected to the House of Commons. In this respect, the British system is similar to the American system. Once the parliament has been elected, however, the selection of Prime Minister and the formation of a government is similar to the procedures in Israel. The leader of the largest party is typically appointed Prime Minister and asked to form the government. It can be seen that although the British voter casts his ballot for a given candidate, his vote at the same time determines the party that will be in power. It is thus possible for the British voter to find himself in the uncomfortable position in which a vote for the candidate he likes most contributes to the formation of a government by a party he dislikes. Consider, for example, a voter who would like to see a Labour government but whose attitude toward the Liberal candidate is more favorable than his attitudes toward the other candidates in his constituency. In fact, he may actively dislike the Labour candidate. Within the British system it is quite possible that by helping to elect the Liberal candidate he likes, the voter would at the same time undermine the Labour Party's strength. His vote for the Liberal candidate might thus contribute to the formation of a Conservative government.

It is therefore unclear what role partisan attitudes and party identification will play in the context of the British electoral system. In contrast, the application of our theory to British elections is again quite straightforward. Voting choice should be a function of choice intentions which, in this case, will be based on the voters' intentions to vote for each of the candidates in their constituencies. The intention to vote for a given candidate is in turn determined by attitudes toward voting for the candidate and by subjective norms, and a consideration of the underlying cognitive structure should provide an explanation of an individual's voting decision.

The beliefs that influence a British voter's attitude toward voting for a given candidate are likely to differ in important respects from the beliefs of his American counterpart. Clearly, some of the beliefs that are most salient in the British electorate have to do with the consequences of voting choice for the formation of the national government. As a result, the British voter's attitude toward voting for a given candidate may have little to do with his attitude toward the candidate as such. It follows that although both American and British voters cast their votes for candidates (rather than for parties), the British voters' attitudes toward these candidates need not be consistently related to their voting decisions. However, since under the British system each candidate is pledged to support his party's position on the issues, voters will tend to believe that voting for a given candidate will increase the likelihood that his party's policies will be implemented. Consequently, the voter's attitude toward a given party should be related to his attitude toward voting for the candidate of that party and, hence, to his voting decision.

## A STUDY OF THE 1974 GENERAL ELECTION IN GREAT BRITAIN[2]

Some of the preceding points can be illustrated by considering a study of voting choice in the 1974 general parliamentary election in Great Britain. During the week prior to the election, a total of 376 voting age residents in four different constituencies (approximately 90 in each) were interviewed in their homes. In

[2]This study was supported in part by the Survey Research Unit of Great Britain's Social Science Research Council. For a complete description, see Fishbein, Thomas and Jaccard (1976).

each of these constituencies, only three candidates, representing the three major parties, were contesting the seat. One third of the respondents in each constituency identified with the Labour Party, one third with the Conservative Party, and one third with the Liberal Party. The study was primarily concerned with the beliefs that determine the British voters' attitudes toward the parties, toward the candidates in their constituencies, and toward the party leaders. In addition, attitudes and subjective norms with respect to voting for each candidate, as well as several external variables, were assessed. It was possible to recontact 328 of the respondents in the week following the election, at which time they were asked to reveal their voting choices.

One of the issues raised earlier concerns the prediction of voting behavior from attitudes toward candidates, parties, and party leaders. Consistent with our discussion, attitudes toward a given party were more strongly related to voting for the candidate of that party than were attitudes toward the candidate. For example, attitudes toward the Conservative Party had a correlation of .74 with whether or not the voters cast their votes for the Conservative candidate in their constituency, while attitudes toward that candidate correlated only .64 with this behavior. The relationship between voting for a given candidate and attitudes toward the leaders of the candidate's party was of intermediate magnitude. For example, attitudes toward Edward Heath (who was then the leader of the Conservative Party) correlated .67 with whether or not a person voted for the Conservative candidate in his constituency. More important, consideration of all three attitudes simultaneously did not lead to more accurate prediction of whether or not a person would vote for a given candidate than the prediction based on the attitudes toward the candidate's party alone. That is, in Great Britain, party attitudes are good predictors of voting behavior, and little is to be gained by the additional consideration of attitudes toward candidates or party leaders. In contrast, in the United States attitudes toward candidates are typically found to predict voting behavior quite well, and little is gained by also considering attitudes toward parties.

Clearly, then, the explanatory value of such variables as attitudes toward candidates and toward parties varies considerably as we go from one electoral system to another. This becomes even more evident when we consider the concept of party identification. As we saw in chapter 13, the concept of party identification has played a prominent role in most analyses of American voting behavior. Let us now examine to what extent this concept contributes to our understanding of voting decisions in Great Britain.

Party identification is usually defined as the individual's sense of personal or psychological attachment to the party of his choice and, according to Campbell (1964), a person's party identification is "remarkably constant through the life of the individual." It might appear that long-standing party loyalties also exist in Great Britain. For example, Butler and Stokes (1969) reported that over the course of three elections in both Britain (1963, 1964, 1966) and in the United States (1956, 1958, 1960), about 80% of the voters cast their votes for candidates of a single party and maintained stable party identifications. Some European scholars, however, have questioned the utility of the party identification concept, pointing out that long-term partisan attachments are not evident in their particular countries. In fact, examination of the British voters who cast their votes for candidates of different parties suggests that, in contrast to their American counterparts, British voters change their party identifications as easily as they change their voting choices. While only 27% of the American voters with bipartisan voting patterns reported changes in their party identifications, fully 62% of the British voters with changing voting patterns reported shifts in party identification. Thus, as Butler and Stokes (1969) pointed out, "in transferring their vote from one party to another [British voters] are less likely to retain a conscious identification with a party other than the one they currently support" (p. 43). In other words, while the American voter seems to maintain identification with a given party even when he intends to vote for the candidate of the opposition party, the British voter apparently identifies (or reports identification) with the party of the candidate for whom he intends to vote at the time he is interviewed.

Consistent with these arguments, our data showed that in the 1974 general election in Great Britain party identification provided highly accurate prediction of voting choice ($r$ = .89). Indeed, at the time of an election, a British voter's party identification appears to be little more than a reflection of his intention to vote for the candidate of that party.[3] While party identification is a useful concept for *predicting* voting decisions in Great Britain, it should be clear that this concept does not contribute much to an *understanding* of British voting behavior.

In sum, attitudes toward parties and candidates, and the voters' party identification, seem to play different roles in American and British elections. Although these variables can be used to predict voting choice in both countries, the way in which these variables influence voting decisions varies considerably. Among the external variables that have been considered, attitude toward the candidates seems to contribute most to our understanding of voting behavior in the United States, whereas in Great Britain, attitude toward the parties seems to contribute most. Further, while the concept of party identification provides some insight into the determinants of American voting behavior, in Britain its utility is limited to the prediction of voting choice.

### Determinants of Voting Behavior in Great Britain

According to the theory of reasoned action, a person's intention to vote for any given candidate, and her actual voting for that candidate, is a function of her attitude toward and her subjective norm with respect to voting for the candidate.

[3]Although there is indirect evidence to support this argument (Fishbein, Thomas & Jaccard, 1976) we cannot report the correlation between intentions and party identification because, as we shall see, measures of intention were not obtained in this study.

Unfortunately, due to a clerical error, measures of voting intention were inadvertently omitted from the questionnaire in the British voting study. However, it seems reasonable to assume that in Great Britain, as in the United States, people vote in accordance with their intentions. Consistent with this assumption, voting for a given candidate could be predicted very accurately from the attitudinal and normative components of our theory. For example, attitudes toward voting for the Labour candidate, and subjective norms with respect to this behavior, were found to have a multiple correlation of .85 with actual voting for that candidate. The attitude toward voting for the Labour candidate correlated .85 with actual vote, and the correlation for the subjective norm was .63. Therefore, as in the American election study described in chapter 13, the attitudinal component was again found to carry more weight ($w$ = .77) than the normative component ($w$ = .12). Similarly, the correlations of voting for the Conservative candidate with attitudes toward this behavior and subjective norms were .81 and .69, respectively; the multiple correlation was .84. The attitudinal component was again a more important determinant of voting ($w$ = .64) than was the normative component ($w$ = .27).[4]

In fact, consistent with expectations and the findings in the American election, attitudes toward voting for a given candidate were the most important determinants of voting, and they predicted an actual vote for the candidate more accurately than did attitudes toward the candidate as such. Thus, we again find that the attitude toward a behavior is a better predictor of that behavior than is the attitude toward the target at which the behavior is directed. Moreover, attitudes toward voting for a candidate also provided more accurate prediction of actual voting for the candidate than did attitudes toward the parties or toward the party leaders.

Note, however, that the preceding analyses were concerned with only a single alternative, namely, voting or not voting for a given candidate. It is also possible to use our attitudinal and normative measures to predict choice among the three candidates. For each respondent we obtained three scores by summing his attitude and subjective norm with respect to voting for each of the three candidates. We then predicted that the respondent would vote for the candidate with the highest score.

Table 14.1 shows the relation between predicted and actual voting choice. Each cell in the table shows the number of respondents who were predicted to vote for a given candidate and the candidate for whom they actually voted. It can be seen that our theory led to very accurate prediction of voting choice. Of the 299 respondents who reported voting, we were able to correctly predict the vote of 266 or 89%.

These findings suggest that the British voter, like his American counterpart,

---

[4]Since there were three major candidates in each constituency, we could not use differential measures of attitude and subjective norm. Instead, our model was used to predict voting behavior separately with respect to each candidate (i.e., respondents were classified as having voted or not voted for each of the three candidates).

**TABLE 14.1**
Relation Between Predicted and Actual Voting Choice[a]

| | PREDICTED VOTING CHOICE | | |
|---|---|---|---|
| ACTUAL VOTING CHOICE | *Conservative Candidate* | *Liberal Candidate* | *Labour Candidate* |
| Conservative candidate | 91 | 4 | 1 |
| Liberal candidate | 9 | 86 | 9 |
| Labour candidate | 2 | 8 | 89 |

[a]Only the 299 respondents who reported voting for one of the three candidates were included in this analysis.

arrives at his voting decision primarily by considering the relative advantages and disadvantages of casting his vote for each of the candidates in his constituency. This conclusion derives from the finding that voting for a given candidate was determined in large part by attitudes toward voting for that candidate and, as we saw in chapter 13, such attitudes are a function of beliefs about and evaluations of the likely consequences of voting for the candidate in question.

We noted earlier in this chapter that the British voter may find himself in a position where he is most attracted to one candidate but where he also recognizes that voting for that candidate could result in the formation of a government he opposes. That is, in contrast to his American counterpart, the British voter should be aware of the tactical implications of his vote. Among his salient beliefs about voting for a given candidate should be the belief that voting for the candidate in question is likely to result in the formation of a certain government. Although salient beliefs about voting for the different candidates were not elicited in this study, an attempt was made to examine at least some of the voters' tactical beliefs. Specifically, respondents were asked to indicate their beliefs that casting their vote for a given candidate would increase the chances of six possible electoral outcomes: a Labour government, a Liberal government, a Conservative government, and three types of coalition governments.

Table 14.2 shows the average tactical beliefs for the total sample of respondents. Generally speaking, people viewed a vote for the Labour candidate as quite likely to increase the chances of a Labour government and, at the same time, such a vote was seen as quite unlikely to increase the chances of any other electoral outcomes. In a somewhat similar fashion, a vote for the Conservative candidate was viewed as quite likely to increase the chances of a Conservative government, but people also believed that voting for the Conservative candidate had a small likelihood of increasing the chances of a Conservative-Liberal coalition government. Other types of electoral outcomes were believed to be unlikely consequences of casting one's vote for the Conservative candidate. Finally, voting for the Liberal candidate was expected to increase the likelihood of a Liberal government only slightly. Perhaps more important, casting a vote for the Liberal

TABLE 14.2
Beliefs that Casting a Vote for a Given Candidate Will Increase the
Chances of Each of the Six Possible Electoral Outcomes

| | VOTING FOR THE | | |
| OUTCOME | Liberal Candidate | Conservative Candidate | Labour Candidate |
| --- | --- | --- | --- |
| Liberal Government | 0.32 | −1.78 | −1.77 |
| Conservative Government | −0.85 | 1.42 | −1.68 |
| Labour Government | −0.49 | −1.43 | 1.79 |
| Labour-Liberal Government | −0.94 | −1.61 | −1.19 |
| Conservative-Liberal Government | 0.09 | 0.29 | −1.17 |
| Three Party Coalition Government | −0.71 | −0.71 | −1.30 |

Note: Scores can range from −3 (extremely unlikely to increase the chances of the outcome) to +3 (extremely likely to increase the chances of the outcome).

candidate was viewed as significantly more harmful to the chances of a Conservative government than to the chances of a Labor government. Finally, a three-
party coalition was seen as quite unlikely, irrespective of one's voting decision.

Although it is beyond the scope of this chapter, it was also found that these
tactical considerations are affected by, and take account of, the particular circumstances of a voter's constituency. In forming their beliefs about the consequences of voting for a given candidate, voters take into consideration whether
the candidate is an incumbent or a challenger and the incumbent's margin of
victory in the preceding election.

The tactical beliefs measured in this study will, of course, constitute only
some of the voter's salient beliefs about voting for a particular candidate. Nevertheless, we would expect the tactical beliefs to be related to attitudes toward
voting for the candidate in question. The results were consistent with these expectations. Generally speaking, people held favorable attitudes toward voting for
a given candidate if they believed that voting for the candidate would promote
the type of government they most desired and would prevent the formation of
governments they opposed. For example, there was general agreement that
voting for the Labour candidate would increase the chances of a Labour government. Consequently, people who favored a Labour government tended to hold
positive attitudes toward voting for the Labour candidate, while those opposed
to a Labour government were usually found to have negative attitudes toward
voting for the Labour candidate.[5]

In conclusion, our theory was shown to be as applicable to the analysis of
voting in Great Britain as it was to the analysis of voting in the United States.
Despite some major differences in the electoral systems of these two countries,

[5]These findings help explain the effects of attitudes toward the parties and of party
identification on voting decisions.

voting decisions in each case could be explained in terms of attitudes and subjective norms with respect to voting for the candidates. Moreover, by examining the cognitive structures underlying these variables it was possible to identify the specific considerations that ultimately determine a person's voting decision. Although the data obtained in the British study did not permit a complete analysis of this kind, we were able to show the effects of certain tactical considerations on attitudes toward voting for candidates and, hence, on voting choice.

The major point to be made, however, is that we were able to predict and explain voting decisions without reference to such external variables as partisan attitudes and party identification. To be sure, these variables are often related to some of the beliefs that provide the basis for the attitudinal and normative components of our theory, and, for this reason, they are often related to actual voting behavior. We have seen, however, that the effects of these and other external variables are not consistent across different electoral systems, and variables of this kind thus fail to make a systematic contribution to our understanding of voting decisions. The advantage of our approach to voting behavior can be seen perhaps most clearly in the following section, which deals with voting in nonpartisan referenda.

## NONPARTISAN VOTING BEHAVIOR

In recent years, the general public has taken an increasingly active role in the political decision-making process. No longer content to leave decisions that impact on their lives solely in the hands of their elected representatives, individuals and interest groups have turned to the use of referenda as a means of expressing their concerns. For example, dissatisfied with their government's failure to enact tax reform and legislation to protect the environment, voters have initiated propositions to greatly reduce property taxes and bar the use of disposable soft drink bottles. Similarly, concerned with the possible consequences of granting equal rights to homosexuals, voters have introduced propositions to rescind prior legislation guaranteeing those rights. Given the potential impact of such measures on the government as well as on the public, it is important to understand the factors that influence people's voting behavior in public referenda.

From our point of view, the decision to vote *yes* or *no* on a given proposition is reached on the basis of the same process that leads to the decision to vote for or against a given candidate. As a result of exposure to the mass media, campaign literature, and discussions with various people, the voter forms beliefs that voting for (or against) the proposition would lead to certain outcomes and that certain individuals or groups think he should vote for (or against) the proposition. By considering the relative advantages and disadvantages of voting for the proposition, he forms an attitude toward this behavior. Similarly, his normative beliefs and motivations to comply lead to the formation of a generalized belief that most important others think he should or should not vote for the proposition (i.e., the subjective norm). The person's intention to vote for (or against) the proposition is based on these attitudinal and normative considerations and ultimately determines his actual vote.

In comparison to the ease with which our theory can be applied to this new voting situation, consider the problems that would be encountered by a more conventional approach. Obviously, attitudes toward candidates and parties are largely irrelevant in this context. Instead, a conventional approach would probably rely on numerous demographic characteristics, personality factors, and measures of attitudes toward various elements in the voting situation. A major problem with such an approach is that we have no theory to guide our selection of variables and must rely on our intuitive understanding of the forces that operate in the situation. Although there is only a limited set of demographic characteristics that are usually considered (e.g., age, sex, race, religion, socioeconomic status, education, and perhaps party identification), there is virtually no limit to the number of personality traits or attitudes one could assess.

Consider, for example, a referendum designed to restrict construction of nuclear power plants. One investigator might focus on such personality variables as liberalism-conservatism, neuroticism, and aggression, while another might be more interested in Strong's vocational interest measure, scientific-humanistic orientation, fear of dying, and locus of control. On the attitudinal side, one study might examine attitudes toward nuclear power, energy conservation, and pollution, while another study might be more concerned with attitudes toward some of the groups that may support or oppose passage of the proposition, including the power companies, the Alternative Energy Coalition, and the Sierra Club. Still another investigator might assess attitudes toward the issue itself, namely the policy of placing restrictions on the construction of nuclear power plants, attitudes toward the energy crisis, and attitudes toward one or more alternative sources of energy.

It stands to reason that in each of these studies, at least some variables will turn out to have statistically significant relations to voting in the referendum. Consequently, different investigators are likely to identify different "determinants" of the voting decision and will thus arrive at very different accounts of the voting process. No matter how reasonable these accounts may appear, it is highly unlikely that the particular set of demographic, personality, or attitude variables found to be related to voting in one referendum will also account for, or even be appropriate to, voting decisions in another referendum concerning a different proposition. The investigator would therefore have to intuitively select a new set of variables for every referendum. Clearly, such an approach cannot contribute much to our understanding of the process whereby people reach a decision to vote for or against a referendum, let alone contribute to our understanding of the voting process in general.

As a result of the 1973 oil embargo, questions concerning energy production and conservation have become the focus of considerable attention. Politicians are debating appropriate means to meet current and future energy needs and are considering the relative emphasis to be placed on various ways of producing energy (e.g., nuclear fission, solar, geothermal). Key issues in this decision-making process concern the role to be accorded conservation, the amount of energy needed in the future, the safety of various alternatives, and the economic and technical feasibility of particular energy production methods.

Political leaders cannot make these decisions in a vacuum. The public has become quite vocal in expressing its concerns about the impact of energy decisions upon the price of energy, the safety and environmental consequences of the power production methods proposed, and the requirements for a change in lifestyle. Public acceptance of an energy proposal is vital to its success.

Nuclear energy in particular has aroused a great deal of public concern. This concern has increased to the point where it threatens to restrict or halt the expansion of the nuclear industry. In 1976, a number of states scheduled voter referenda that would place restrictions upon the operation and construction of nuclear power plants. One of these, California's Proposition 15, if passed, would have made the construction of new plants and the operation of existing ones contingent upon the removal of utility liability limits and the legislative approval of safety and waste disposal systems. Although the measures proposed in 1976 were defeated, a nuclear referendum held in Austria in 1978 was supported. The issues surrounding the use of nuclear power continue to be debated and it is quite likely that voter referenda on nuclear power will be held in the future. Thus the views held by the general public toward specific legislative proposals will have great impact on the continued growth and existence of the nuclear program and the fate of other energy proposals. It would appear to be beneficial to this nation's energy program, its leaders, and the public, if we could develop a better understanding of the process by which people come to accept or reject a particular energy proposal. In this section we will try to show how our theory can help achieve this aim.

## A STUDY OF THE 1976 OREGON NUCLEAR SAFEGUARDS REFERENDUM[6]

Among the various voting decisions that confronted Oregon voters in the election of 1976 was Ballot Measure No. 9—The Oregon Nuclear Safeguards Initiative. This measure, like California's Proposition 15, was designed to place restrictions on the construction of nuclear power plants.

[6]This study was supported in part by an NSF postdoctoral energy research fellowship to Carol Bowman No. HES 75-199936. For a complete discussion of the study, see Bowman and Fishbein (1978).

Prior to the election, interviews were conducted by telephone with 19 potential voters in order to elicit salient outcomes and referents associated with voting for the proposition. Since at the time of the interview public opinions on the issue were just beginning to crystallize, it was decided to supplement the obtained outcomes and referents with information from newspaper items and the campaign literature. A content analysis of all the materials yielded lists of 20 salient consequences and 7 referents that were used to construct a standard questionnaire.[7] The outcomes and referents are shown in Tables 14.3 and 14.4 (p. 211 and p. 213).

Just prior to the election, 89 respondents completed and returned a questionnaire they had received through the mail.[8] The respondent's voting intention was assessed by means of the following scale:

I intend to vote *yes* on the Oregon Nuclear Safeguards Initiative—Ballot Measure No. 9.

likely ____ : ____ : ____ : ____ : ____ : ____ : ____ unlikely

In addition, the questionnaire also assessed the following variables: attitudes and subjective norms with respect to voting *yes* on the proposition, beliefs that voting *yes* would lead to each of the 20 outcomes and that each of the seven referents thought the respondent should vote *yes,* as well as evaluations of each outcome and motivations to comply with each referent. Finally, measures were obtained of several demographic characteristics, including party identification and attitudes toward four nuclear concepts (the construction of more nuclear power plants, a halt in the operation of all nuclear power plants, the use of nuclear energy, and nuclear power).

In the week following the election, follow-up telephone calls were made to all respondents in order to ascertain their actual voting behavior. Of the 89 respondents, 39 voted *yes* (in favor of placing restrictions on nuclear power plant construction), 38 voted *no*, 4 did not vote in the referendum, 4 refused to reveal their votes, and 4 could not be contacted.

The results of the study provided strong support for our theory. Consistent with findings in other voting situations, a person's intention to vote *yes* on the nuclear safeguards proposition accurately predicted actual voting behavior ($r$ = .89). In turn, voting intentions were strongly related to attitudes and subjective norms with respect to voting *yes* on the proposition ($R$ = .92). Although

[7]Relevant parts of this questionnaire constitute the sample questionnaire in appendix B.

[8]Questionnaires were mailed to 500 addressees randomly selected from the 1976 telephone directory for Portland, Oregon. Of the 500 questionnaires, 47 were returned by the post office as undeliverable, 12 were returned unanswered, and 92 were returned answered, but three of these had been completed after the respondent had voted in the election. Viewed within the context of comparable mail surveys with no special incentive for responding, this response rate of 18% is not atypical, although it is slightly lower than average (see, for example, Kanuk & Berenson, 1975).

both components made significant contributions to the prediction of intentions, the attitude toward the act of voting *yes* was the more important of the two determinants. Finally, both the attitude and the subjective norm were accurately predicted from considerations of their underlying cognitive structures. These relationships are summarized in Figure 14.1.

The preceding findings demonstrate that the salient beliefs considered in this study ultimately determined how a person voted on the Oregon nuclear safeguards initiative. To gain insight into the considerations that led people to vote *yes* or *no* on the proposition, we divided the respondents into those who intended to and actually did vote *yes* and those who intended to and actually did cast a *no* vote. Since the attitudinal component carried more weight in the prediction of intentions than did the normative component, let us first examine the behavioral beliefs and outcome evaluations that contributed to the attitude toward voting *yes* on the proposition.

**Behavioral beliefs underlying attitudes toward voting yes.** The average behavioral beliefs and outcome evaluations for the proponents and opponents of the measure are shown in Table 14.3. For ease of discussion we have arranged the outcomes into two groups: outcomes for which both groups of voters held similar beliefs (numbers 1 to 9) and outcomes for which the two groups held significantly different beliefs ($p < .01$) about casting a *yes* vote (numbers 10 to 20).

The first nine beliefs are important since they indicate that the voters in our sample were very well informed about the issues involved in the referendum. They realized, among other things, that adoption of the proposition (i.e., a *yes*

**FIGURE 14.1**
Relations among beliefs, attitudes, subjective norms, intentions, and voting behavior in the 1976 Oregon Nuclear Safeguards Referendum.

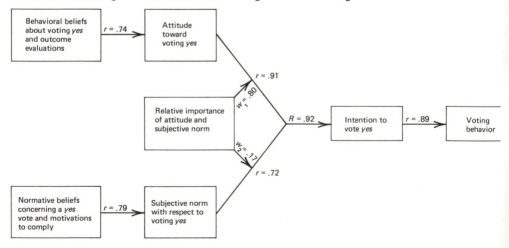

TABLE 14.3

Mean Behavioral Beliefs and Outcome Evaluations for Proponents and Opponents of the Nuclear Safeguards Proposition

| OUTCOME OF VOTING YES ON THE PROPOSITION | BEHAVIORAL BELIEF STRENGTH | | OUTCOME EVALUATION | |
|---|---|---|---|---|
| | *Proponents* | *Opponents* | *Proponents* | *Opponents* |
| 1. Require new tests of nuclear safety systems | 2.58 | 1.95 | 2.55 | 1.46* |
| 2. Require a decision on a permanent nuclear waste disposal method | 2.32 | 1.77 | 2.82 | 1.81* |
| 3. Increase public participation in nuclear decisions | 1.45 | .54 | 2.18 | .65* |
| 4. Make it easy for companies to obtain legislative approval for new nuclear power plants | −1.71 | −1.79 | −2.32 | − .14* |
| 5. Make nuclear power plant operators fully responsible financially for nuclear accidents | 1.21 | .18 | 2.21 | 1.11 |
| 6. Deny full compensation to the victims of a nuclear accident | −1.84 | −1.33 | −2.50 | −2.11 |
| 7. Give regulatory control of nuclear power to state legislators | 1.50 | 1.54 | − .32 | −1.43 |
| 8. (Lead to) court battles over the ballot measure's constitutionality | 1.32 | 1.62 | .13 | − .57 |
| 9. Maintain Oregon's present system for regulating nuclear power | −1.08 | −1.33 | −1.29 | .95* |
| 10. A ban on more nuclear power plants | .37 | 2.21* | .84 | −2.38* |
| 11. Ensure low-cost electricity | −1.13 | −2.23* | 1.71 | 2.32 |
| 12. Help state's economic development | − .18 | −2.33* | .89 | 2.11 |
| 13. Increase unemployment | −1.13 | .41* | −1.39 | − .70 |
| 14. Reduce funds for development of alternative energy sources | −1.92 | .36* | −2.68 | −2.24 |
| 15. Eliminate a needed energy source | −1.16 | 1.05* | −1.13 | −1.70 |
| 16. (Lead to) a future energy shortage | − .61 | 1.79* | −1.45 | −1.46 |
| 17. Set up realistic standards for nuclear waste management | 1.58 | −1.26* | 2.58 | 2.38 |
| 18. Decrease danger from radioactive materials and wastes | 2.05 | − .69* | 2.84 | 2.27 |
| 19. Reduce the threat of nuclear theft and sabotage | .74 | −1.10* | 2.71 | 2.51 |
| 20. Make new nuclear plants safer than present ones | 1.97 | − .23* | 2.42 | 2.14 |

*Significant difference between proponents and opponents of the proposition ($p < .01$)

vote) would mean a change in Oregon's present system for regulating nuclear power and would require new tests of nuclear safety systems and a decision on a permanent nuclear waste disposal method. Further, they also knew that passage of the proposition would give regulatory control of nuclear power to state legislators, would make nuclear power plant operators financially responsible for nuclear accidents, and would essentially give full compensation to victims of such accidents. Finally, although not directly part of the referendum proposal, media coverage and general public debate had made it clear to most voters that passage of the proposition would not ensure low-cost electricity and would probably lead to a court battle over the constitutionality of the proposition.

These findings demonstrate that a concerned public is much better informed than it has usually been given credit for, and that irrespective of their eventual voting decisions, respondents recognized some of the advantages and disadvantages of the proposed measure.

Thus far we have outlined areas of belief where the two groups of voters agreed and where this consensus realistically reflected the issues at stake. Differences in the evaluations of outcomes 1 through 4 begin to shed some light on differential voting behavior. Note, however, that of the 20 outcomes considered in this study, only 3 were evaluated in opposite directions by the two groups of voters (numbers 8 to 10), and in only two cases (numbers 9 and 10) was this qualitative difference statistically significant. Not surprisingly, respondents who favored a ban on more nuclear power plants and who negatively evaluated the current regulatory system in Oregon were likely to vote *yes* on the proposition while respondents who opposed a ban and who favored the current system were likely to vote *no*.

In addition to these evaluative differences, the major factors that distinquished between *yes* and *no* voters were differences in beliefs concerning the likelihood of the last nine outcomes in Table 14.3. It can be seen that there were considerable disagreements about some of the consequences of casting a *yes* vote. These disagreements are related to three basic issues: the state's economy, the energy crisis, and the safety of nuclear power plants.

Some people believed that adoption of the proposed measure (a *yes* vote) would hurt economic development in Oregon and increase unemployment, while others were uncertain about its effects on economic development and believed it would *not* increase unemployment. The first group of respondents was likely to vote *no* while the second was likely to vote *yes*.

There was also considerable disagreement about the effects of the proposition on the energy crisis in general. There were some who believed that passage of the proposal (a *yes* vote) would reduce funds for the development of alternative energy sources, would eliminate a needed energy source, and would ultimately lead to a future energy shortage. Others felt these outcomes were unlikely. Those in the former group were more likely to vote *no* on the proposition than those in the latter group.

The final area of disagreement concerned the likelihood that passage of the proposition (a *yes* vote) would make new nuclear power plants safer than present ones, would set up realistic standards for nuclear waste management, would decrease danger from radioactive materials and waste, and would reduce the threat of nuclear sabotage. In general, if a person believed that voting *yes* would lead to the outcomes listed, he or she was very likely to cast a *yes* vote. On the other hand, people who felt that risk reductions were unlikely outcomes of voting *yes* typically cast their votes against the proposition.

In sum, respondents who believed that a *yes* vote would reduce nuclear hazard and increase safety *without* harming the economy or increasing the probability of an energy crisis supported the proposed measure (i.e., voted *yes*). In contrast, respondents who believed that a *yes* vote would harm the economy and increase the likelihood of a future energy shortage without reducing nuclear risk or increasing safety voted against the proposition.

**Normative beliefs underlying subjective norms concerning a *yes* vote.** Although of less importance, normative considerations were also found to contribute significantly to the voting decision, and it is therefore of interest to briefly examine the determinants of the subjective norm. Table 14.4 presents the mean values of the normative beliefs that each referent would advocate a *yes* vote and the motivations to comply with each referent.

It can be seen that there were significant differences in the voters' beliefs concerning their personal referents (family, friends, and co-workers). Although the two groups of voters did not differ in their motivations to comply with their personal referents, each group believed that their positions on the referendum were supported by these referents.

For the four public referents, both *yes* and *no* voters believed that the power companies, most government officials, and most nuclear experts thought they should vote *no* and believed that the environmentalists thought they should vote *yes*. There was, however, a significant difference between the two groups of voters in the strength of the normative belief concerning the nuclear experts.

**TABLE 14.4**

Mean Normative Beliefs and Motivations to Comply for Proponents and Opponents of the Nuclear Safeguards Proposition

| REFERENTS | NORMATIVE BELIEF | | MOTIVATION TO COMPLY | |
|---|---|---|---|---|
| | *Proponents* | *Opponents* | *Proponents* | *Opponents* |
| Most members of my family | 1.27 | −1.85* | 3.49 | 3.26 |
| My close friends | 1.62 | −1.51* | 2.68 | 3.05 |
| My co-workers | .81 | −1.80* | 2.62 | 2.85 |
| The power companies | −2.59 | −2.17 | 1.41 | 3.64* |
| The environmentalists | 2.27 | 1.83 | 4.73 | 3.28 |
| Most government officials | − .73 | − .93 | 2.05 | 3.51* |
| Most nuclear experts | − .43 | −2.20* | 3.30 | 5.36* |

*Significant difference between proponents and opponents of the proposition ($p < .05$).

Respondents who ultimately voted *no* believed that this position was strongly supported by the nuclear experts, whereas those who ultimately voted *yes* were less sure that the nuclear experts advocated a *no* vote.

While agreeing as to the positions advocated by the four public referents, the two groups of voters differed in their motivations to comply. Predictably, those who were more motivated to comply with the power company, the government, and most nuclear experts (all of whom opposed the proposition) and were less motivated to comply with the environmentalists were more likely to cast a *no* vote.

### Effects of External Variables

In keeping with a conventional approach, a limited number of demographic characteristics and more traditional attitudinal variables were also assessed. The demographic characteristics considered were the respondents' sex, age, and education. Additionally, given the political nature of the behavior under investigation, respondents were asked to indicate their party affiliations.

The results showed that these variables were largely irrelevant to a person's voting decisions; neither sex nor age or education could be used to predict whether a person would vote for or against the nuclear safeguards referendum. Party identification was found to be a somewhat better predictor, with Democrats and Independents more likely to vote *yes* than Republicans. Although the correlation was significant, it was of relatively low magnitude ($r = .37$). Moreover, consideration of party identification in addition to voting intentions did not appreciably improve the prediction of behavior beyond the level obtained by using intentions alone.

The traditional attitudes assessed in this study were selected to be relevant to the nuclear safeguards referendum. It seems reasonable to assume that a person's vote in the referendum would be related to his attitude toward nuclear power, the use of nuclear energy, the construction of more nuclear power plants, and a halt in the operation of all nuclear power plants. In fact, each of these attitudes was found to be strongly related to voting behavior; the correlation ranged from .60 to .70. However, their consideration in addition to intentions again failed to improve prediction of voting behavior. In fact, each of the four traditional attitudes was found to be highly related to intentions as well as to attitudes toward voting *yes* and to subjective norms. Thus, it may be argued that traditional attitudes predicted voting behavior because they were related to the more immediate determinants of that behavior. Although it is beyond the scope of this chapter, an analysis of the beliefs that underlie attitudes toward voting *yes* and subjective norms concerning such a vote supports this argument. For example, the more positive a voter's attitude was toward nuclear power, the more likely he was to believe that a *yes* vote would harm the economy and increase the likelihood of a future energy shortage, and the less likely he was to believe that a *yes* vote would reduce nuclear risk or increase safety.[9]

To summarize briefly, when confronted with the decision to support or oppose the Oregon Nuclear Safeguards Referendum, voters considered the likely consequences of voting *yes* and, to a lesser extent, the normative prescriptions of important referents. Attitudes and subjective norms based on these beliefs led to accurate predictions of intentions, and these intentions were, in turn, highly related to actual voting behavior. By examining the beliefs of supporters and opponents of the initiative, we were able to account for their differential voting behavior. Although voters were in general agreement about the legislative and legal implications of the proposition, they disagreed markedly in their beliefs concerning the effects of a *yes* vote on the economy, on the energy shortage, and on nuclear safety.

## SUMMARY AND CONCLUSION

The data presented in this and the previous chapters provide a good illustration of the way in which the same fundamental set of variables can be used to analyze voting behavior in very different contexts. To be sure, comparing different types of elections uncovers some very important substantive differences. In an American presidential election, voting behavior is strongly influenced by beliefs that voting for a given candidate will lead to the implementation of certain policies. British voters are influenced not only by policy considerations of this kind but also by the tactical implications of their votes. That is, voting behavior in Great Britain is determined in part by beliefs that voting for a certain candidate will influence the composition of the government. Still different considerations are involved in the case of voting in a referendum. Here the voter appears primarily concerned with the consequences of implementing the proposed policy.

To illustrate these different types of considerations, in the American presidential election of 1976, some of the salient beliefs that influenced voting choice had to do with the likelihood that voting for Carter or Ford would lead to tax reforms, a reduction in the defense budget, and a national health care system. In our British election study we found that voters were guided in part by their beliefs that voting for a candidate in their constituency would raise or lower the chances of a Labour government, a Liberal government, a Conservative government, or some form of coalition government. Finally, in the Oregon Nuclear

---

[9]This does not necessarily imply that attitudes toward nuclear power determined beliefs about a *yes* vote. It is conceivable that a different set of beliefs provided the basis for both the attitude toward nuclear power and the beliefs (or outcome evaluations) concerning a *yes* vote.

Safeguards Referendum, salient beliefs distinguishing between supporters and opponents of the initiative included beliefs that casting a *yes* vote would help the state's economy and increase nucelar safety.

Even within a given type of voting situation, the content of the particular beliefs that are salient will vary from election to election. These beliefs will reflect the concerns of the public at the time of the election and the issues that are raised in the course of the campaign. Some of the salient beliefs in past presidential elections have concerned civil rights, relations with Cuba, and the wars in Korea and Viet Nam, while more recently questions concerning unemployment, inflation, and honesty in government have become salient issues. Even more obvious, the particular beliefs that are salient in a given referendum depend on the proposition under consideration. Different issues are raised by initiatives dealing with nucelar energy, gay rights, or legalized gambling.

External variables, such as demographic characteristics, party identification, global attitudes, and personality traits may be related to some of the beliefs that are salient in one campaign but unrelated to the salient beliefs in another campaign. As a result, the relation of any given external variable to voting behavior may differ from election to election. For example, we saw that party identification was virtually identical to voting intention in Great Britain and had a strong relation to voting behavior in an American presidential election but was only moderately related to voting in the Oregon Nuclear Safeguards Referendum. Clearly, then, the conventional approach with its reliance on external variables cannot provide a systematic explanation of voting behavior.

According to the theory of reasoned action, voting choice can ultimately be explained only by examining the content of the beliefs that are salient in a given election. Although these beliefs differ from election to election, they all represent beliefs about the act of casting a vote, be it a vote for a given candidate or a vote for or against a proposition. These beliefs provide the basis for the voter's attitude toward the vote, and, in conjunction with the subjective norm, this attitude leads to the formation of a voting intention and eventually determines the voting choice. Although the explanation of voting behavior differs substantively from one election to another, the basic psychological processes underlying the vote are identical.

# CHAPTER 15

Changing the
Behavior of
Alcoholics:
Effects of
persuasive
communication

Martin Fishbein
Icek Ajzen
Judy McArdle

Thus far in part 2 of this book we have shown how the theory of reasoned action can be used to explain and predict behavior in various applied settings. We saw that outcomes such as weight loss or childbirth are influenced by appropriate behaviors, although other factors must also be taken into account. In contrast, we provided evidence to show that a given behavior, be it avoiding snacks between meals, purchasing a product, or voting for a candidate, is determined by the person's intention to perform the behavior in question. Several chapters demonstrated that these intentions can be predicted from corresponding measures of attitude toward performance of the behaviors and subjective norms with respect to their performance. We also showed that attitudes toward a behavior are determined by behavioral beliefs and outcome evaluations and that subjective norms are a function of normative beliefs and motivations to comply. Finally, we presented data which showed that by examining this cognitive foundation we obtain a more detailed, substantive explanation of the behavior under consideration. Within our theory, the beliefs underlying attitudes and subjective norms represent the basic determinants of any behavior.

In many applied areas, we are interested not only in the prediction and understanding of certain behaviors but also in the development of programs to influence their likelihood of occurrence. It is beyond the scope of this chapter to review the various strategies that have been used in attempts to influence people's behavior. Suffice it to note that the majority of persuasive attempts provide individuals with information which, it is hoped, will induce them to behave in the desired manner. For example, educational programs contain information designed to get people to undertake a proper diet or to employ birth control methods; advertising is designed to influence buying behavior; political campaigns involve speeches, debates, and distribution of campaign literature, all designed to get people to vote for a given candidate or to vote for or against a certain proposition in a referendum. To state this in different terms, most strate-

This chapter is based in part on the third author's doctoral dissertation, Department of Psychology, University of Illinois at Champaign-Urbana, 1972.

gies of behavior change involve the use of one or more persuasive communications.[1]

In discussing the application of our approach to weight reduction and family planning, we described some of the implications of our theory for the development of effective programs of change. In this chapter we will discuss these implications in greater detail and try to demonstrate the utility of our approach for understanding the persuasion process and for designing effective persuasive communications.

## TRADITIONAL APPROACH TO PERSUASION

Most research on communication and persuasion can be traced to the Yale Communication Research Program under the direction of Carl I. Hovland (cf. Hovland, Janis, & Kelley, 1953; Hovland, 1957; Hovland & Janis, 1959; Hovland & Rosenberg, 1960; Sherif & Hovland, 1961). In their extended research program, Hovland and his associates investigated factors influencing the effectiveness of persuasive communication. Defining communication as "the process by which an individual (the communicator) transmits stimuli (usually verbal) to modify the behavior of other individuals (the audience)," they viewed their research task as the investigation of *who* says *what* to *whom* with *what effect*. Most research thus explored how "attitude change" (the effect) is influenced by variations in the characteristics of the *source* of the communication (who), the *message* (what), and the *audience* (whom).

One basic assumption underlying this research is that the effect of a given communication depends on the extent to which it is *attended to, comprehended,* and *accepted.* Figure 15.1 summarizes the major factors identified by Hovland and his associates in their analysis of the communication and persuasion process. Note that primary concern is with "attitude change," but many different variables are subsumed under this label. The effects of source, message, and audience factors on attitude change are assumed to be mediated by attention, comprehension, and acceptance. One implication of this conceptualization is that a given manipulation may both facilitate and inhibit attitude change. A high-fear appeal, for example, may reduce attention but increase acceptance.

According to the Yale approach, "attention and comprehension determine what the recipient will *learn* concerning the content of the communicator's message; other processes, involving changes in motivation, are assumed to determine whether or not he will accept or adopt what he learns" (Hovland & Janis, 1959, p. 5). The effects of a communication, then, depend on two factors: learn-

[1]For a general discussion of change strategies, see Fishbein and Ajzen (1975, chaps. 9-11).

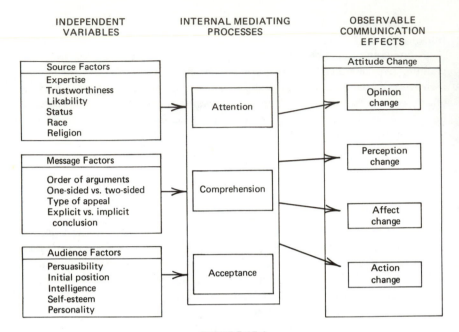

| INDEPENDENT VARIABLES | INTERNAL MEDIATING PROCESSES | OBSERVABLE COMMUNICATION EFFECTS |

**FIGURE 15.1**
Yale approach to communication and persuasion.
(Based on Janis and Hovland, 1959.)

ing of message content and acceptance of what is learned. Consistent with this approach, McGuire (1968) developed a two-factor model of persuasion which combines attention and comprehension into a single factor of reception. According to McGuire's model, the process of persuasion involves two basic steps: "reception of the message content and yielding to what is comprehended."

Many studies have thus obtained some measure of reception, usually in the form of a multiple-choice or recall test dealing with the content of the message. The second mediating factor, acceptance or yielding, has not been directly measured. Instead, the usual argument is that in the absence of differences in reception, the effect of a given manipulation on "attitude change" is due to its effect on acceptance.

Although concentrating on reception (attention and comprehension) and yielding, McGuire (1968, 1969) suggested two additional steps in the persuasion process: *retention* of the position agreed with and *action* in accordance with the retained agreement. "Attitude change" is thus regarded as a process involving five steps: *attention, comprehension, yielding, retention,* and *action.* "The receiver must go through each of these steps if communication is to have an ultimate persuasive impact, and each depends on the occurrence of the preceding step" (McGuire, 1969, p. 173). Each step is viewed as a possible dependent measure of "attitude change" in a communication and persuasion study. These *destination* variables constitute one component of the communication process. The remaining components in McGuire's analysis are *source, message, channel,* and *receiver.* Thus, following Laswell (1948) and using an approach similar to the earlier Yale analysis, he conceptualized the communication process in terms of who (source) says what (message) to whom (receiver) how (channel) and with what effect (destination).

## Behavior Change Within the Traditional Approach

Information is the essence of the persuasion process. Receivers are exposed to a persuasive communication in the hope that they will be influenced by the information it contains. The effectiveness of the message depends in large measure on the nature of this information. Since the present chapter focuses primarily on change in behavior, the first issue that must be addressed concerns the type of information required to produce the desired change. Unfortunately, the traditional approach has virtually nothing to say on this topic. In fact, it is disconcerting to find that message content has rarely been the focus of much attention. Construction of an effective message has been left largely to the intuitive devices of the investigator, while most communication and persuasion research has been devoted to the discovery of factors that influence the effectiveness of the message as constructed.

For example, there have been literally hundreds of studies conducted to investigate the effects of "communicator credibility." Typically, the experimenter constructs a message that he assumes will produce attitude change. Once the message has been constructed, the actual experiment is relatively straightforward: the same message is given to two groups of subjects; one group is told that the communicator is a "high credibility source" (an expert) and the other is told the communicator is a "low credibility source" (a charlatan). The two groups are then compared in terms of the amount of change the message produced. Other studies have investigated "audience effects." A given message is presented to receivers who are high or low in self-esteem, intelligence, anxiety, or need for achievement. Here, the investigator's interest is in the relative amount of change the message produces in the different audiences.

Clearly, in studies of this kind message content is largely irrelevant. To be sure, global features of the message, such as order of presentation and type of appeal (e.g., high versus low fear appeal), have not escaped scrutiny, but few attempts have been made to take account of the items of information actually contained in the message. It follows that the traditional approach provides little guidance as to the information that should be included in a message designed to change people's behavior.

Unfortunately, research in the tradition of the Yale communication program has also failed to provide much information about the factors that influence the effectiveness of a *given* message. Indeed, the concerted efforts of many able and well-trained investigators have produced an accumulation of largely contradictory and inconsistent research findings with few, if any, generalizable principles of effective communication. The literature on communication and persuasion reveals virtually no consistent findings concerning the effects of any given manipulation on attitude change. For example, communicator credibility has been found to increase persuasion in some studies but not in others. Studies on such message factors as fear appeals, order of presentation, and one-sided versus two-sided messages have yielded equally inconsistent results: Variations in order of presentation sometimes produce recency effects, sometimes primacy effects, and sometimes no effects at all; a high-fear message is sometimes found to increase persuasion, sometimes to decrease persuasion, and sometimes to have the same effect as a low-fear message. The results are no more consistent when individual difference variables are considered: Chronic anxiety is sometimes found to have a positive relation, sometimes a negative relation, and sometimes no relation to the amount of persuasion. Other variables, such as distracting subjects or forewarning them that they will be exposed to a persuasive appeal, have also led to inconsistent and contradictory findings.[2]

This state of affairs may be due in part to the fact that in the traditional approach, the term *attitude* is used in a generic sense to refer not only to a person's affective feelings toward some object, but also to his cognitions or beliefs about the object, and to his conations or behavioral tendencies and actions with respect to the object (see Figure 15.1). Given this all-inclusive definition of attitude, investigators have felt free to select their dependent measures in an arbitrary fashion, so long as the measure appeared to be related to the issue under consideration. In marked contrast, throughout this book we have advocated a clear distinction between belief, attitude, intention, and behavior and we have tried to show that, although interrelated, these variables have very different determinants. The inconsistent findings in research on persuasive communication confirm this view by demonstrating that a given manipulation can have different effects on measures of belief, attitude, intention, or behavior.

Another fundamental difficulty inherent in this research may also be responsible for many of the conflicting findings reported in the literature. As we have emphasized already, investigators of the persuasion process have, with a few notable exceptions (e.g., McGuire, 1960; Wyer & Goldberg, 1970), tended to neglect the content of the message. It is our contention that the effect of varying a source, message, or receiver factor cannot be understood in isolation from the content of the message. An independent variable found to be positively related to the effectiveness of one message may be found to have little influence on, or be negatively related to, the effectiveness of another message.

Consider, for example, the case of communicator credibility. Some support for our line of reasoning can be found in a study by McCroskey (1970) who

---

[2]For reviews of this literature, see McGuire (1969), Fishbein and Ajzen (1972, 1975), and Himmelfarb and Eagly (1974).

attempted to change attitudes toward federal control of education. In one experimental condition, the message provided strong supportive evidence for its main arguments, and in another condition the arguments were stated with minimal supportive evidence. Variations in source credibility had a significant effect on attitude change only when minimal evidence was provided. When the message contained strong supportive evidence, equal amounts of attitude change were observed. It may be argued that in this latter condition the information contained in the message was sufficient to produce the desired change irrespective of the source's credibility.

As another example, consider the audience variable of self-esteem. It is conceivable that a receiver of low self-esteem will, in comparison to a high self-esteem individual, yield more to forcefully stated arguments but would yield less to arguments stated in a qualified manner. For still other arguments we may find little or no difference between high and low self-esteem receivers.

In conclusion, two problems are inherent in the traditional approach to persuasive communication: this approach fails to distinguish among beliefs, attitudes, intentions, and behavior and, for all practical purposes, it neglects the content of the message. These problems take on particular importance when our ultimate goal is to influence people's behavior. Before we can provide guidelines for the formulation of persuasive communications that will be effective in changing behavior, we must have an understanding of the factors that determine behavior. The traditional approach, however, is not based on any systematic theory of behavior. Instead, it assumes that if we can get receivers to yield to the message, they will change their beliefs, feelings, intentions, and actions; that is, they will change their attitudes (see Figure 15.1). This view of attitude change follows naturally from the multi-component conception of attitude described in chapter 2. There we saw that the multi-component view is inadequate as a basis for predicting and understanding behavior. Since this approach tells us little about the determinants of behavior, it cannot help us identify the information to which receivers of a communication must be exposed if we wish to change their behavior.

## AN ALTERNATIVE APPROACH TO BEHAVIOR CHANGE[3]

In the introduction to this chapter we reiterated our view that beliefs are the basic determinants of any behavior. It follows that, in the final analysis, behavior change is brought about by producing changes in beliefs. By influencing beliefs about the consequences of performing the behavior we can produce change in the attitude toward the behavior, and by influencing beliefs about the expecta-

[3]The discussion on the following pages draws heavily upon our previous publications (Fishbein & Ajzen, 1975, 1980).

tions of specific referents we can affect the subjective norm.[4] A change in the attitudinal or normative component is likely to be reflected in the person's intention and behavior, provided that the component affected carries a significant weight in the prediction of the intention. Two possible strategies suggest themselves with regard to the beliefs that are singled out for change: We can try to influence some of the beliefs that are salient in a subject population or try to introduce novel, previously nonsalient, beliefs.

A concrete example may be instructive. Suppose that a communicator would like to induce receivers of his message to donate blood. If he used our approach, he would assess the salient beliefs held by members of his target population, obtaining a set of behavioral beliefs concerning the perceived consequences of donating blood (e.g., "donating blood is painful," "donating blood helps save lives") and a set of normative beliefs with respect to this behavior (e.g., "my spouse thinks I should not donate blood," "my friends think I should donate blood"). In constructing his message, the communicator could attempt to change any one of these salient beliefs in the appropriate direction. Thus, in an attempt to produce more favorable attitudes toward this behavior, he could try to decrease the receivers' subjective probabilities that donating blood is painful. Alternatively, he could try to induce a more favorable subjective norm by increasing the receivers' subjective probabilities that their spouses think they should donate blood.

The second strategy open to the communicator involves the introduction of previously nonsalient beliefs or of beliefs that were salient for only a minority of the target population. For example, the communicator might induce the receivers to believe that donating blood will assure them of access to the blood bank should they ever need it and that the President of the United States thinks they should donate blood. Assuming that receivers positively evaluate having access to the blood bank, this communication should produce more favorable attitudes toward donating blood. In the same manner, if the receivers are highly motivated to comply with the President, the communication should result in more favorable subjective norms.

In conclusion, to influence an intention or the corresponding behavior, it is necessary to change either behavioral beliefs or normative beliefs or both. From our point of view, a message can be effective in changing a behavior only if it influences these *primary beliefs,* that is, the beliefs that, from a theoretical point

---

[4]Note that attitudes toward the behavior can also be influenced by changing outcome evaluations and that subjective norms can also be influenced by changing motivations to comply with specific referents. However, in both cases we must ultimately again change beliefs. Since the evaluation of an outcome is nothing but the person's attitude toward that outcome, influencing the evaluation requires changing beliefs about the outcome. Although the determinants of motivation to comply are less well understood, it seems clear that a person's motivation to comply with a given referent is some function of his beliefs about that referent and, in particular, beliefs about the referent's power, expertise, trustworthiness, etc.

of view, are functionally related to (or are primary determinants of) the behavior in question. To be effective, therefore, a persuasive communication designed to change intentions or overt behavior should contain information linking the behavior to various positive or negative outcomes, or it should provide information about the normative expectations of specific referents.[5]

It is important to note that the attitude toward a behavior is based on the *total set* of beliefs about performing the behavior and that the subjective norm is similarly determined by the *total set* of normative beliefs. Although a message that is successful in changing one or two behavioral beliefs concerning the behavior's consequences may at times influence the person's attitude toward the behavior, it will often have little or no effect since the changes produced as intended may be offset by unexpected changes in other relevant beliefs. For the same reason, a message that influences one or two normative beliefs may also have little effect on the subjective norm. Only when the message brings about a shift in the summed products across the total set of underlying beliefs can it be expected to influence attitudes or subjective norms and, hence, intentions and behavior.

## Structure and Content of a Persuasive Communication

From our point of view, the purpose of a persuasive communication is to change the primary beliefs that underlie one or more behaviors. The present section deals with the cognitive processes that mediate the message's effects on primary beliefs. Before turning to this analysis, however, we must take a brief look at the structure of a persuasive communication.

**Structure of a message**. As a general rule, a message consists of two parts: a set of *arguments* and factual *evidence* designed to support the arguments. When the aim of the message is to change intention or behavior, the message will often also include one or more recommended actions.

As an illustration, consider the persuasive communication used by Eagly (1974) in a series of experiments dealing with, among other things, the discrepancy of the source's position from that of the receiver.[6] In one study, this message was used in an attempt to change receivers' acceptance of the conclusion that either 6, 4, or 2 hours of sleep were desirable for the average adult for maximum happiness, well-being, and success in life. In a second study, the same mes-

---

[5]It is of the utmost importance to realize that the primary beliefs determining specific intentions and behaviors differ greatly from the beliefs that are functionally related to attitude toward a target and that both types of beliefs may bear little resemblance to the primary beliefs that are inferentially related to a conclusion. In the case of attitude toward a target, the appropriate primary beliefs are beliefs linking the target to various positive or negative attributes, and if the aim of the message is to change a belief or conclusion, other beliefs that are inferentially related to the conclusion have to be changed.

[6]We are grateful to Alice Eagly for providing us with the text of her message.

sage was used to change the conclusion that the *receiver* (rather than the average adult) should get 6 hours or 1 hour of sleep.

After stating the general conclusion, the message proceeded with a series of six arguments, each supported by several items of "factual" evidence. The six arguments can be paraphrased as follows:

1. The amount we sleep is culturally determined and arbitrary.
2. How rested a person feels when he wakes up depends on how much "rapid eye movement" sleep he gets rather than his total amount of sleep.
3. A person can sleep fewer hours per day if he learns to take naps rather than sleep for one 8-hour period.
4. Sleeping for long periods is bad for a person physically.
5. People often sleep as a defensive escape from their problems.
6. Many successful people sleep considerably less than 8 hours.

To bolster these arguments, the message provided various factual items of evidence. For example, the argument that the amount we sleep is culturally determined and arbitrary was supported by the following set of statements:

People believe that 8 hours are necessary because they have been told this is so and have been taught to sleep a lot when they were children. A University of California anthropologist pointed out that in some cultures the norm is markedly less sleep than 8 hours, while in other cultures people are expected to sleep even more than in our society. Also, anthropologists point out that the amount of sleep people get varies with the season, especially for primitive and peasant people who live close to the land—they sleep when it is dark, so sleep more in the winter. Northern people, like Lapplanders and Eskimos, sleep, according to one study, 1.8 times more in the winter than in the summer. In industrialized civilizations, we are not so affected by these rhythms of nature; sleep patterns become more purely cultural.

In constructing a message of this kind, two basic assumptions are made: first, that acceptance of the supportive evidence will result in acceptance of the arguments and, second, that acceptance of the arguments will lead to a change in the conclusion. Unfortunately, these assumptions are rarely, if ever, tested. Although the investigator will usually try his best to construct an effective message, we saw earlier that he has no clear guidelines to aid him in the selection of arguments and appropriate evidence. As a result, he may select arguments and evidence that fail to meet the two preceding assumptions and, thus, the message may be ineffective.

Some of the difficulties created by this state of affairs can be illustrated with respect to Eagly's sleep communication described earlier. She used the same set of six arguments in attempts to change quite different conclusions. Clearly, however, an argument or set of arguments perceived to be supportive of one conclusion may not be perceived as supportive of some other conclusion. For example, an argument which leads to a change in the conclusion that "6 hours of sleep are desirable for the average adult for maximum happiness, well-being, and success in life" may have much less effect on the conclusion advocating 2 hours of sleep for the same goals, or on the conclusion that the *receiver* should get 6 hours of sleep. The situation would have been even more problematic if the dependent variable had been attitude toward sleep, intention to sleep less, or actual sleeping behavior. The reason is that these variables are increasingly removed from the arguments contained in the communication. The belief that a certain amount of sleep is necessary is only one of the beliefs that may determine attitude toward sleeping less, which in turn is only one of the two major determinants of sleeping intention and behavior. Yet, since the traditional approach considers all of these variables to be expressions of attitude, it would have to assume that they would all be equally affected by the communication.

## Processing of Message Content

According to our approach, the first step in the construction of a persuasive communication for the purpose of changing behavior is the selection of an appropriate set of arguments; that is, the arguments selected should either constitute some of the primary beliefs underlying the behavior, or they should be known to determine or influence those primary beliefs.

One of the problems in research on communication and persuasion is that arguments are usually selected not on the basis of a systematic and empirically validated theory but quite arbitrarily on the basis of often fallacious assumptions and intuition. This can be seen most clearly in many messages designed to change one or more specific behaviors. Throughout this book we have seen that the assumption of a strong relation between a person's attitude toward a target and any given behavior with respect to that target is clearly unwarranted. Still, the arguments of a message intended to influence a specific behavior are often belief statements that link the target of the behavior to various positive or negative attributes. Such a message may be quite effective in changing the receiver's attitude toward the target, since the arguments it contains constitute primary beliefs for this variable; but it is unlikely to have the desired effect on behavior.[7] In short, to produce a change in behavior or behavioral intention, the arguments included in the message must attack primary beliefs about performance of the behavior and not about the attributes of the target of the behavior.

**Acceptance, yielding, and impact effects**. The mere presentation of an argument (without any supportive evidence) may lead to a change in the corresponding belief of the receiver, particularly if it is a novel, previously nonsalient argument. It

[7]As we saw in our discussion of consumer and political behavior (chapters 12 and 13), exceptions to this rule occur when the arguments influence not only beliefs about the target but also beliefs about the behavior.

is important, however, to distinguish between *acceptance* of an argument and *yielding*, that is, change in the corresponding belief.[8] Consider, for example, the argument that "smoking is hazardous to your health." A person may strongly believe (i.e., accept) that smoking is hazardous to health without ever having been exposed to the message containing the argument in question. Yielding, on the other hand, refers to the change in acceptance of the belief statement resulting from exposure to the message. Thus, a receiver who shifted her subjective probability that smoking is dangerous to health from .40 to .70 would exhibit yielding of 30 percentage points on the probability scale.

In addition to acceptance of, and yielding to, a persuasive argument, the presentation of an argument may have indirect effects; that is, it may have *impact effects* on one or more other beliefs that were not explicitly mentioned. For example, suppose that a television commercial contains the statement, "Detergent $X$ is strong." Apart from any possible yielding to this argument, the receiver may also infer that "detergent $X$ is harmful to clothes," and the persuasive effect of the message may be very different from that intended. Clearly, to fully understand the effects of a persuasive communication it is important to assess not only the receiver's acceptance of and yielding to the arguments it contains but also its impact effects on other, unmentioned, primary beliefs.

To summarize briefly, we postulate that it is possible to specify a set of primary beliefs that serve as the potential determinants of a given behavior. These beliefs concern the consequences of performing the behavior and the normative prescriptions of relevant referents. To be effective, a message must influence these primary beliefs. The effects of the message can be direct in that it can produce acceptance of and yielding to the arguments it contains. Equally important, the message may have indirect effects by its impact on primary beliefs not explicitly mentioned in the communication. Some of these impact effects may, of course, be intended, but others may not have been foreseen and they may produce unexpected results. Changing a few primary beliefs, however, may not be enough to bring about change in behavior. To be effective, the persuasive communication must change a sufficient number of primary beliefs to influence the attitude toward the behavior or the subjective norm. Further, a change in either component will influence the intention only if it carries a significant weight in the prediction of that intention. Finally, the extent to which a change in intention will result in behavioral change depends on the strength of the intention-behavior relation. The main point to be made is that many steps intervene between the presentation of information and change in behavior. A complete account of persuasive communication must consider all of these processes that intervene between exposure to information and behavioral change.

---

[8]The term *yielding* is used here in a more restricted sense than is usually implied (e.g., McGuire, 1968). We use it to refer solely to change in the subjective probability associated with a belief corresponding directly to a statement contained in the message.

## AN EMPIRICAL STUDY OF BEHAVIOR CHANGE

Many issues raised in the preceding discussion are highlighted in a study conducted in a V.A. hospital. In this hospital, only 50% of the patients diagnosed as alcoholic were willing to be transferred to the hospital's Alcoholic Treatment Unit (ATU). A decision was made to use persuasive communication in order to encourage more alcoholics to sign up for the unit.

It is often assumed that behavioral change of this kind can be brought about by a persuasive communication based on the "health-belief model." This model, as described by Rosenstock (1974), states that an individual should be most likely to take action to avoid a disease if he believes that 1) he is personally *susceptible* to the disease, 2) that the occurrence of the disease would have at least *moderately severe negative consequences* on some aspect of his life, and 3) that taking a particular action would be *beneficial* to reducing his susceptibility.

An appeal based on this model would emphasize the dangers of a given course of action, suggest how this action can be avoided, and recommend an alternative course of action. In the present context, the message would 1) emphasize the negative consequences of continued drinking, 2) tell the patients that they can gain control over their drinking by joining the ATU's program, and 3) recommend that they sign up for the Alcoholic Treatment Unit.

From our point of view, such a message can only be of questionable effectiveness. According to the theory of reasoned action, to increase the likelihood that a person will sign up for the ATU, we have to change the primary beliefs that are functionally related to this behavior. Ideally, we would conduct a pilot study in which salient beliefs are elicited and a standard questionnaire based on these beliefs is constructed and administered.[9] Responses to the questionnaire are used to confirm the validity of our theory within the behavioral domain under consideration. At the same time, this pilot study provides information about the relative weights of the attitudinal and normative components and permits us to identify the salient beliefs that best discriminate between respondents who intend and those who do not intend to perform the behavior in question. On the basis of this information we can decide which of the two components to attack and then construct a message (or messages) containing information designed to change the primary beliefs underlying the component (or components) selected.[10]

As we shall see, signing up for the ATU was found to be under somewhat more attitudinal than normative control and a decision was therefore made to attack the attitudinal component in our attempts to change the behavior. Gener-

---

[9] The questionnaire would contain measures of all the components in our theory: belief strength, outcome evaluations, motivations to comply, attitude toward the behavior, subjective norm, and intention (see appendix A).

[10] Recall that the message can either attempt to change salient beliefs or provide information about primary beliefs that are not salient.

ally speaking, in order to make a patient more favorable toward signing up, we can provide him with information that either will increase his beliefs that signing up for the ATU will lead to positive consequences or will decrease his beliefs that signing up for the ATU will lead to negative consequences. Alternatively, we can try to convince him that not signing up for the ATU would lead to negative consequences or prevent the occurrence of positive consequences.

The main point to be made is that in order to be effective a persuasive communication must change the receivers' primary beliefs about signing up or not signing up for the ATU. In contrast, the appeal based on the health-belief model provides information about continued drinking, and although it does state that one can gain control over drinking by joining the ATU, it never directly attacks the receiver's beliefs about signing up for the ATU. At best, the receiver might *infer* that signing up for the ATU will prevent the negative consequences of continued drinking described in the message or that not signing up will lead to those negative consequences. In other words, even if the message based on the health-belief model were accepted and yielded to, it would change the patient's behavior only if it had an impact effect on beliefs about signing up or not signing up. From our point of view there is no reason to rely on such indirect effects when it is possible to design a communication that directly attacks the receiver's beliefs concerning the consequences of signing up or not signing up for the ATU.

The Persuasive Appeals

To be able to test these ideas, we constructed three persuasive communications. The first, which we shall call the *traditional appeal,* was based on the health-belief model and was comprised of 10 major arguments, each linking continued drinking to a different negative consequence (e.g., deterioration of physical health, deterioration of relationships with family, and less freedom within the hospital). The message then argued that the ATU had a program that could help patients gain control over their drinking, and, finally, it recommended that they "sign up for the ATU now." The second message, which we shall call the *negative appeal,* was also comprised of 10 major arguments. Here, however, each statement linked not signing up for the ATU with a different negative consequence. In fact, not signing up for the ATU was linked with the same 10 negative consequences that appeared in the traditional appeal (e.g., not signing up for the ATU will lead to a deterioration of your physical health and it will lead to less freedom within the hospital). The negative message also ended with the recommendation to "sign up for the ATU now." The third message, which we shall call the *positive appeal,* was the mirror image of the negative message. It, too, was comprised of 10 major arguments, but each linked signing up for the ATU with a positive consequence. These consequences were the direct opposites of the negative consequences (e.g., signing up for the ATU will improve your physical health, will give you more freedom within the hospital, etc.). Once again, the positive message also ended with the specific recommendation to "sign up for the ATU now."

Note that the information contained in the three messages was virtually identical, except that the traditional appeal focused on "continued drinking," the negative appeal on "not signing up for the ATU," and the positive appeal on "signing up for the ATU." The comparability of the three messages can be seen in Table 15.1, which presents the closing paragraph of each message. This paragraph summarizes the 10 basic arguments contained in each message and states the specific recommendation to "sign up for the ATU now."

### TABLE 15.1
#### Closing Paragraphs Summarizing the Content of the Traditional, Negative, and Positive Appeals

TRADITIONAL APPEAL

So, in closing, I would like to stress that continuing to drink alcohol means that you are not only refusing to face reality but that you are also losing the opportunity of ever solving your basic problem. In fact, continued drinking, in itself, will lead to ruined physical and mental health as well as to a poorer relationship with your family and your employer. Also, as long as you stay *in* the hospital, your continued drinking means that you will receive less personal attention from the hospital staff, less help with your personal problems, less self-government, less freedom to leave the hospital, and less opportunity to be with men who, like yourself, are in good contact with reality. I believe you now understand that you will only be hurtung yourself if you continue drinking alcohol. Joining the ATU will give you the opportunity to solve your drinking problem. Therefore, I *urge* you to sign up for the ATU *now!*

NEGATIVE APPEAL

So, in closing, I would like to stress that by not signing up for the ATU, you are not only refusing to face reality but you also are losing the opportunity to learn to control your drinking. Thus, not signing up for the ATU will lead to ruined physical and mental health as well as to a poorer relationship with your family and your employer. Also, as long as you stay *in* the hospital, your not signing up for the ATU means that you will receive less personal attention from the hospital staff, less help with your personal problems, less self-government, less freedom to leave the hospital, and less opportunity to be with men who, like yourself, are in good contact with reality. I believe you now understand that you will only be hurting yourself if you don't sign up for the ATU. Therefore, I *urge* you to sign up for the ATU *now!*

POSITIVE APPEAL

So, in closing, I would like to stress that signing up for the ATU is a step in the right direction since the ATU gives you the opportunity to learn to control your drinking. Thus, signing up for the ATU will lead to improved physical and mental health, as well as to a better relationship with your family and your employer. Also, as long as you stay *in* the hospital, your signing up for the ATU means that you will receive more personal attention from the hospital staff, more help with your personal problems, more self-government in the hospital, more freedom to leave the hospital, and more opportunity to be with men who, like yourself, are in good contact with reality. I believe you now understand that you will be helping yourself if you sign up for the ATU. Therefore, I *urge* you to sign up for the ATU *now!*

The participants in the study were 160 male patients between the ages of 20 and 65 who were admitted to the Danville Veteran's Administration Hospital and who were diagnosed as alcoholics.[11] Within one to four days after being admitted to the hospital, each participant was approached individually and informed that the ATU offers a program to help those men for whom alcohol is in some way a problem. They were then asked to complete a short questionnaire containing, among other things, standard measures of intention to sign up for the ATU, attitudes toward signing up and toward not signing up for the ATU, and subjective norm with respect to signing versus not signing up.[12] After completing the survey, each patient was presented a preliminary sign-up sheet for admission to the ATU and asked to sign his name and circle "Do" or "Do Not," depending upon whether or not he wanted to be transferred to the ATU. This pretest behavioroid measure was used to categorize the patients into those who, before exposure to a persuasive appeal, were willing or were unwilling to be transferred. Half of the subjects were initially willing and half were initially unwilling to be transferred to the ATU.

The relations among behavior, intention, differential attitude (attitude toward signing up minus attitude toward not signing up), and the differential measure of subjective norm are shown in Figure 15.2. It can be seen that the patient's intention to sign up for the ATU was a highly accurate predictor of the behavioroid sign-up measure. This intention could in turn be predicted with a high degree of accuracy from the theory's two components, although the differential attitude toward signing up carried somewhat more weight in the prediction than did the differential subjective norm. These findings indicate that a change in attitude toward signing up or not signing up should influence the intention to sign up as well as actual sign-up behavior.

### Presentation of the Persuasive Appeal

One to four days after the pretest, small groups of patients (one to six) were assembled in a room and told that they were being screened as possible candidates for the ATU. They were assigned to one of four conditions: three experimental conditions where subjects were exposed to one of the three persuasive appeals and a no-message control. This procedure resulted in four groups of 40 patients each, half of whom had, in the pretest, indicated their willingness to be

[11]We are indebted to Dr. Paul Haskin, Director of the ATU, Danville V.A. Hospital, for his general cooperation as well as for making the tapes. We also wish to express our appreciation to the administration and staff of the Danville V.A. for their cooperation.

[12]The intention was measured on a 7-point *likely-unlikely* scale, each attitude on a 7-point *good-bad* scale, and the subjective norm was the sum over five normative beliefs, each multiplied by the motivation to comply with the referent in question (wife or ex-wife, doctor, parents, minister or priest, close friends).

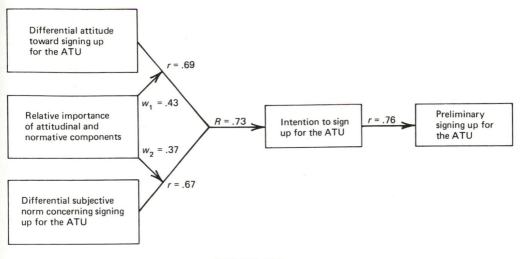

**FIGURE 15.2**
Relations among differential attitudes and subjective norms,
intentions, and preliminary sign-up behavior.

transferred to the ATU and half of whom had refused to join. At this point, the control group was given a final official sign-up sheet for admission to the ATU. The experimental groups, however, were asked to listen to one of the three tape-recorded messages presented by the director of the ATU. Immediately after the appeal, the official sign-up sheet for admission to the ATU was passed to each participant in the experimental groups. All participants were instructed to sign the sheet and to circle "Do" or "Do Not," depending on how they now felt about being transferred to the ATU.

Beliefs

Following presentation of the appeal and the sign-up for the ATU, participants were asked to help evaluate the hospital's new method of selecting men for the ATU (i.e., testing them in a group rather than individually). As part of this evaluation, they completed a posttest questionnaire which, among other things, measured their beliefs about continued drinking, about signing up as well as about not signing up for the ATU, and their attitudes toward these three behaviors. In all, 30 beliefs were assessed: 10 beliefs corresponding to the 10 main arguments in the traditional appeal, 10 beliefs corresponding to the main arguments in the negative appeal, and 10 beliefs corresponding to the main arguments in the positive appeal.

For example, with respect to the argument concerning personal attention from the hospital staff, three measures of belief were obtained at different places in the questionnaire.

1. Continuing to drink alcohol will lead to my receiving *less* personal attention from the hospital staff.

_____ : _____ : _____ : _____ : _____
I myself     I myself     undecided     I myself     I myself
strongly     disagree                   agree        strongly
disagree                                             agree

2. *Not* signing up for the Alcoholic Treatment Unit will lead to my receiving *less* personal attention from the hospital staff.

_____ : _____ : _____ : _____ : _____
I myself     I myself     undecided     I myself     I myself
strongly     disagree                   agree        strongly
disagree                                             agree

3. Signing up for the Alcoholic Treatment Unit will lead to my receiving *more* personal attention from the hospital staff.

_____ : _____ : _____ : _____ : _____
I myself     I myself     undecided     I myself     I myself
strongly     disagree                   agree        strongly
disagree                                             agree

Similar sets of three beliefs each were assessed with respect to the remaining nine major arguments. Each belief scale was scored from $-2$ (strongly disagree) through 0 (undecided) to $+2$ (strongly agree).

**Acceptance of message content.** The first question to be asked concerns the degree to which the patients accepted (i.e., believed) the 10 major arguments contained in the message to which they were exposed. Table 15.2 shows average acceptance scores for these 10 arguments; the scores could range from $-20$ to $+20$. It can be seen that, in terms of overall acceptance, there were no significant differences between the three appeals, although there was a tendency for receivers of the traditional appeal to agree more with the 10 arguments contained in their message. Predictably, participants who were initially willing to sign up for the ATU were significantly more likely to believe the content of the message they heard than were initially unwilling participants ($M = 12.77$ vs. 3.20). Perhaps most important, even participants who were initially unwilling to be transferred revealed quite strong acceptance of the 10 arguments contained in the traditional appeal ($M = 7.10$). That is, unwilling participants exposed to the traditional appeal were likely to agree that continued drinking would lead to negative consequences. In contrast, unwilling patients exposed to the positive or negative appeals were unlikely to believe the arguments concerning positive consequences of signing up or negative consequences of not signing up, respectively.[13]

[13]Statistically, this was revealed in a significant interaction between initial willingness and type of appeal.

**TABLE 15.2**
Acceptance of Message Content: Average Belief Strength

| INITIAL WILLINGNESS TO SIGN UP | TYPE OF APPEAL | | | |
|---|---|---|---|---|
| | Traditional | Negative | Positive | Total |
| Willing | 12.45 | 11.95 | 13.90 | 12.77 |
| Unwilling | 7.10 | 2.50 | .00 | 3.20 |
| Overall acceptance | 9.78 | 7.23 | 6.95 | |

**Yielding and impact**. From our point of view, however, the effectiveness of a given message depends not so much on the degree to which its content is accepted, but on its ability to produce *changes* in primary beliefs—in the present case, beliefs about signing up and about not signing up for the ATU. To obtain estimates of change in those beliefs, we compared the beliefs of patients who were exposed to one of the messages with the corresponding beliefs of patients in the no-message control group.

Table 15.3 shows the average estimated change in primary beliefs about signing up for the ATU and about not signing up that resulted from exposure to each message. First, in contrast to acceptance (see Table 15.2), there was no significant difference in the amount of belief change for respondents initially willing or unwilling to sign up for the ATU. There were, however, marked differences in amount of primary belief change produced by the different messages. With respect to beliefs about both signing up and not signing up, the negative appeal was most effective, followed by the positive appeal. The traditional appeal, however, had unanticipated and undesirable effects. In comparison to the control group, patients exposed to the traditional appeal were actually *less* likely to believe that signing up would lead to positive consequences or that not signing up would lead to negative consequences.

It is important to realize that these effects of the traditional appeal represent *impact effects* (rather than yielding to the message) since none of the beliefs in question were contained in the traditional message.[14] For the same reason, the effects of the negative appeal on beliefs about signing up, as well as the effects of the positive appeal on beliefs about not signing up, also represent impact effects. In contrast, the effects of the positive appeal on beliefs about signing up and the effects of the negative appeal on beliefs about not signing up represent *yielding* to arguments actually contained in the message. Table 15.3 shows that patients not only yielded most to the content of the negative appeal but that this appeal also had a substantial impact on unmentioned beliefs.

In sum, then, all three appeals produced significant changes in primary beliefs about signing up and not signing up. As a result of both yielding and impact

[14]In contrast to the strong acceptance of arguments about continued drinking contained in the traditional appeal, there was only relatively little *yielding* to (i.e., change in acceptance of) these arguments. This shows that a message will usually produce little change in beliefs if the receivers already agree with most of the arguments it contains.

**TABLE 15.3**

**Mean Change in Beliefs About Signing Up and Not Signing Up for the ATU**

| INITIAL WILLINGNESS TO SIGN UP | BELIEFS ABOUT SIGNING UP: TYPE OF APPEAL | | | BELIEFS ABOUT NOT SIGNING UP: TYPE OF APPEAL | | | Total |
|---|---|---|---|---|---|---|---|
| | Traditional[b] | Negative[b] | Positive[a] | Traditional[b] | Negative[a] | Positive[b] | |
| Willing | −1.65 | 3.65 | 3.55 | −.80 | 5.70 | 3.80 | 2.38 |
| Unwilling | −2.00 | 6.45 | .80 | −1.30 | 6.95 | .85 | 1.96 |
| Overall change | −1.83 | 5.04 | 2.17 | −1.05 | 6.35 | 2.33 | |

[a]Means in these columns reflect yielding to message content.
[b]Means in these columns reflect impact effects on unmentioned beliefs.

effects, the negative and positive appeals strengthened the patient's beliefs that signing up would lead to desirable consequences and that not signing up would lead to undesirable consequences; the effect of the negative appeal on these beliefs was found to be significantly greater than that of the positive appeal. The traditional appeal also had a significant impact on the primary beliefs, but in this case the direction of change was opposite to the purpose of the communication.

### Attitude Change

Given these changes in primary beliefs, we would expect corresponding changes in the differential attitude toward signing up (i.e., attitude toward signing up for the ATU minus attitude toward not signing up). Specifically, while attitudes should remain relatively stable in the no-message control group, the differential attitudes toward signing up should become more favorable as a result of exposure to the negative and positive appeals but less favorable as a result of exposure to the traditional appeal.

Table 15.4 shows that the obtained changes in differential attitudes were consistent with these expectations. Note also that as in the case of change in primary beliefs, there were no significant differences in attitude change between patients initially willing or unwilling to sign up for the ATU.

The effects of the persuasive appeals on differential attitude change can be clearly seen in Figure 15.3, which shows the pretest and posttest attitudes in the four experimental conditions.

### Behavior Change

Signing up for the Alcoholic Treatment Unit was found to reflect the changes in differential attitudes. Table 15.5 presents the percentage of patients who signed up for the ATU following the persuasive appeal. As might be expected, participants who initially expressed willingness to be transferred were significantly more likely to actually sign up for the ATU (82.5%) than were the initially unwilling participants (13.7%).

**TABLE 15.4**
Mean Change in Differential Attitude Toward Signing up for the ATU

| INITIAL WILLINGNESS TO SIGN UP | TYPE OF APPEAL | | | | |
|---|---|---|---|---|---|
| | Traditional | Negative | Positive | Control | Total |
| Willing | −.80 | 1.20 | 1.30 | .50 | .55 |
| Unwilling | −.80 | 1.15 | .40 | .05 | .20 |
| Overall change | −.80 | 1.18 | .85 | .28 | |

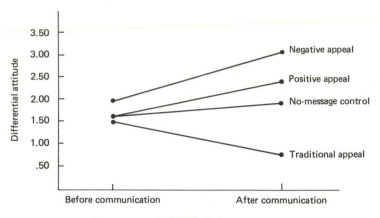

**FIGURE 15.3**
Changes in differential attitudes toward signing up for the ATU.

Considering only those patients who initially indicated that they were not willing to transfer to the ATU, none in the no-message control group changed their mind. The traditional appeal was unsuccessful in increasing the signing rate appreciably (5% signed) but both the positive message (20%) and the negative message (30%) significantly increased signing behavior. Turning to the participants who were initially willing to be transferred to the ATU, one in the no-message control (5%), one receiving the positive appeal (5%), and none receiving the negative appeal changed their minds. In marked contrast, 50% of the initially willing patients who received the traditional appeal did not sign up for the ATU. This "boomerang effect" was highly significant ($p < .01$). Overall, therefore, the posttest behavior of patients in the no-message control group was consistent with their pretest behavior; the negative and positive appeals significantly increased signing behavior, while the traditional appeal significantly reduced signing behavior. These effects of the different appeals on actual behavior are shown in Figure 15.4.

**TABLE 15.5**
Percentage of Participants Who Signed up for the ATU

| INITIAL WILLINGNESS TO SIGN UP | TYPE OF APPEAL | | | | |
|---|---|---|---|---|---|
| | *Traditional* | *Negative* | *Positive* | *Control* | *Total* |
| Willing | 50% | 100% | 95% | 95% | 82.5% |
| Unwilling | 5% | 30% | 20% | 0% | 13.7% |
| Overall percentage | 27.5% | 65% | 57.5% | 47.5% | |

238

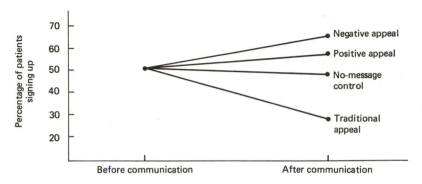

**FIGURE 15.4**
Effects of different appeals on actual signing up for the ATU.

## SUMMARY AND CONCLUSION

In this chapter we have tried to show how the theory of reasoned action can be applied to the problem of changing behavior through persuasive communication. According to the theory, the ultimate determinants of any behavior are behavioral beliefs concerning its consequences and normative beliefs concerning the prescriptions of relevant others. To influence a person's behavior, therefore, it is necessary to change these primary beliefs. By producing sufficient change in primary beliefs we should be able to influence the person's attitude toward performing the behavior or her subjective norm with respect to it. Depending on their relative weights, changes in these components should then lead to changes in intentions and actual behavior.

The first step toward producing behavioral change is the identification of a set of primary beliefs relevant for the behavior in question. Once identified, these beliefs can serve as the basic arguments in a persuasive communication. Alternatively, the message can attempt to change primary beliefs indirectly by presenting other arguments known to be related to the primary beliefs.[15] Thus, one advantage of our approach is that it provides guidelines for the construction of a persuasive communication.

The effectiveness of a message depends on the extent to which it produces the desired changes in primary beliefs and on the degree to which the assumptions linking these beliefs to attitudes, subjective norms, intentions, and behavior

[15]See for example McGuire (1960) and Wyer and Goldberg (1970) on the change of beliefs through the use of arguments based on syllogistic reasoning.

are met. Acceptance of arguments contained in the message does not guarantee the desired change in primary beliefs. Even if the arguments correspond to primary beliefs, their acceptance does not necessarily indicate *change,* that is, yielding to message content. Moreover, whether or not the message is accepted, it may have impact effects on unmentioned primary beliefs. To fully understand the effects of a message, therefore, it is important to distinguish between acceptance, yielding, and impact. We can then trace the changes in primary beliefs to changes in attitudes and subjective norms, and further to changes in intentions and behavior.

We illustrated our approach by describing a study which attempted to encourage alcoholics to sign up for a treatment program. Three persuasive communications were constructed. Two were based on our approach in that they used arguments corresponding to primary beliefs about signing up for the program (positive appeal) or not signing up (negative appeal). The third, based on the "health-belief model," pointed to the dangers of continued drinking and argued that patients could gain control over drinking by signing up for the program. This traditional appeal could at best have had impact effects since it did not directly attack the primary beliefs. The results of the study showed that the positive and negative appeals increased the number of patients who signed up for the treatment program while the traditional appeal actually lowered that number.

We described the traditional approach to persuasive communication and we noted that it was not based on a systematic theory of behavior and, hence, could not provide guidelines for formulating the arguments of a persuasive message. It is interesting to note that the traditional approach cannot account for the findings of our study. According to this approach, the superiority of the positive and negative appeals must be due either to greater reception of these messages or to greater acceptance of their contents. These mediating processes are in turn assumed to be influenced by such factors as interest in the message, arousal, and communicator credibility.

To test these ideas, participants were asked to rate their interest in the message they had heard, the credibility of the communicator, and the amount of arousal created by the message. In addition, they were given a reception test in which they were asked whether the communication had contained each of 15 statements—the 10 major arguments that had actually been part of their communication and 5 additional arguments. Interest in the message and perceived communicator credibility did not differ significantly as a function of the type of appeal to which patients were exposed. These factors therefore cannot account for the persuasive effects of the three appeals.

The three appeals did, however, produce different degrees of reported arousal. Greatest arousal was produced by the negative message, followed closely by the traditional appeal; least arousal was produced by the positive appeal. Message type also had a significant effect on reception, with the positive appeal resulting in most accurate reception (correct on 11.85 items out of the possible 15), followed by the traditional appeal (11.10 correct), and the negative appeal (10.43 correct). Consistent with expectations based on the traditional approach, increased arousal was associated with less accurate reception ($r = -.26$).

Again, however, these effects cannot account for the differences in behavioral change. Whereas the traditional appeal was intermediate in both arousal and reception, it had the least desirable persuasive effect. Since neither arousal nor reception can explain the obtained results, a traditional analysis must assume that they are due to differences in acceptance of message content. A direct measure of acceptance showed, however, that this was not the case; all three messages were accepted to the same degree.[16] Clearly, then, the traditional approach is of little help in understanding communication and persuasion processes.

In marked contrast, the effects of the three appeals are easily understood within the framework of our approach. We showed that the negative message had the strongest effects on primary beliefs, in terms of both yielding and impact. Not only did receivers of the negative appeal yield to the arguments that not signing up for the treatment program would lead to negative consequences; they also inferred that signing up would lead to positive consequences. Although the effects were not as strong, the positive appeal also changed primary beliefs in the desired direction by means of both yielding to arguments contained in the message and impact on unmentioned primary beliefs.

The traditional appeal had unanticipated impact effects on primary beliefs. Receivers exposed to arguments that continued drinking leads to negative consequences inferred that they had little to gain by signing up for the treatment program and that they had little to lose by not signing up.

These changes in primary beliefs were reflected in changes in attitudes and behavior. Patients exposed to the negative appeal become most favorable to signing up for the treatment program and they were, in fact, most likely to do so. Those exposed to the positive appeal also became more favorable toward signing up, although to a lesser degree, and this change in attitude was also reflected in their behavior. Participants exposed to the traditional appeal, however, actually lowered their attitudes toward signing up, and, consistent with this change in attitude, more than half of the patients who were initially willing to sign up for the program eventually decided against it.

In sum, our approach provided the guidelines that enabled us to construct persuasive communications effective in producing behavioral change. To be sure, the most effective (negative) appeal was found to persuade only 30% of the initially unwilling patients to change their minds and sign up for the treatment program. It must be realized, however, that small as it may appear, this effect is

---

[16]McGuire (1968) replaced the term *acceptance* with *yielding*, but it is not clear whether a different process was intended. We have made a distinction between acceptance of message content and yielding to it. While there was, in fact, most yielding to the negative appeal and least to the traditional appeal, this finding cannot explain the boomerang effect of the traditional appeal.

really quite remarkable. Not only was it produced by a single exposure to a message that lasted a mere 10 minutes, but the behavior involved was far from trivial. By agreeing to be transferred to the treatment unit, patients committed themselves to take part in an eight-week program that separated them from family and friends and, in some cases, entailed a loss of income. It also had important psychological implications since it involved an admission on the part of the patient that he was an alcoholic who could not cope with his drinking problem.

# CHAPTER
# 16

## Some Final
## Comments

In this book we have described an approach to the prediction and understanding of human behavior and we have illustrated its application in a variety of behavioral domains. Basic to this approach is the view that people use the information available to them in a reasonable manner to arrive at their decisions. This is not to say that their behavior will always be reasonable or appropriate from an objective point of view. People's information is often incomplete and at times also incorrect. But we would argue that a person's behavior follows quite logically and systematically from whatever information he happens to have available.

Within our approach, this information constitutes the person's beliefs. Of the many different kinds of beliefs a person holds, we have identified two types as underlying any given action: behavioral beliefs and normative beliefs. We have tried to show that systematic processes link these beliefs to behavior by way of attitude toward the behavior, subjective norm, and intention. Each stage in the sequence follows reasonably from the preceding stage. For example, it is reasonable to feel positively about performing a behavior if you believe that its performance will lead to more good than bad outcomes. It is also reasonable to feel social pressure to not perform a behavior if you believe that people with whom you are motivated to comply think you should not perform it. Finally, it is reasonable to weigh your personal feelings (attitude) and the perceived social pressure (subjective norm) in arriving at and carrying out your intention. Taken together, the processes involved in this sequence comprise a *theory of reasoned action.*

In part 2 of this book we showed that this theory can account for behavior in such diverse areas as weight reduction, occupational choice, family planning, brand choice, voting in American and British elections as well as in referenda, and voluntary treatment programs. The studies described, however, served merely as illustrations. The theory has been applied in other domains, including use of public transportation (Thomas, 1976; Thomas, Bull, & Clark, 1978), reenlistment in military organizations (Hom, Katerberg, & Hulin, 1978; Keenan, 1976), church attendance, (King, 1975), drug abuse (Pomazal & Brown, 1977), and blood donation (Pomazal & Jaccard, 1976). Although the substantive explanation of behavior provided by the theory of reasoned action varies from one content area to another, the same basic constructs and psychological processes are involved. Moreover, we tried to show that the effects of variables external to the theory, such as demographic characteristics, personality traits, and traditional measures of attitudes toward objects, can be explained by examining their effects on beliefs, attitude toward the behavior, subjective norm, and intention. The theory of reasoned action thus provides a comprehensive framework that can help explain many of the inconsistent findings in applied social research.

At this point, some words of caution are in order. It should be clear that there are likely to be some human behaviors that cannot be explained by a theory of reasoned action. Among these behaviors are emotional outbursts and performance of well-learned skills, such as turning the pages of a book or driving a car. There may also be certain individuals for whom the theory does not apply; some people may arrive at their decisions in different ways. The accumulating evidence suggests, however, that the theory is useful for most individuals and with respect to most social behaviors. In our opinion, many behaviors which appear unplanned turn out, on closer examination, to be quite intentional. We saw in chapter 4 that low intention-behavior relations may often reflect changes in intentions rather than evidence for unplanned behavior.

A related issue concerns use of the theory as a description of human information processing. Although we take the position that beliefs determine attitudes and subjective norms and that these in turn influence intentions, we do not mean to imply that prior to performing each and every action, people systematically scrutinize the determinants of their behavior. Rather, we view the processes involved as largely automatic or implicit, and only in rare cases do we become fully aware of these processsses. Consider, for example, a person's attitude toward smoking cigarettes. As the person forms beliefs that smoking has certain advantages or disadvantages, she simultaneously and automatically also acquires a positive or negative attitude toward smoking.[1] When confronted with the opportunity to smoke, this favorable or unfavorable feeling toward smoking is directly aroused without any need on the part of the person to systematically review her beliefs about the behavior and, together with her subjective norm, the attitude influences her decision to smoke or to not smoke. Only when asked to explain her intention or behavior is she likely to become fully aware of her feelings toward smoking, of the social pressure to smoke or to not smoke, and of her behavioral and normative beliefs underlying these determinants of her decision.[2]

It may also be useful in this concluding chapter to address a different issue

---

[1] For detailed discussions of attitude formation, see Fishbein (1967b) and Fishbein and Ajzen (1975, chap. 6).

[2] In contrast, recent research (Nisbett & Wilson, 1977) suggests that even when asked, people are often unaware of *external* variables (demographic characteristics, situational factors) that influence their beliefs, attitudes, intentions, and actions.

that is frequently raised with respect to the theory of reasoned action. The issue is typically viewed in terms of general versus specific attitude measures. It is sometimes mistakenly assumed that the theory of reasoned action involves highly specific attitudes that are relevant only for a single, unique behavior. Since the theory does refer to attitude toward a behavior (rather than attitude toward an object or target), this impression is understandable. We have tried to make it clear, however, that the theory of reasoned action can be applied at any level of generality. The behavioral criterion selected by the investigator determines how specific or general his measure of attitude (as well as his measures of beliefs, intention, and subjective norm) has to be. If, for whatever reason, he is interested in predicting and understanding a single action, directed at a certain target, in a specific context, and at a given time, then of course his measure of attitude must correspond to his criterion in all of these elements. Usually, however, our interest is in much more global behaviors which are general at least with respect to context and time and often with respect to target or action as well. Thus, we may want to understand the factors determining cigarette smoking (irrespective of the brand of cigarettes, the context, the time) or discrimination against members of a minority group regardless of the specific form this discrimination takes. Here very specific attitudes would be inappropriate. Instead, we would have to assess attitudes toward smoking cigarettes or toward the minority group in question. Similarly, intentions, subjective norms, behavioral and normative beliefs would also have to correspond in their levels of generality to the behavioral criterion as defined by the investigator. The theory of reasoned action thus requires not that we assess specific attitudes but rather that our measures of attitude always correspond to our measures of behavior.

Finally, we would like to make it clear that the theory formulated in this book is still in the process of development. Many years of intensive work on attitude theory and measurement have given us a good understanding of the ways attitudes are formed and of how they can best be measured. Many questions, however, remain with respect to the normative component in our theory.

First, we are not at all certain that the measure of subjective norm proposed in this book is the best way of directly assessing perceived social pressure to perform or to not perform a behavior. Although we are convinced that perceived social pressure must be taken into account in order to explain social behavior, alternative ways of assessing that pressure might be developed. For example, research currently in progress is exploring the utility of asking people whether their important others perform the behavior under consideration instead of (or in addition to) asking them whether these important others think they should perform the behavior. The same question also applies at the level of normative beliefs, that is, the perceived normative prescription of a given individual or group.

Closely related to the latter question, there are many unresolved issues with respect to the concept of motivation to comply. For example, in this book we have conceptualized and measured motivation to comply at a very general level:

motivation to comply with a given referent irrespective of the particular behavior under consideration. We have previously argued against tying this concept to a specific behavioral prescription (Fishbein & Ajzen, 1975, p. 306) since we see such a measure of motivation to comply as playing a role similar to the weight of the normative component which is also behavior-specific. It could be argued, however, that motivation to comply is best measured at an intermediate level, that is, at the level of complying with a referent within a behavioral domain. For example, instead of asking people how much, *in general,* they want to do what, say, their friends think they should do, they could be asked how much they want to do what their friends think they should do when it comes to family planning or to politics. Here, too, research is in progress to answer these and other questions concerning the concept of motivation to comply.

Some theorists (e.g., Schwartz & Tessler, 1972; Pomazal & Jaccard, 1976) have argued that in addition to perceived social pressures, we must take into account the individual's own feeling of moral obligation or responsibility to perform the behavior under investigation. They have suggested that a measure of moral norm be added as a third component in the theory of reasoned action.[3] Similarly, Triandis (1967, 1977) has developed a theory of interpersonal behavior that may also be classified as a theory of reasoned action. In some respects, the theory is quite similar to our own, but as Triandis (1977, pp. 231-232) noted himself, it makes no attempt to be parsimoneous. In addition to attitude toward a behavior, it includes a separate measure of the perceived consequences of performing the behavior. Moreover, Triandis recognizes the importance of social determinants, but within his theory this construct involves the separate measurement of norms, roles, self-concept, moral norm, ideals, and contractual agreements.

We realize, of course, that future research may demonstrate the need to consider additional factors in our attempts to predict and understand behavior. In this book we have tried to show, however, that, when appropriately measured, attitudes and subjective norms are sufficient to predict intentions, and, at least at the present time, we see no need to expand our theory of reasoned action.

---

[3]In fact, the original statement of our theory (Fishbein, 1967a) included personal normative beliefs in addition to attitude and social normative beliefs. Research led us to drop the third component from the theory since it seemed to be little more than an alternative way of measuring behavioral intention.

# References

ABELSON, R. P. Are attitudes necessary? In B. T. King, & E. McGinnies (Eds.), *Attitudes, conflict, and social change.* New York: Academic Press, 1972, pp. 19-32.

ABELSON, R. P., ARONSON, E., McGUIRE, W. J., NEWCOMB, T. M. ROSEN-BERG, M. J., & TANNENBAUM, P. H. (Eds.), *Theories of cognitive consistency: A sourcebook.* Skokie, Ill.: Rand McNally, 1968.

AJZEN, I., & FISHBEIN, M. The prediction of behavior from attitudinal and normative variables. *Journal of Experimental Social Psychology,* 1970, *6,* 466-487.

AJZEN, I., & FISHBEIN, M. Factors influencing intentions and the intention-behavior relation. *Human Relations,* 1974, *27,* 1-15.

AJZEN, I., & FISHBEIN, M. Attitude-behavior relations: A theoretical analysis and review of empirical research. *Psychological Bulletin,* 1977, *84,* 888-918.

ALLPORT, G. W. Attitudes. In C. Murchinson (Ed.), *A handbook of social psychology.* Worchester, Mass.: Clark University Press, 1935, pp. 798-844.

BALDWIN, J. M. *Dictionary of philosophy and psychology* (3 vols.). New York: Macmillan, 1901-1905.

BASS, F. M., & TALARZYK, W. W. An attitude model for the study of brand preferences. *Journal of Marketing Research,* 1972, *9,* 93-96.

BERELSON, B., LAZARSFELD, P. F., & McPHEE, W. N. *Voting: A study of opinion formation in a presidential campaign.* Chicago: University of Chicago Press, 1954.

BETTELHEIM, G., & JANOWITZ, M. *Dynamics of prejudice: A psychological and sociological study of veterans.* New York: Harper & Row, Pub., 1950.

BIRD, C. *Social psychology.* Englewood Cliffs, N.J.: Prentice-Hall, Inc., 1940.

BOWMAN, C. H., & FISHBEIN, M. Understanding public reactions to energy proposals: An application of the Fishbein model. *Journal of Applied Social Psychology,* 1978, *8,* 319-340.

BRANNON, R. Attitudes and the prediction of behavior. In B. Seidenberg, and A. Snadowsky (Eds.), *Social psychology: An introduction.* New York: Free Press, 1976.

BUMPASS, L., & WESTOFF, C. *The later years of child bearing.* Princeton, N.J.: Princeton University Press, 1969.

BUTLER, D., & STOKES, D. *Political change in Britain: Forces shaping electoral choice.* New York: St. Martin's Press, 1969.

CALDER, B. J., & ROSS, M. *Attitudes and behavior.* Morristown, N.J.: General Learning Press, 1973.

CAMPBELL, A. Voters and elections: Past and present. *Journal of Politics,* 1964, *26,* 745-757.

CAMPBELL, A., CONVERSE, P. E., MILLER, W. E., & STOKES, D. E. *The American voter.* New York: John Wiley, 1960.

CAMPBELL, A., GURIN, G., & MILLER, W. E. *The voter decides.* Evanston, Ill.: Row, Peterson, 1954.

CAMPBELL, D. T. The generality of a social attitude. Unpublished doctoral dissertation, University of California, Berkeley, 1947.

CAMPBELL, D. T. Social attitudes and other acquired behavioral dispositions. In S. Koch (Ed.), *Psychology: A study of a science* (Vol. 6). New York: McGraw-Hill, 1963, pp. 94-172.

CARTWRIGHT, D. Some principles of mass persuasion: Selected findings of research on the sale of United States War Bonds. *Human Relations,* 1949, *2,* 253-267.

COHEN, J. B., FISHBEIN, M., & AHTOLA, O. T. The nature and uses of expectancy-value models in consumer attitude research. *Journal of Marketing Research,* 1972, *9,* 456-460.

COLLDEWEIH, J. H. The effects of mass media consumption on accuracy of beliefs about the candidates in a local congressional election. Unpublished doctoral dissertation, University of Illinois, 1968.

COLLINS, B. E. Four components of the Rotter internal-external scale: Belief in a difficult world, a just world, a predictable world, and a politically responsive world. *Journal of Personality and Social Psychology,* 1974, *29,* 381-391.

COREY, S. M. Professed attitudes and actual behavior. *Journal of Educational Psychology,* 1937, *28,* 271-280.

DAVIDSON, A. R., & JACCARD, J. J. Population psychology: A new look at an old problem. *Journal of Personality and Social Psychology,* 1975, *31,* 1073-1082.

DAY, G. S. Evaluating models of attitude structure. *Journal of Marketing Research,* 1972, *9,* 279-286.

DeFLEUR, M. L., & WESTIE, F. R. Attitude as a scientific concept. *Social Forces,* 1963, *42,* 17-31.

DEUTSCHER, I. Words and deeds: Social science and social policy. *Social Problems*, 1966, *13*, 235-254.

DOOB, L. W. The behavior of attitudes. *Psychological Review*, 1947, *54*, 135-156.

EAGLY, A. H. The comprehensibility of persuasive arguments as a determinant of opinion change. *Journal of Personality and Social Psychology*, 1974, *29*, 758-773.

EDWARDS, A. L. *Techniques of attitude scale construction.* Englewood Cliffs, N.J.: Prentice-Hall, Inc., 1957.

EDWARDS, C. N. Cultural values and role decisions: A study of educated women. *Journal of Counseling Psychology*, 1969, *16*, 36-40.

EHRENBERG, A. S. C. *Repeat-buying, theory and applications.* Amsterdam and New York: North Holland Publishing Co., 1972.

EHRLICH, H. J. Attitudes, behavior, and the intervening variables. *American Sociologist*, 1969, *4*, 29-34.

ENGEL, J. F., KOLLAT, D. T., & BLACKWELL, R. D. *Consumer behavior* (2nd Ed.) New York: Holt, Rinehart & Winston, 1975.

FAWCETT, J. T., & ARNOLD, F. S. The value of children: Theory and method. *Representative Research in Social Psychology*, 1973, *4*, 23-36.

FAZIO, R. H., & ZANNA, M. Attitudinal qualities relating to the strength of the attitude-behavior relationship. *Journal of Experimental Social Psychology*, 1978, *14*, 398-408.

FERBER, R. The role of planning in consumer purchases of durable goods. *American Economics Review*, 1954, *44*, 854-874.

FESTINGER, L. *A theory of cognitive dissonance.* Evanston, Ill.: Row, Peterson, 1957.

FESTINGER, L. Behavioral support for opinion change. *Public Opinion Quarterly*, 1964, *28*, 404-417.

FISHBEIN, M. An investigation of the relationships between beliefs about an object and the attitude toward that object. *Human Relations*, 1963, *16*, 233-240.

FISHBEIN, M. The relationship of the behavioral differential to other attitude instruments. *American Psychologist*, 1964, *19*, 540 (reference).

FISHBEIN, M. Sexual behavior and propositional control. Paper presented at the annual meeting of the Psychonomic Society, 1966.

FISHBEIN, M. Attitude and the prediction of behavior. In M. Fishbein (Ed.), *Readings in attitude theory and measurement.* New York: John Wiley, 1967, pp. 477-492. (a)

FISHBEIN, M. A behavior theory approach to the relation between beliefs about an object and the attitude toward the object. In M. Fishbein (Ed.), *Readings in attitude theory and measurement.* New York: John Wiley, 1967, pp. 389-400. (b)

FISHBEIN, M. A consideration of beliefs and their role in attitude measurement. In M. Fishbein (Ed.), *Readings in attitude theory and measurement.* New York: John Wiley, 1967, pp. 257-266. (c)

FISHBEIN, M. Some comments on the use of "models" in advertising research. In *Seminar on "Translating advanced advertising theories into research reality."* Amsterdam, Netherlands: ESOMAR, 1971, pp. 297-318.

FISHBEIN, M. The prediction of behavior from attitudinal variables. In C. D. Mortensen, & K. K. Sereno (Eds.), *Advances in communication research.* New York: Harper and Row, Pub., 1973, pp. 3-31.

FISHBEIN, M. A theory of reasoned action: Some applications and implications. In H. Howe, & M. Page (Eds.), *Nebraska symposium on motivation, 1978.* Lincoln, Neb.: University of Nebraska Press. In press.

FISHBEIN, M., & AJZEN, I. Attitudes and opinions. *Annual Review of Psychology,* 1972, *23,* 487-544.

FISHBEIN, M., & AJZEN, I. Attitudes toward objects as predictors of single and multiple behavioral criteria. *Psychological Review,* 1974, *81,* 59-74.

FISHBEIN, M., & AJZEN, I. *Belief, attitude, intention and behavior: An introduction to theory and research.* Reading, Mass.: Addison-Wesley, 1975.

FISHBEIN, M., & AJZEN, I. Misconceptions about the Fishbein model: Reflections on a study by Songer-Nocks. *Journal of Experimental Social Psychology,* 1976, *12,* 579-584.

FISHBEIN, M., & AJZEN, I. Acceptance, yielding, and impact: Cognitive processes in persuasion. In R. E. Petty, T. M. Ostrom, & T. C. Brock (Eds.), *Cognitive responses in persuasion.* Hillsdale, N.J.: Erlbaum, 1980.

FISHBEIN, M., & COOMBS, F. S. Basis for decision: An attitudinal analysis of voting behavior. *Journal of Applied Social Psychology,* 1974, *4,* 95-124.

FISHBEIN, M., & JACCARD, J. J. Theoretical and methodological considerations in the prediction of family planning intentions and behavior. *Representative Research in Social Psychology,* 1973, *4,* 37-51.

FISHBEIN, M., LOKEN, B., CHUNG, J., & ROBERTS, S. *Smoking behavior among college women.* Report prepared for the Federal Trade Commission, University of Illinois, 1978.

FISHBEIN, M., & RAVEN, B. H. The AB scales: An operational definition of belief and attitude. *Human Relations,* 1962, *15,* 35-44.

FISHBEIN, M., THOMAS, K., & JACCARD, J. J. Voting behavior in Britain: An attitudinal analysis. *Occasional Papers in Survey Research,* 1976, *7,* SSRC Survey Unit, London, England.

FREEDMAN, J. L., CARLSMITH, J. M., & SEARS, D. O. *Social psychology.* Englewood Cliffs, N.J.: Prentice-Hall, Inc., 1970.

FREEDMAN, R. American studies of family planning and fertility: A review of major trends and issues. In C. Kiser (Ed.), *Research in family planning*. Princeton, N.J.: Princeton University Press, 1962, pp. 211-227.

FREEDMAN, R., WHELPTON, P., & CAMPBELL, A. *Family planning, sterility, and population growth*. New York: McGraw-Hill, 1959.

FRIEDAN, B. *The feminine mystique*. New York: Dell Pub. Co., Inc., 1970.

GREEN, B. F. Attitude measurement. In G. Lindzey (Ed.), *Handbook of social psychology* (Vol. 1). Reading, Mass.: Addison-Wesley, 1954, pp. 335-369.

GREEN, P. E., & WIND, Y. Recent approaches to the modeling of individuals' subjective evaluations. In P. Levine (Ed.), *Attitude research bridges the Atlantic*. Chicago, Ill.: American Marketing Association, 1975.

GUTTMAN, L. A basis for scaling qualitative data. *American Sociological Review*, 1944, *9*, 139-150.

GYSBERS, N. C., JOHNSTON, J. A., & GUST, T. Characteristics of homemaker- and career-oriented women. *Journal of Counseling Psychology*, 1968, *15*, 541-546.

HALL, S. M., & HALL, R. G. Outcome and methodological considerations in behavioral treatment of obesity. *Behavior Therapy*, 1974, *5*, 352-364.

HEIDER, F. Social perception and phenomenal causality. *Psychological Review*, 1944, *51*, 358-374.

HEIDER, F. *The psychology of interpersonal relations*. New York: John Wiley, 1958.

HELSON, R. The changing image of the career woman. *Journal of Social Issues*, 1972, *28*, 33-46.

HIMMELFARB, S., & EAGLY, A. H. Orientations to the study of attitudes and their change. In S. Himmelfarb, & A. H. Eagly (Eds.), *Readings in attitude change*. New York: John Wiley, 1974, pp. 2-49.

HOM, P. W., KATERBERG, R., Jr., & HULIN, C. L. The prediction of employee turnover in a part-time military organization. Technical Report 78-2. University of Illinois, 1978.

HORN, D. The smoking problem in 1971. Unpublished paper presented at the American Cancer Society's 13th Annual Science Writers Seminar, Phoenix, Arizona, April 6, 1971.

HOVLAND, C. I. (Ed.), *The order of presentation in persuasion*. New Haven, Conn.: Yale University Press, 1957.

HOVLAND, C. I., & JANIS, I. L. (Eds.), *Personality and persuasibility*. New Haven, Conn.: Yale University Press, 1959.

HOVLAND, C. I., JANIS, I. L., & KELLEY, H. H. *Communication and persuasion*. New Haven, Conn.: Yale University Press, 1953.

HOVLAND, C. I., & ROSENBERG, M. J. (Eds.), *Attitude organization and change*. New Haven, Conn.: Yale University Press, 1960.

HOWARD, J. A., & SHETH, J. N. *The theory of buyer behavior.* New York: John Wiley, 1969.

HOYT, D. P., & KENNEDY, C. E. Interest and personality correlates of career-oriented and homemaking-oriented college women. *Journal of Counseling Psychology,* 1958, *5,* 44-48.

JACCARD, J. J. Predicting social behavior from personality traits. *Journal of Experimental Research in Personality,* 1974, *7,* 358-367.

JACCARD, J. J., & DAVIDSON, A. R. Toward an understanding of family planning behaviors: An initial investigation. *Journal of Applied Social Psychology,* 1972, *2,* 228-235.

JAFFE, F. S., & GUTTMACHER, A. F. Family planning programs in the U.S. *Demography,* 1968, *5,* 910-923.

JANIS, I. L., & HOVLAND, C. I. An overview of persuasibility research. In C. I. Hovland, & I. L. Janis (Eds.), *Personality and persuasibility.* New Haven, Conn.: Yale University Press, 1959, pp. 1-26.

JEFFREY, D. B. Some methodological issues in research on obesity. *Psychological Reports,* 1974, *35,* 623-626.

KANUK, L., & BERENSON, C. Mail surveys and response rates: A literature review. *Journal of Marketing Research,* 1975, *12,* 440-453.

KATONA, G. Contribution of psychological data to economic analysis. *Journal of the American Statistical Association,* 1947, *42,* 449-459.

KATONA, G. *Psychological analysis of economic behavior.* New York: McGraw-Hill, 1951.

KATZ, D., & STOTLAND, E. A preliminary statement to a theory of attitude structure and change. In S. Koch (Ed.), *Psychology: A study of a science* (Vol. 3). New York: McGraw-Hill, 1959, pp. 423-475.

KEENAN, K. M. Reasons for joining and early termination of service in WRAC. Report No. 24/75, Ministry of Defense Personnel Research Establishment, Farnsborough, Hauts, 1976. Also described in M. Tuck, *How do we choose? A study in consumer behavior.* London: Methuen, 1976.

KELLEY, S., Jr., & MIRER, T. W. The simple act of voting. *American Political Science Review,* 1974, *68,* 572-591.

KIESLER, C. A., COLLINS, B. E., & MILLER, N. *Attitude change.* New York: John Wiley, 1969.

KING, G. W. An analysis of attitudinal and normative variables as predictors of intentions and behavior. *Speech Monographs,* 1975, *42,* 237-244.

KISER, C. The Indianapolis study of social and psychological factors affecting fertility. In C. V. Kiser (Ed.), *Research in family planning.* Princeton, N.J.: Princeton University Press, 1962.

KISER, C., & WHELPTON, P. K. Social and psychological factors affecting fertility. *Milbank Memorial Fund Quarterly,* 1958, *36,* 282-329.

KRECH, D., & CRUTCHFIELD, R. S. *Theory and problems in social psychology.* New York: McGraw-Hill, 1948.

KRECH, D., CRUTCHFIELD, R. S., & BALLACHEY, E. L. *Individual in society.* New York: McGraw-Hill, 1962.

LANGE, L. Neue Experimente über den Vorgang der einfachen Reaktion auf Sinneseindrücke. *Philosophische Studien,* 1888, *4,* 479-510.

LaPIERE, R. T. Attitudes vs. actions. *Social Forces,* 1934, *13,* 230-237.

LASWELL, H. D. The structure and function of communication in society. In L. Bryson (Ed.), *The communication of ideas.* New York: Harper & Row, Pub., 1948, pp. 37-51.

LAZARSFELD, P. F., BERELSON, B., & GAUDET, H. *The people's choice: How the voter makes up his mind in a presidential campaign.* New York: Columbia University Press, 1944.

LIKERT, R. A technique for the measurement of attitudes. *Archives of Psychology,* 1932, No. 140.

LISKA, A. E. (Ed.), *The consistency controversy: Readings on the impact of attitude on behavior.* New York: John Wiley, 1975.

LOKEN, B., & FISHBEIN, M. The relationship between occupational variables and child bearing intentions: Fact or artifact? Unpublished manuscript, Department of Psychology, University of Illinois at Champaign-Urbana, 1978.

MACHNIK, W. J. Einstellung und Verhalten: Welche Bedeutung haben eigentlich Image-Studien? *ZV + ZV,* No. 5-6, 1976.

MATHEWS, E., & TIEDEMAN, D. V. Attitudes toward career and marriage in the development of life styles of young women. *Journal of Counseling Psychology,* 1964, *11,* 375-384.

MAULDIN, W. P. Fertility studies: Knowledge, attitude and practice. *Studies in Family Planning,* 1965, *1* (No. 7), 1-10.

MAZIS, M. B., AHTOLA, O. T., & KLIPPEL, R. E. A comparison of four multi-attribute models in the prediction of consumer attitudes. *Journal of Consumer Research,* 1975, *2,* 38-52.

McCROSKEY, J. C. The effects of evidence as an inhibitor of counter persuasion. *Speech Monographs,* 1970, *37,* 188-194.

McGUIRE, W. J. A syllogistic analysis of cognitive relationships. In C. I. Hovland, & M. J. Rosenberg (Eds.), *Attitude organization and change.* New Haven, Conn.: Yale University Press, 1960, pp. 65-111.

McGUIRE, W. J. Personality and susceptibility to social influence. In E. F. Borgatta, & W. W. Lambert (Eds.), *Handbook of personality theory and research.* Skokie, Ill.: Rand McNally, 1968, pp. 1130-1187.

McGUIRE, W.J. The nature of attitudes and attitude change. In G. Lindzey, & E. Aronson (Eds.), *The handbook of social psychology* (2nd ed., Vol. 3). Reading, Mass.: Addison-Wesley, 1969, pp. 136-314.

McKEE, M., & ROBERTSON, I. *Social problems*. New York: Random House, 1975.

McNEIL, J. Federal programs to measure consumer purchase expectations, 1946-1973: A post-mortem. *Journal of Consumer Research*, 1974, *1*, No. 3, 1-15.

NICOSIA, F. M. *Consumer decision processes: Marketing and advertising implications*. Englewood Cliffs, N.J.: Prentice-Hall, Inc., 1966.

NISBETT, R. E., & WILSON, T. D. Telling more than one can know: Verbal reports on mental processes. *Psychological Review*, 1977, *84*, 231-259.

OSGOOD, C. E., SUCI, G. J., & TANNENBAUM, R. H. *The measurement of meaning*. Urbana, Ill.: University of Illinois Press, 1957.

OSTROM, T. M. The relationship between the affective, behavioral, and cognitive components of attitude. *Journal of Experimental Social Psychology*, 1969, *5*, 12-30.

POHLMAN, E. *The psychology of birth planning*. Cambridge, Mass.: Schenkman, 1969.

POMAZAL, R. J., & BROWN, J. D. Understanding drug use motivation: A new look at a current problem. *Journal of Health and Social Behavior*, 1977, *18*, 212-222.

POMAZAL, R. J., & JACCARD, J. J. An informational approach to altruistic behavior. *Journal of Personality and Social Psychology*, 1976, *33*, 317-326.

RAINWATER, L. *Family design*. Chicago: Aldine, 1965.

RAND, L. Masculinity or femininity? Differentiating career-oriented and home-making-oriented college freshmen women. *Journal of Counseling Psychology*, 1968, *15*, 444-449.

REGAN, D. T., & FAZIO, R. H. On the consistency between attitudes and behavior: Look to the method of attitude formation. *Journal of Experimental Social Psychology*, 1977, *13*, 28-45.

ROSENBERG, M. J. Cognitive structure and attitudinal affect. *Journal of Abnormal and Social Psychology*, 1956, *53*, 367-372.

ROSENBERG, M. J., & HOVLAND, C. I. Cognitive, affective, and behavioral components of attitudes. In C. I. Hovland, & M. J. Rosenberg (Eds.), *Attitude organization and change*. New Haven, Conn.: Yale University Press, 1960, pp. 1-14.

ROSENSTOCK, I. M. Historical origins of the Health Belief Model. *Health Education Monographs*, 1974, *2*, 409-419.

RYDER, N. B., & WESTOFF, C. F. *Reproduction in the United States, 1965*. Princeton, N.J.: Princeton University Press, 1971.

SALBER, E. J., & ABELIN, T. Smoking behavior of Newton school children—5 year follow-up. *Pediatrics*, 1967, *40*, 363-372.

SCHLEGEL, R. P., CRAWFORD, C. A., & SANBORN, M. D. Correspondence and mediational properties of the Fishbein model: An application to adolescent alcohol use. *Journal of Experimental Social Psychology*, 1977, *13*, 421-430.

SCHNEIDER, D. J. *Social psychology*. Reading, Mass.: Addison-Wesley, 1976.

SCHUMAN, H., & JOHNSON, M. P. Attitudes and behavior. *Annual Review of Sociology*, 1976, *2*, 161-207.

SCHWARTZ, S. H., & TESSLER, R. C. A test of a model for reducing measured attitude-behavior discrepancies. *Journal of Personality and Social Psychology*, 1972, *24*, 225-236.

SHERIF, M., & HOVLAND, C. I. *Social judgment: Assimilation and contrast effects in communication and attitude change*. New Haven, Conn.: Yale University Press, 1961.

SHETH, J. N., & TALARZYK, W. W. Perceived instrumentality and value importance as determinants of attitudes. *Journal of Marketing Research*, 1972, *9*, 6-9.

SMITH, M. B. The personal setting of public opinions: A study of attitudes toward Russia. *Public Opinion Quarterly*, 1947, *11*, 507-523.

SPENCER, H. *First principles*. New York: Burt, 1862.

STUART, R. B., & DAVIS, B. *Behavioral techniques for the management of obesity*. Champaign, Ill.: Research Press, 1971.

STUNKARD, A., & McLAREN-HUME, M. The results of treatment for obesity. *Archives of International Medicine*, 1959, *103*, 79-85.

TANGRI, S. S. Determinants of occupational role innovation among college women. *Journal of Social Issues*, 1972, *28*, 177-199.

THOMAS, K. A reinterpretation of the "attitude" approach to transport-mode choice and an exploratory empirical test. *Environment and Planning*, 1976, *8*, 793-810.

THOMAS, K., BULL, H. C., & CLARK, J. Attitude measurement in the forecasting of off-peak travel behavior. In P. W. Bonsall, Q. Dalvi, & P. J. Hills (Eds.), *Urban transportation planning: Current themes and future prospects*. Turnbridge Wells: Abacus, 1978.

THOMAS, W. I., & ZNANIECKI, F. *The Polish peasant in Europe and America* (Vol. 1). Boston: Badger, 1918.

THURSTONE, L. L. Theory of attitude measurement. *Psychological Bulletin*, 1929, *36*, 222-241.

THURSTONE, L. L. The measurement of attitudes. *Journal of Abnormal and Social Psychology*, 1931, *26*, 249-269.

THURSTONE, L. L., & CHAVE, E. J. *The measurement of attitude*. Chicago: University of Chicago Press, 1929.

TRIANDIS, H. C. Exploratory factor analysis of the behavioral component of social attitudes. *Journal of Abnormal and Social Psychology,* 1964, *68,* 420-430.

TRIANDIS, H. C. Toward an analysis of the components of interpersonal attitudes. In C. W. Sherif, & M. Sherif (Eds.), *Attitudes, ego involvement, and change.* New York: John Wiley, 1967, pp. 227-270.

TRIANDIS, H. C. *Interpersonal behavior.* Monterey, Calif.: Brooks/Cole, 1977.

TUCK, M. *How do we choose? A study in consumer behavior.* London: Methuen, 1976.

TYLER, L. E. The antecedents of two varieties of vocational interest. *Genetic Psychology Monographs,* 1964, *70,* 203-212.

VINOKUR-KAPLAN, D. To have—or not to have—another child: Family planning attitudes, intentions, and behavior. *Journal of Applied Social Psychology,* 1978, *8,* 29-46.

WAGMAN, M. Interests and values of career and homemaking oriented women. *Personnel and Guidance Journal,* 1966, *44,* 794-801.

WATLEY, D. J., & KAPLAN, R. Career or marriage: Aspirations and achievements of able young women. *Journal of Vocational Behavior,* 1971, *1,* 29-43.

WATSON, J. B. *Behaviorism.* New York: W. W. Norton & Co., Inc., 1925.

WEBSTER, M., Jr. *Actions and actors: Principles of social psychology.* Cambridge, Mass.: Winthrop, 1975.

WEISSTEIN, N. Psychology constructs the female. In V. Gornick, & B. K. Moran (Eds.), *Woman in sexist society.* New York: Basic Books, 1971.

WESTOFF, C. F. The modernization of U.S. contraceptive practice. *Family Planning Perspectives,* 1972, *4,* 9-19.

WESTOFF, C., MISHLER, E., & KELLEY, E. Preferences in size of family and eventual fertility 20 years after. *American Journal of Sociology,* 1957, *62,* 491-497.

WESTOFF, C., POTTER, R., & SAGI, P. *The third child: A study in the prediction of fertility.* Princeton, N.J.: Princeton University Press, 1963.

WESTOFF, C., POTTER, R., SAGI, P., & MISHLER, E. *Family growth in metropolitan America.* Princeton, N.J.: Princeton University Press, 1961.

WESTOFF, C., & RYDER, N. United States: The Papal Encyclical and Catholic practice and attitudes, 1969. *Studies in Family Planning,* 1970, *50,* 1-7.

WESTOFF, C., & RYDER, N. *The contraceptive revolution.* Princeton N.J.: Princeton University Press, 1977.

WHELPTON, P. K., CAMPBELL, A., & PATTERSON, J. E. *Fertility and family planning in the United States.* Princeton, N.J.: Princeton University Press, 1966.

WICKER, A. W. Attitudes vs. actions: The relationship of verbal and overt behavioral responses to attitude objects. *Journal of Social Issues,* 1969, *25,* 41-78.

WILKIE, W. L., & PESSEMIER, E. A. Issues in marketing use of multi-attribute attitude models. *Journal of Marketing Research,* 1973, *10,* 428-441.

WILSON, D. T., MATHEWS, H. L., & HARVEY, J. W. An empirical test of the Fishbein behavioral intention model. *Journal of Consumer Research,* 1975, (March), *1,* 39-48.

WYATT, F. Clinical notes on the motives of reproduction. *Journal of Social Issues,* 1967, *23,* 29-56.

WYER, R. S., Jr., & GOLDBERG, L. A probabilistic analysis of relationships among beliefs and attitudes. *Psychological Review,* 1970, *77,* 100-120.

ZAJONC, R. B. Structure of the cognitive field. Unpublished doctoral dissertation, University of Michigan, 1954.

# APPENDIX A

## Steps in the Construction of a Standard Questionnaire

1. Define the *behavior* of interest in terms of its action, target, context, and time elements (see chapter 3).
   *Example:* Voting in the next presidential election.
   In this example action (voting), target (presidential election), and time (the next election) are specified. Make sure that your criterion measure corresponds exactly to the behavior you have in mind.
2. Define the corresponding behavioral *intention* (see chapter 4).
   *Example:* Intention to vote in the next presidential election

Proposed measurement format

I intend to vote in the next presidential election.

likely _____:_____:_____:_____:_____:_____:_____ unlikely
    extremely  quite   slightly  neither  slightly   quite  extremely

3. Define the corresponding *attitude* and *subjective norm* (see chapter 5).
   *Examples:* (a) Attitude toward voting in the next presidential election
                 (b) Subjective norm with respect to voting in the next presidential election

Proposed measurement format

(a) *Attitude*[1]

My voting in the next presidential election is

harmful _____:_____:_____:_____:_____:_____:_____ beneficial
    extremely  quite   slightly  neither  slightly   quite  extremely

[1]Any standard scaling procedure can be used to measure attitude toward the behavior. If the semantic differential is used, the adjective scales included must be evaluative in nature. The four scales listed in 3(a) are merely illustrations.

good \_\_\_\_\_:\_\_\_\_\_:\_\_\_\_\_:\_\_\_\_\_:\_\_\_\_\_:\_\_\_\_\_:\_\_\_\_\_ bad
    extremely   quite   slightly   neither   slightly   quite   extremely

rewarding \_\_\_\_\_:\_\_\_\_\_:\_\_\_\_\_:\_\_\_\_\_:\_\_\_\_\_:\_\_\_\_\_:\_\_\_\_\_ punishing
    extremely   quite   slightly   neither   slightly   quite   extremely

unpleasant \_\_\_\_\_:\_\_\_\_\_:\_\_\_\_\_:\_\_\_\_\_:\_\_\_\_\_:\_\_\_\_\_:\_\_\_\_\_ pleasant
    extremely   quite   slightly   neither   slightly   quite   extremely

(b) *Subjective norm*

Most people who are important to me think

I should \_\_\_\_ : \_\_\_\_ : \_\_\_\_ : \_\_\_\_ : \_\_\_\_ : \_\_\_\_ : \_\_\_\_ I should not
vote in the next presidential election.

Steps 1 through 3 permit prediction and explanation of behavior at a general level. To obtain substantive information about the cognitive foundation underlying the behavior, it is necessary to complete Steps 4 and 5.

4. Elicit salient outcomes and referents (see chapter 6).
   *Examples:* A sample of respondents, representative of the population studied, is asked the following questions.
   (a) *Salient outcomes*

   (1) What do you see as the advantages of your voting in the next presidential election?
   (2) What do you see as the disadvantages of your voting in the next presidential election?
   (3) Is there anything else you associate with your voting in the next presidential election?

   (b) *Salient referents*

   (1) Are there any groups or people who would approve of your voting in the next presidential election?
   (2) Are there any groups or people who would disapprove of your voting in the next presidential election?
   (3) Are there any other groups or people who come to mind when you think about voting in the next presidential election?

Responses to these questions are used to identify modal salient outcomes and referents. Construct behavioral beliefs statements linking the behavior to each salient outcome and normative belief statements with respect to each salient referent.

5. Define *behavioral beliefs, outcome evaluations, normative beliefs,* and *motivation to comply.*

*Examples:*  (a)  Behavioral belief: My voting in the next presidential election will help Candidate $X$ get elected.

(b)  Normative belief: My parents think I should vote in the next presidential election.

Proposed measurement format

(a)  *Behavioral beliefs*

My voting in the next presidential election will help Candidate $X$ get elected.

likely _____:_____:_____:_____:_____:_____:_____ unlikely
       extremely   quite    slightly    neither   slightly    quite   extremely

(b)  *Outcome evaluations*

Helping Candidate $X$ get elected is

good _____:_____:_____:_____:_____:_____:_____ bad
      extremely   quite    slightly    neither   slightly    quite   extremely

(c)  *Normative beliefs*

My parents think

I should ____ : ____ : ____ : ____ : ____ : ____ : ____ I should not
             vote in the next presidential election.

(d)  *Motivations to comply*

Generally speaking, how much do you want to do what your parents think you should do?

Not at all ____ : ____ : ____ : ____ : ____ : ____ : ____ Very much

Notes

1. Except for the motivation to comply scales, which are scored from 1 (not at all) to 7 (very much), all scales described in this outline are scored from $-3$ (unlikely, bad, harmful, punishing, unpleasant) to $+3$ (likely, good, beneficial, rewarding, pleasant).
2. It is possible to employ variations of the graphic scales described in this outline. For examples of somewhat different formats for measuring subjective norms, normative beliefs, and motivations to comply, see appendix B.

# APPENDIX
# B

## Sample
## Questionnaire

Following is a slightly modified version of the questionnaire used in the study of voting in the 1976 Oregon Nuclear Safeguards Referendum (see chapter 14). Only the parts directly relevant to the theory of reasoned action are reproduced.

General Instructions[1]

In the questionnaire you are about to fill out we ask questions which make use of rating scales with seven places; you are to make a check mark in the place that best describes your opinion. For example, if you were asked to rate "The Weather in Portland" on such a scale, the seven places should be interpreted as follows:

The Weather in Portland is

good _____:_____:_____:_____:_____:_____:_____ bad
    extremely   quite   slightly   neither   slightly   quite  extremely

If you think the Weather in Portland is *extremely good*, then you would place your mark as follows:

The Weather in Portland is

good \_\_\_X\_\_\_:_____:_____:_____:_____:_____:_____ bad
    extremely   quite   slightly   neither   slightly   quite  extremely

If you think the Weather in Portland is *quite bad*, then you would place your mark as follows:

The Weather in Portland is

good _____:_____:_____:_____:_____:\_\_\_X\_\_\_:_____ bad
    extremely   quite   slightly   neither   slightly   quite  extremely

[1]These headings are for illustrative purposes only. They do not appear on the questionnaire.

If you think the Weather in Portland is *slightly good,* then you would place your mark as follows:

### The Weather in Portland is

good _____:_____:\_\_\_X\_\_\_:_____:_____:_____:_____ bad
　　　　extremely　quite　slightly　neither　slightly　quite　extremely

If you think the Weather in Portland is *neither good nor bad,* then you would place your mark as follows:

### The Weather in Portland is

good _____:_____:_____:\_\_\_X\_\_\_:_____:_____:_____ bad
　　　　extremely　quite　slightly　neither　slightly　quite　extremely

You will also be using a rating scale with likely-unlikely as endpoints. This scale is to be interpreted in the same way. For example, if you were asked to rate "The Weather in Portland is cold in January" on such a scale, it would appear as follows:

### The Weather in Portland is Cold in January

likely _____:_____:_____:_____:_____:_____:_____ unlikely
　　　　extremely　quite　slightly　neither　slightly　quite　extremely

If you think that it is *extremely likely* that The Weather in Portland is cold in January, you would make your mark as follows:

### The Weather in Portland is Cold in January

likely \_\_\_X\_\_\_:_____:_____:_____:_____:_____:_____ unlikely
　　　　extremely　quite　slightly　neither　slightly　quite　extremely

In making your ratings please remember the following points:

(1) Place your marks in the *middle of spaces,* not on the boundaries:

　　　　　　　this　　　　　　　　　　　　　　　　　　not this

(2) Be sure you answer all items—please do not omit any.
(3) Never put more than one check mark on a single scale.

In this particular questionnaire we are mainly concerned with people's views toward the regulation of nuclear power plants and related facilities.

In addition to a few general questions, we would like to ask you about one of the statewide propositions which will appear on the November general election ballot—the Oregon Nuclear Safeguards Initiative—Ballot Measure No. 9 that "Regulates nuclear power plant construction approval."

Do you have any questions?

## Intention

I intend to vote "Yes" on the Oregon Nuclear Safeguards Initiative—Ballot Measure No. 9

likely \_\_\_\_:\_\_\_\_:\_\_\_\_:\_\_\_\_:\_\_\_\_:\_\_\_\_:\_\_\_\_ unlikely
extremely  quite  slightly  neither  slightly  quite  extremely

## Attitude toward the behavior

My voting "Yes" on the Oregon Nuclear Safeguards Initiative—Ballot Measure No. 9

good \_\_\_\_:\_\_\_\_:\_\_\_\_:\_\_\_\_:\_\_\_\_:\_\_\_\_:\_\_\_\_ bad
extremely  quite  slightly  neither  slightly  quite  extremely

wise \_\_\_\_:\_\_\_\_:\_\_\_\_:\_\_\_\_:\_\_\_\_:\_\_\_\_:\_\_\_\_ foolish
extremely  quite  slightly  neither  slightly  quite  extremely

harmful \_\_\_\_:\_\_\_\_:\_\_\_\_:\_\_\_\_:\_\_\_\_:\_\_\_\_:\_\_\_\_ beneficial
extremely  quite  slightly  neither  slightly  quite  extremely

## Outcome evaluations

1. Requiring new tests of nuclear safety systems

good \_\_\_\_:\_\_\_\_:\_\_\_\_:\_\_\_\_:\_\_\_\_:\_\_\_\_:\_\_\_\_ bad
extremely  quite  slightly  neither  slightly  quite  extremely

2. Requiring a decision on a permanent nuclear waste disposal method

good \_\_\_\_:\_\_\_\_:\_\_\_\_:\_\_\_\_:\_\_\_\_:\_\_\_\_:\_\_\_\_ bad
extremely  quite  slightly  neither  slightly  quite  extremely

3. Increasing public participation in nuclear decisions

good \_\_\_\_:\_\_\_\_:\_\_\_\_:\_\_\_\_:\_\_\_\_:\_\_\_\_:\_\_\_\_ bad
extremely  quite  slightly  neither  slightly  quite  extremely

4. Reducing the threat of nuclear theft and sabotage

good _____:_____:_____:_____:_____:_____:_____ bad
      extremely  quite   slightly  neither  slightly  quite  extremely

5. Ensuring low-cost electricity

good _____:_____:_____:_____:_____:_____:_____ bad
      extremely  quite   slightly  neither  slightly  quite  extremely

6. Eliminating a needed energy source

good _____:_____:_____:_____:_____:_____:_____ bad
      extremely  quite   slightly  neither  slightly  quite  extremely

7. Court battles over Ballot Measure No. 9's constitutionality

good _____:_____:_____:_____:_____:_____:_____ bad
      extremely  quite   slightly  neither  slightly  quite  extremely

8. Giving regulatory control of nuclear power to state legislators

good _____:_____:_____:_____:_____:_____:_____ bad
      extremely  quite   slightly  neither  slightly  quite  extremely

9. Helping the state's economic development

good _____:_____:_____:_____:_____:_____:_____ bad
      extremely  quite   slightly  neither  slightly  quite  extremely

10. Setting up realistic standards for nuclear waste management systems

good _____:_____:_____:_____:_____:_____:_____ bad
      extremely  quite   slightly  neither  slightly  quite  extremely

11. Making nuclear power plant operators fully responsible financially for nuclear accidents

good _____:_____:_____:_____:_____:_____:_____ bad
      extremely  quite   slightly  neither  slightly  quite  extremely

12. Making it easy for companies to obtain legislative approval for new nuclear power plants

good _____:_____:_____:_____:_____:_____:_____ bad
      extremely  quite   slightly  neither  slightly  quite  extremely

13. Increasing unemployment

good _____:_____:_____:_____:_____:_____:_____ bad
      extremely  quite   slightly  neither  slightly  quite  extremely

14. Maintaining Oregon's present system for regulating nuclear power

good _____:_____:_____:_____:_____:_____:_____ bad
     extremely   quite    slightly   neither   slightly    quite   extremely

15. A future energy shortage

good _____:_____:_____:_____:_____:_____:_____ bad
     extremely   quite    slightly   neither   slightly    quite   extremely

16. A ban on more nuclear power plants

good _____:_____:_____:_____:_____:_____:_____ bad
     extremely   quite    slightly   neither   slightly    quite   extremely

17. Making new nuclear plants safer than present ones

good _____:_____:_____:_____:_____:_____:_____ bad
     extremely   quite    slightly   neither   slightly    quite   extremely

18. Denying full compensation to the victims of a nuclear accident

good _____:_____:_____:_____:_____:_____:_____ bad
     extremely   quite    slightly   neither   slightly    quite   extremely

19. Reducing funds for the development of alternative energy sources

good _____:_____:_____:_____:_____:_____:_____ bad
     extremely   quite    slightly   neither   slightly    quite   extremely

20. Decreasing the danger from radioactive materials and wastes

good _____:_____:_____:_____:_____:_____:_____ bad
     extremely   quite    slightly   neither   slightly    quite   extremely

Behavioral beliefs

(*Note:* For convenience and time's sake, we are asking you only about voting "Yes." We could just as easily have asked you about voting "No." Our choice between the two was essentially arbitrary.)

1. My voting "Yes" on the Oregon Nuclear Safeguards Initiative, Ballot Measure No. 9, would require new tests of nuclear safety systems.

likely _____:_____:_____:_____:_____:_____:_____ unlikely
     extremely   quite    slightly   neither   slightly    quite   extremely

2. My voting "Yes" on the Oregon Nuclear Safeguards Initiative, Ballot Measure No. 9, would require a decision on a permanent nuclear waste disposal method.

likely _____:_____:_____:_____:_____:_____:_____ unlikely
extremely  quite  slightly  neither  slightly  quite  extremely

3. My voting "Yes" on the Oregon Nuclear Safeguards Initiative, Ballot Measure No. 9, would increase public participation in nuclear decisions.

likely _____:_____:_____:_____:_____:_____:_____ unlikely
extremely  quite  slightly  neither  slightly  quite  extremely

4. My voting "Yes" on the Oregon Nuclear Safeguards Initiative, Ballot Measure No. 9, would reduce the threat of nuclear theft and sabotage.

likely _____:_____:_____:_____:_____:_____:_____ unlikely
extremely  quite  slightly  neither  slightly  quite  extremely

5. My voting "Yes" on the Oregon Nuclear Safeguards Initiative, Ballot Measure No. 9, would ensure low-cost electricity.

likely _____:_____:_____:_____:_____:_____:_____ unlikely
extremely  quite  slightly  neither  slightly  quite  extremely

6. My voting "Yes" on the Oregon Nuclear Safeguards Initiative, Ballot Measure No. 9, would eliminate a needed energy source.

likely _____:_____:_____:_____:_____:_____:_____ unlikely
extremely  quite  slightly  neither  slightly  quite  extremely

7. My voting "Yes" on the Oregon Nuclear Safeguards Initiative, Ballot Measure No. 9, would result in court battles over Ballot Measure No. 9's constitutionality.

likely _____:_____:_____:_____:_____:_____:_____ unlikely
extremely  quite  slightly  neither  slightly  quite  extremely

8. My voting "Yes" on the Oregon Nuclear Safeguards Initiative, Ballot Measure No. 9, would give regulatory control of nuclear power to state legislators.

likely _____:_____:_____:_____:_____:_____:_____ unlikely
extremely  quite  slightly  neither  slightly  quite  extremely

9. My voting "Yes" on the Oregon Nuclear Safeguards Initiative, Ballot Measure No. 9, would help the state's economic development.

likely _____:_____:_____:_____:_____:_____:_____ unlikely
extremely  quite  slightly  neither  slightly  quite  extremely

10. My voting "Yes" on the Oregon Nuclear Safeguards Initiative, Ballot Measure No. 9, would set up realistic standards for nuclear waste management systems.

likely _____:_____:_____:_____:_____:_____:_____ unlikely
    extremely   quite   slightly   neither   slightly   quite   extremely

11. My voting "Yes" on the Oregon Nuclear Safeguards Initiative, Ballot Measure No. 9, would make nuclear power plant operators fully responsible financially for nuclear accidents.

likely _____:_____:_____:_____:_____:_____:_____ unlikely
    extremely   quite   slightly   neither   slightly   quite   extremely

12. My voting "Yes" on the Oregon Nuclear Safeguards Initiative, Ballot Measure No. 9, would make it easy for companies to obtain legislative approval for new nuclear power plants.

likely _____:_____:_____:_____:_____:_____:_____ unlikely
    extremely   quite   slightly   neither   slightly   quite   extremely

13. My voting "Yes" on the Oregon Nuclear Safeguards Initiative, Ballot Measure No. 9, would increase unemployment.

likely _____:_____:_____:_____:_____:_____:_____ unlikely
    extremely   quite   slightly   neither   slightly   quite   extremely

14. My voting "Yes" on the Oregon Nuclear Safeguards Initiative, Ballot Measure No. 9, would maintain Oregon's present system for regulating nuclear power.

likely _____:_____:_____:_____:_____:_____:_____ unlikely
    extremely   quite   slightly   neither   slightly   quite   extremely

15. My voting "Yes" on the Oregon Nuclear Safeguards Initiative, Ballot Measure No. 9, would result in a future energy shortage.

likely _____:_____:_____:_____:_____:_____:_____ unlikely
    extremely   quite   slightly   neither   slightly   quite   extremely

16. My voting "Yes" on the Oregon Nuclear Safeguards Initiative, Ballot Measure No. 9, would result in a ban on more nuclear power plants.

likely _____:_____:_____:_____:_____:_____:_____ unlikely
    extremely   quite   slightly   neither   slightly   quite   extremely

17. My voting "Yes" on the Oregon Nuclear Safeguards Initiative, Ballot Measure No. 9, would make new nuclear plants safer than present ones.

likely _____:_____:_____:_____:_____:_____:_____ unlikely
    extremely   quite   slightly   neither   slightly   quite   extremely

18. My voting "Yes" on the Oregon Nuclear Safeguards Initiative, Ballot Measure No. 9, would deny full compensation to the victims of a nuclear accident.

likely _____:_____:_____:_____:_____:_____:_____ unlikely
　　　extremely　quite　slightly　neither　slightly　quite　extremely

19. My voting "Yes" on the Oregon Nuclear Safeguards Initiative, Ballot Measure No. 9, would reduce funds for the development of alternative energy sources.

likely _____:_____:_____:_____:_____:_____:_____ unlikely
　　　extremely　quite　slightly　neither　slightly　quite　extremely

20. My voting "Yes" on the Oregon Nuclear Safeguards Initiative, Ballot Measure No. 9, would decrease the danger from radioactive materials and wastes.

likely _____:_____:_____:_____:_____:_____:_____ unlikely
　　　extremely　quite　slightly　neither　slightly　quite　extremely

Now we would like to know how you think other people would like you to vote.

Subjective norm

Most people who are important to me think I should vote "Yes" on the Oregon Nuclear Safeguards Initiative—Ballot Measure No. 9.

likely _____:_____:_____:_____:_____:_____:_____ unlikely
　　　extremely　quite　slightly　neither　slightly　quite　extremely

Normative beliefs

1. Most members of my family think I should vote "Yes" on the Oregon Nuclear Safeguards Initiative—Ballot Measure No. 9.

likely _____:_____:_____:_____:_____:_____:_____ unlikely
　　　extremely　quite　slightly　neither　slightly　quite　extremely

2. My close friends think I should vote "Yes" on the Oregon Nuclear Safeguards Initiative—Ballot Measure No. 9.

likely _____:_____:_____:_____:_____:_____:_____ unlikely
　　　extremely　quite　slightly　neither　slightly　quite　extremely

3. My coworkers think I should vote "Yes" on the Oregon Nuclear Safeguards Initiative—Ballot Measure No. 9.

likely _____:_____:_____:_____:_____:_____:_____ unlikely
　　　extremely　quite　slightly　neither　slightly　quite　extremely

4. The power companies think I should vote "Yes" on the Oregon Nuclear Safeguards Initiative—Ballot Measure No. 9.

likely _____:_____:_____:_____:_____:_____:_____ unlikely
     extremely  quite  slightly  neither  slightly  quite  extremely

5. The environmentalists think I should vote "Yes" on the Oregon Nuclear Safeguards Initiative—Ballot Measure No. 9.

likely _____:_____:_____:_____:_____:_____:_____ unlikely
     extremely  quite  slightly  neither  slightly  quite  extremely

6. Most government officials think I should vote "Yes" on the Oregon Nuclear Safeguards Initiative—Ballot Measure No. 9.

likely _____:_____:_____:_____:_____:_____:_____ unlikely
     extremely  quite  slightly  neither  slightly  quite  extremely

7. Most nuclear experts think I should vote "Yes" on the Oregon Nuclear Safeguards Initiative—Ballot Measure No. 9.

likely _____:_____:_____:_____:_____:_____:_____ unlikely
     extremely  quite  slightly  neither  slightly  quite  extremely

Motivation to comply

1. Generally speaking, I want to do what most members of my family think I should do.

likely _____:_____:_____:_____:_____:_____:_____ unlikely
     extremely  quite  slightly  neither  slightly  quite  extremely

2. Generally speaking, I want to do what my close friends think I should do.

likely _____:_____:_____:_____:_____:_____:_____ unlikely
     extremely  quite  slightly  neither  slightly  quite  extremely

3. Generally speaking, I want to do what my coworkers think I should do.

likely _____:_____:_____:_____:_____:_____:_____ unlikely
     extremely  quite  slightly  neither  slightly  quite  extremely

4. Generally speaking, I want to do what the power companies think I should do.

likely _____:_____:_____:_____:_____:_____:_____ unlikely
     extremely  quite  slightly  neither  slightly  quite  extremely

5. Generally speaking, I want to do what the environmentalists think I should do.

likely _____:_____:_____:_____:_____:_____:_____ unlikely
        extremely   quite   slightly   neither   slightly   quite   extremely

6. Generally speaking, I want to do what most government officials think I should do.

likely _____:_____:_____:_____:_____:_____:_____ unlikely
        extremely   quite   slightly   neither   slightly   quite   extremely

7. Generally speaking, I want to do what most nuclear experts think I should do.

likely _____:_____:_____:_____:_____:_____:_____ unlikely
        extremely   quite   slightly   neither   slightly   quite   extremely

# AUTHOR INDEX